THE YOUNG GEORGE DU MAURIER

GEORGE DU MAURIER
Unfinished self-portrait in oils, painted in Paris, 1856 or 1857

THE YOUNG GEORGE DU MAURIER

A SELECTION OF HIS LETTERS, 1860-67

EDITED BY

DAPHNE DU MAURIER

With a biographical appendix by

DEREK PEPYS WHITELEY

and illustrations from contemporary drawings by du Maurier

1952

DOUBLEDAY & COMPANY, INC.

Garden City, New York

LIBRARY OF CONGRESS CATALOG CARD NUMBER: 52-5613
FIRST PUBLISHED, 1952, IN THE UNITED STATES

PRINTED IN THE UNITED STATES
FIRST EDITION

[redacted]

CONTENTS

ILLUSTRATIONS

N.B.—In addition to the above reproductions in half-tone, many of the little drawings with which du Maurier embellished the letters here printed will be found incorporated in the text, as near as possible to their positions in the original letters.

INTRODUCTION

by DAPHNE DU MAURIER

WHEN George du Maurier died in October, 1896, at the age of sixty-two, he was mourned not only by his family and his friends, but by a wide circle of people who had come to know him through his drawings and his novels, and who felt, although they had never met him, that here was an artist and a writer who had expressed for many years all of the graces of the world they knew.

If the characters that he drew, and wrote about, were a little larger than life, the men almost too tall, the women more than beautiful, this was seen not as a fault but as a virtue; for du Maurier was a man who worshipped beauty and was not ashamed to put his ideals upon paper, which was something that his generation understood.

To him, as to his contemporaries, beauty was an end in itself. Whether it was the turn of a woman's head, her smooth dark hair parted in the centre with the low knot behind, and the curve of her shoulder; or the way a man stood, the way his shoulders were set; the sudden smile of a child, and the quiet grave patience of old people—these were things to be revered and loved, and later reproduced with tenderness. Even when pulling jokes and poking fun, and as a humorous draughtsman for nearly thirty years he had full measure of this, du Maurier was never malicious or unkind. He mocked at many, but with a twinkle in the eye. Never from him the sneer, the acid half-truth behind an innuendo, the damning Judas-thrust that passes for wit.

He laughed at people because he loved them, because he understood and shared their little weaknessess, their foibles; their snobbery was his snobbery, their sudden social gaffes and faux pas were misfortunes committed all too often by himself, a bohemian at heart on the fringe of High Society.

The mistress of the house caught unexpectedly in disarray by unwelcome callers; the precocious child who faces a visitor with great innocent eyes and lets fall a blast of candour; the odd-man-out at a dinner-party way above his milieu, the one cricketer among musicians, the one musician among cricketers; the bore who talks too much, the dullard who talks too little, the woman who laughs too loudly and too long—all these were targets for his pencil in those pages of *Punch* some sixty and seventy years ago, and no one appreciated the fact more than the delighted butts who recognised themselves.

It was the fashion once to decry the late Victorians, their pictures and their novels. They seemed hide-bound and intolerant to a later age that promised freedom. Not so to-day. We have learnt our lesson. Looking back, separated from them by more than half a century, the years they graced and the world they delighted in appear to us now as things lovely and precious, lost by our own fault.

Not the mere picture post-card charm of crinolines and carriages, which du Maurier drew with his pencil and saw with his own eyes. Nor the lamp-light that he knew, and the un-busy streets. Nor the houses new-painted for a London season, the window-boxes gay with geraniums, and the water-cart that came early on a June morning to sprinkle the fresh sand. Not the croquet that he played on a summer afternoon, nor the leisurely lawn tennis. Not the young man that he sketched, who would be leaning on his croquet mallet asking a question of someone whose muslin dress swept the ground, and who smiled for one brief moment under her sunshade and then turned away. Nor the small boys in sailor suits, nor the little long-haired girls in pinafores, nor the husband and wife reading aloud in turn, upon a winter's evening. Nor the grandmother and the unmarried sister living in the house, or written to each day and visited; nor the new baby that came every spring. These things were as natural to du Maurier and to his contemporaries as the air they breathed and the ground they walked upon. But with them went deference and courtesy, fidelity and faith, a belief in a man's work and the pride that goes hand-in-hand with that belief. These fundamental standards wove the pattern of a Victorian day, and the writers and artists of that day became part of the pattern and echoed it in print or upon canvas, stamping it with their own individuality, their own genius, creating an era that was at once warm and colourful and prosperous, an age away from our present world of meagre mediocrity.

We who are offered to-day a so-called wealth of literature from the bookstalls of stations and air-ports, pulpy pages known as digests or potted shorts, find it hard to understand the part played by *Punch* in the latter half of the nineteenth century.

It stood alone, the only weekly paper of its kind.

A gibe at the government from *Punch* in 1870, and worried members of Parliament would be discussing the fact in the lobbies the same day. A cool criticism of a picture or a poem, and the luckless author hung his head in shame. Only the best draughtsmen of the day contributed to *Punch*, and with them the wittiest writers, the ablest critics. A successful future was assured to whoever was lucky enough to obtain a permanent place on the *Punch* staff. And George du Maurier was so lucky. When the well-known illustrator Leech died in 1864 he succeeded to his place, although only thirty years old. His weekly drawing on the left-hand page, opposite the cartoon on the right, soon became the most talked-of page in *Punch*, and had he ended his days as a draughtsman only, he would long have been remembered and loved for this work alone.

But in late middle-age he wrote two novels, *Peter Ibbetson* and *Trilby*, which somehow found their way into the hearts of his contemporaries in a way few novels have done before or since.

The word hearts is used intentionally, because the critical mind cannot admit that George du Maurier was a great novelist, in the sense of a Dickens or a Thackeray. As a writer he was careless, and knew little of style or form, and the plots of his novels can be called fantastic, melodramatic, even absurd. Yet these two stories, *Peter Ibbetson* and *Trilby*, sounded such an echo in the emotions of the men and women of his day, both in this country and throughout the United States of America, that they were read, and re-read, and thumbed again, year after year, down to our time; and not only read but in some inexplicable fashion, deeply loved. When a novel can affect the human heart in such a way it seems to mean one thing only. Not that the tale is exceptional in itself, but that the writer has so projected his personality on to the printed page that the reader either identifies himself with that personality, or becomes fascinated by it, and in a sense, near hypnotised.

It so happened that the personality of George du Maurier, though never forceful in a strong or domineering way, held great attraction. He radiated a kind of warmth that made people turn to him on sight with sympathy, and as they came to know him better this quality of warmth caught at their hearts, just as his novels caught his readers. It is true to say he had no enemies. He was a man well loved. His charm—most wretched word too often overdone—was never forced, and never insincere. It was a gift from God.

His feeling for family was deep, and strong, and very French. It was not only affection for his wife, and his five children; but to him the ties of blood stretched far beyond, to nephews, nieces, cousins and second cousins, so that any who needed help were not afraid to come to him. Ancestors, long buried in French soil and never known, were dear to him; and dearer still the grandchildren and the great-grandchildren he did not live to see.

He was a man of very simple tastes. He loved his home. He had no wish to travel, except to France, or to the Yorkshire fishing port of Whitby, and when his novels made him famous he found himself embarrassed by his fame.

"Perhaps Papa will now put electric light in the lumber-room," said Gerald, his younger son, when success burst upon his father; but the lumber-room remained unlit. George du Maurier saw no reason to change his way of living because he received hundreds of letters every week from perfect strangers. He smiled to himself, and thought it all very peculiar, and went for a long walk on Hampstead Heath; and when he returned he rolled a cigarette, and went to his easel in the studio, and continued drawing, or writing, with the continual clatter about him of his family and his friends.

If the fortune he received from *Trilby* remained unspent upon himself, it was because he had the forethought to set it all aside for those who came after him. He remembered his own early days, in Paris and in London, and he saw no reason why his descendants should suffer want if by the success of his own efforts, he could make provision for them.

His own father, Louis-Mathurin Busson du Maurier, had not been able to make provision for him, or his mother, brother and sister, and they had suffered much in consequence. His father had been a delightful, engaging man of many talents, with a beautiful singing voice which his son inherited, and although he was a scientist by profession his inventions always failed, in spite of which he lived with unfailing confidence and good humour until the day of his death.

He married Ellen Clarke, the daughter of the notorious Mary Anne Clarke whose liaison with the Duke of York at the beginning of the century had caused so much scandal, and possibly the memory of those early days had left a permanent strain upon the daughter, because she possessed a more difficult character than her husband Louis-Mathurin. She was by nature nervy, anxious, and highly-strung. Disappointed in the ability of her husband to make a success of life, she concentrated upon her eldest son, loving him fiercely and possessively, a love which he returned with real feeling, but fortunately for himself, without a sense of strain.

There were three children born of the marriage. George, who was never known as George but always as Kicky, a nickname which he carried to the end of his days, was the eldest, and was born in Paris in 1834. He was brought up there, with his younger brother Eugène, nicknamed Gyggy, and his sister Isobel. His happy childhood and his schooldays he described in *Peter Ibbetson* and in his third not so successful novel, *The Martian*.

In spite of his later success, and his real contentment with his life in Hampstead, he looked back upon those early Paris days with deep nostalgia and almost passionate regret, as though in the depth of him there was a seed of melancholy, a creature unfulfilled, who longing wistfully for what-was-once and cannot-be-again, came to the surface with the written word and vanished at once unseen.

That happy childhood was a memory he clung to all his life, all the more so because his adolescence and early manhood was not so blest. The reason for this was that his father, still seeking the fortune that eluded him, left Paris and settled in London, in Pentonville, and for the next few years, until his father died in 1856, young Kicky, to please him, studied chemistry, a subject he detested and for which he had no aptitude. The younger boy, Gyggy, neglected and misunderstood, had the sense to run away and return to France, where he joined the French army; but his character was lighter and more irresponsible than his brother's, and he never had the energy to rise above the rank of corporal, to the shame of his parents, and to his own indifference.

When Louis-Mathurin died, Kicky persuaded his mother to let him return to Paris and to study art in the studios of the Quartier Latin. He, and his brother and sister, had drawn brilliantly from an early age, and Kicky felt strongly that unless he could develop this gift freely, without restriction, in the city he loved so well, he would never make anything of his life, but would drift into failure, like his father before him. His mother understood him well enough to know that this was true, so Kicky, her first-born and best-beloved, was given her blessing to follow the career he had chosen for himself.

Back in the Paris he loved, young George du Maurier spent eighteen happy months amongst his fellow students, living the life that Little Billee lived in *Trilby*, and his appearance at that time was afterwards described by his great friend Tom Armstrong.

'It is curious,' wrote Armstrong, 'that my recollection of our first meeting should be so vivid, but I suppose his personality from the beginning attracted me. . . . I can revive the picture of him in my mind's eye sitting astride one of the dingy Utrecht velvet chairs, with his elbows on the back, pale almost to sallowness, square-shouldered and very lean, with no hair on his face except a slight moustache. . . . He certainly was very attractive and sympathetic, and the other young fellows with whom I was living felt much as I did. We admired his coats with square shoulders and long skirts after the fashion of the day, and we admired his voice and his singing, his power of drawing portraits and caricatures from memory, his strength and skill with his fists, and above all we were attracted by his very sympathetic manner. I think this certainty of finding sympathy was one of his greatest and most abiding charms. His personality was a very engaging one, and evoked confidence in those who knew him very little. Music was a powerful influence in du Maurier's life. He used to say that literature, painting and sculpture evoked no emotion which could be compared with that felt by a sensitive person on hearing a well trained voice or a violin. . . . In those days he spent much more time at our hired piano than he did before an easel.'

The Little Billee existence might have continued much longer, or at least long enough for Kicky to become a great painter, but this was never to be. For suddenly, in the summer of '58, the tragedy of his life occurred. He lost the sight of his left eye. And for a time it was feared he might lose the sight of both. The agony and misery of the months that followed he described many years later in *The Martian*.

He moved from Antwerp, where he had been sharing a studio with a fellow student, Felix Moscheles, to the little town of Malines, and for a while he felt he would never recover from the blow, and even had dark thoughts of suicide. His mother, who came out to be with him, could not comfort him; for though he made light of the tragedy in public, and laughed and joked about it when his friends came to Malines to see him, showing them his dark glasses and saying he was an *aveugle*, she knew, and they suspected, what his inner suffering must be.

Money was scarce. They had nothing to live upon but the annuity his mother had inherited from Mary Anne Clarke, the original hush-money from the Duke of York. His brother Gyggy was a constant source of worry, always in debt as his father had been, and his sister Isobel, now a pretty girl of nineteen, must also be supported, for although she played the piano beautifully she could hardly earn her living by doing so, nor was she likely to find herself a rich husband.

It seemed to Kicky at that time that he, who had hoped to be the main prop of the family, had become, in a few short months, its greatest liability. It would be better if they were rid of him altogether.

And then Isobel wrote from London, where she was staying with a school friend, Emma Wightwick, to say that Mrs. Wightwick had heard of an oculist at Grafrath, near Dusseldorf, who had cured hundreds of people near to blindness, and who was said in fact to be the finest oculist in Europe. What was more, there was a school for painting in Dusseldorf itself. Why did not Kicky and her mother leave Malines, and Belgium, and try their luck in Germany? This suggestion saved her brother from suicide, and in the spring of '59 George du Maurier and his mother went to Dusseldorf, the charm and gaiety of which went to the young artist's head immediately, and life seemed once more possible. The oculist could not restore the sight of his left eye, but he did promise that, with care, the right one would remain sound to the end of his days; and so, his natural optimism returning, Kicky began to draw again—he even drew a flattering likeness of the oculist himself—and he and his mother plunged into the light-hearted society of Dusseldorf, where life was bohemian, and manners easy, and money did not matter too much because it went so far.

His sister Isobel came out to join them, flirting happily

with all the impecunious German counts and princekins and Kicky did the same with a Miss Lewis, who was the beauty of that particular season, while artist friends drifted down from Paris and Antwerp to join in the fun, and in the work too, which was rather haphazard and not very steady.

There were plenty of sketches lying about in the studio du Maurier shared with a young Swiss friend, all showing promise but few of them finished; and it was not until his closest friend Tom Armstrong came to stay in the spring of 1860, and told him frankly that he was doing no good and allowing himself to drift, that Kicky took stock of himself. Tom was perfectly right. He *was* doing no good. He was living on his mother, he was selling no pictures, and he was getting himself entangled with girls he could not possibly afford to marry, into the bargain. Tom Armstrong showed him *Punch's Almanack*, which he had brought over from London, and pointed out the drawings of Keene and Leech, insisting that if Kicky chose to do so he could draw as well as either. If a fellow wanted to earn his living by the pencil, London was the place to start, Tom Armstrong urged. He was returning himself in May, he could get Kicky introductions to *Punch* and to other weekly illustrated papers; several of their friends had moved from Paris to London; artistic London was a world away from the dreariness of Pentonville and chemical laboratories; there was every reason why the move should be made now, before it was too late, and Kicky had allowed himself to settle to the life of a second-rater in a German provincial town. How about it?

Young du Maurier looked about him. The season in Dusseldorf was beginning once again. The same little narrow circle meeting at the same parties. The same concerts, the same idle chatter, the same frothy flirtations meaning nothing. Amusing last year, coming as it did after the anxiety with his eye, but amusing no longer. He was fit again, he was well, and he wanted to draw, he wanted to be independent, and he wanted to be able to keep his mother, instead of his mother keeping him. He was twenty-six;

if he did not pull himself together he would become another Gyggy, reduced to the ranks in Saumur for bad behaviour.

Once again, as in Malines, it was the influence of the Wightwick family that finally decided him. Not Mrs. Wightwick this time, but the daughter, Emma. She and her mother had come out to Dusseldorf to see Isobel, who had stayed with them in London. Kicky remembered Emma as a long-legged handsome schoolgirl, with a plait swinging from her shoulders. She was now grown-up, and very lovely, with a pair of eyes that made Miss Lewis's seem like boot-buttons. When she looked at him, gravely, yet with understanding, it did something to his heart that no woman had done before.

He decided to go to London.

So in May, 1860, borrowing ten pounds from his mother's annuity, young George du Maurier set forth from Dusseldorf to London, travelling with Tom Armstrong and the Wightwicks, and the story of how he fared there is told in the letters that follow this introduction. The personality that Tom Armstrong found so sympathetic reveals itself clearly enough, with its moods at times sanguine, at times despondent, but more often than not eager for life and for experience, and for what he could contribute towards both.

In those days he used to feel within himself two persons. The one serious, energetic, full of honest ambition and good purpose; the other a wastrel, reckless and careless, easily driven to the devil. It seemed to him, in such a mood, that only the love and influence of Emma Wightwick could save him from disaster. Possibly, like so many young men, he was too introspective. He had yet to learn, and to acquire, the philosophy of the middle years.

He wrote very fully to his mother, as will be seen. He kept little or nothing from her. He shared with her both his gaiety and his disillusions. Some robust quality of understanding in her, inherited surely from Mary Anne, made it easy for him to be frank with her on matters delicate. She even twitted him, during his long engagement, for excessive purity, telling him it was bad for his health, and quite unnecessary. Sure of her faith in him, he could not help showing her, from time to time, a little-boy conceit. He was anxious, so desperately anxious, to do well. Therefore he must pretend sometimes that he had already arrived, that editors were running after him, that critics were open-mouthed, that London society—and especially the women of that society—were kneeling at his feet. This quality of cocksureness, this tendency to show off, to talk big, which will be observed in the letters, only betrayed itself to the mother who bore him as inner doubt and fear of failure, as a sort of bolster to his youthful pride so swiftly wounded by a careless word. Because of it he endeared himself to her all the more, and knowing his faults, unable to help herself, she loved him the better for them.

Emma Wightwick, who was to be his wife, saw no fault in him at all. Except that, when he was not with her, he was inclined to become tipsy at evening parties. Also he smoked over-many cigarettes. And sometimes he worked too hard, and stayed up too late, and was apt to talk nonsense to his friends; besides rather foolishly admiring too many pretty faces, which he would sketch from memory on the backs of old envelopes. She felt that Paris had induced bad ways in him which she must correct, and his tendency to think of himself as a Frenchman, and a bohemian, was something it would be better for him to forget. He must learn to become an Englishman, and a respectable one at that. Which indeed he did, without too much agony of the spirit. But that France and its memories still possessed some part of him, he showed in his novels some thirty years later.

Before turning to the letters, the reader might care to see one more description of him by a contemporary, this time from a daughter of Frith the artist, who writing her memoirs in 1908,[1] remembered young George du Maurier in the 1860's, when he had not been married very long, and was still making his way in the London world. Here is what she says of him.

'When I first knew du Maurier he was living in rooms

[1]Leaves from a Life.

over a shop quite close to the British Museum, and was in daily terror of losing his sight.

'He was never a robust man, but had immense virility, and was one of those charming natures which give out hope, life, and amusement to all who come in contact with them, and I should sum him up in one word—joyous. Naturally he had his dark days and times, but these he never shewed in public. In the days I knew him he was not at all well off, and he had an increasing family, but he had married one of those wives of that period, the women who lived for their homes and their husbands, and there was not a load that Mrs. du Maurier did not take from his shoulders when she could, not a thing she would not do to help him, and see that no small worries stood between him and his work.

'She was one of the loveliest creatures of her time, and from her statuesque beauty her husband drew his inspiration, and has immortalised her over and over again in the pictures in *Punch.* She had quantities of lovely dark hair, and in those days often twisted a yellow riband among her locks with a most ravishing effect. It was always a delight to me to watch du Maurier draw, while Mrs du Maurier sat and sewed, and the children played about the floor unchecked.

'Du Maurier became a rich man, and had a big house, but I question if any days were happier, although all were happy, than those first days when he sang at his work in the front room over the corner shop. . . .

'His talk was most delightful, but above all the delight caused me by his charming singing is a thing I shall never forget.

'He would sit down to the piano, and in a moment the room would be full of divine melody, not loud, not declamatory, but music in the fullest sense of the word; a nightingale singing in an orchard full of apple blossom was not as sweet, and I have heard a sudden hush come over a large assembly should he sing, albeit he liked a small audience. I have only to close my eyes, and I can hear him once more—a perfect silence would fall upon us all.

' "*Den lieben lange Tag*" wailed out across the night,

and I was gazing at the moon across the sea, listening to the mingled ripple of the waves on the shore and the lovely voice in the drawing room, my eyes filling with tears, I do not quite know why, and my heart beating as sentimentally as that of any love-sick maiden in her 'teens. Never did any moon shine before or since as that did, or any sea and voice mingle as did those.

'Then the tune would change; dainty little ripples ran along the keys of the piano; we were in France. Despite the very obvious moonlight on the sea, the sun shone, soldiers clanked along the boulevard, girls came out and beckoned and smiled, the leaves rustled on the trees, and all was Spring, and gaiety, and pleasure. One never had to ask him to continue; one little song after another would make the evening memorable; he knew his audience, knew that we could never have enough, and he played upon us all with his voice, another Orpheus with his lute, until we travelled miles into the country of make-believe, and wandered with him along the myriad roads of fancy. How I wish I could reproduce that *voix d'or*! At any rate, I possess it always, and can never forget the evenings when we were sung to by du Maurier.

'I always think that those who knew and loved such a genius as his can never lose him; he may die, he himself may pass into the shadows, but how much he leaves behind. . . .'

82 Grosvenor Street,
Sunday morning.
[May, 1860]

My dear Mamma

Here we are safe at last, at Mrs. Wightwick's, and it's my private opinion that I have got into very comfortable diggins for kinder people never existed. My head is in such a confused state that I cannot give you a very logical account of the journey. Going down the Rhine the weather was miserable, and I slept on the floor in the cabin, but stood it very well indeed—eyes as well as ever—did not get to Rotterdam till 5. There we walked about and made ourselves very happy, Emma of course in ecstacies at everything as she always is. On Saturday 12 we left Rotterdam in the London boat, with Tom, it was very jolly barring anxieties and regrets etc. Emma was the first to turn up, then Mrs. W. then Tom who was fearfully ill all day and is now completely disfigured by the congestion arising from violent retching—had I suffered as he did I should have been stone blind now. I wasn't sick at all. The blood has sent Tom's eyes quite à fleur de tête. We were up this morning at 4 and breakfasted—jolly again and got in at 9—Douglas[1] met us—great swell, very stout. Armstrong coming here to dine at three.

I am afraid you got very wet going home. I don't think I ever felt more uncomfortable than just when you left, but soon got over it. Emma cried—Mrs. W. and T. drank brandy and water but could not be jolly. I am sure you and Isabel must find it very slow, I hardly like to think of it—by the contrast—had it not been for leaving you and also natural anxiety about getting on in this big place, the trip would have been one of the happiest flutters of this chequered existence. Mrs. W. so very jolly all the way. Didn't she and T. walk into the brandies, that's all. This is such a comfortable home—jolly little room upstairs. Looks as if

[1]Douglas Fisher, Emma's cousin.

I were going to be made a pet of—Emma and I like cousins, Mr. W. not a bit changed. To-day and to-morrow of course I shall have to go about with Tom.

I've put on one of my new shirts; but it doesn't fit, old lady! I know this will make you unhappy in your mind and therefore I had done better not to tell you but the collar comes like this:—  right up to the chin, instead of this 

Do you understand? and do you think I could make the alteration myself? Haven't lost any of our packages; but had another alarm about them at Rotterdam. The Wightwicks such capital people to travel with, so good-tempered. When my hair was turning gray with anxiety about Mrs. W's luggage, and I was flying about the wharves in distraction, she walked quietly after me remarking the officials looked foreign. I do not intend to stop here more than a week, but when gone I shall come here very often, as I feel the welcome so hearty that the most sensitive amour propre couldn't—you know what I want to say.

I hope you will not mope and be grumpy—I can't help feeling very happy and elated *now*. I've had nothing but good omens on the way. My number 48 is now staring at me from the opposite house—and I feel the pluck of the devil. I feel every confidence in the kindness of these jolly genuine people, et je crois savoir comment les prendre—Du reste, tu connais mon tact.

As for E. I'm very sorry for it but I love her with all my heart! She's *so* jolly—not in a way to make you uneasy at all, though.

Oh, hang it, you know, to be in all this life, and to think of Malines, eh? It's enough to unsettle my brain for a week. This letter is not of course to tell you any news, but merely that all is right—as it is written in a great hurry, you may guess. I shall write in my room to you at night and send it when all is covered, in 3 or 4 days or a week. Love and kindest regards to Isabellas 1 and 2[1] and everybody. You shall hear from me again soon. (Wait a week or a fortnight, ould Mammy, when Tom's gone and I in lodgings —shan't I begin to miss you then!) Keep me au courant, write small, but in the kind of hand you wrote to me in Blankenberg—don't cross—but never mind how small.

Lots of things I should have liked to write more and long about—but I give you my word I can't. I'm so ahuri at present. I am looking very well, and quite brown. Adieu pour le moment.

Your ever affectionate son,

K.

Thursday
[May, 1860]

My dear Mamma

Just got your note and enclosure; I see you had not yet received my last; you've no idea how refreshing news from home are—I am glad you are well with everybody. Don't snub the Marryatts, but of course without running too much after them—be very attentive to the C's., and Best.

I must now tell you some news of myself. Tom, who left yesterday, alas! took me to Reade who received me most kindly. I went to him again today with my portfolio, from which he made a selection to show to Leech—gave me letters to the London News Journal, Illustrated times, Mark Lemon, and Ingram and then took me to one Carrick who will give me more useful introductions and so to-morrow I am going to trot about all day with my

[1] *I.e.*, Isabel du Maurier and a friend, Isabella Lewis, who with her sister Louisa, was a close acquaintance of the du Mauriers in Dusseldorf.

portfolio of patterns under my arm. Jemmy[1] is going to introduce me to Keene who is a friend of his, and he says a very nice fellow, with more work on his hands than he can do. Mr. W. also going to introduce me to publishers, ce qu'il en connait.

On Saturday, I think, I shall move into lodgings, very cheap of course—six shillings a week, giving one a good bedroom and no bugs. You've no idea of the kind welcome from O'Connor and Whistler; the others I've not yet seen. I must now tell you about Jemmy since there is not much more to say at present about your unappreciated Kycke. I have seen his picture, out and out the finest thing in the Academy. I have seen his etchings, which are the finest I *ever* saw. The other day at a party where there were swells of all sorts he was introduced to Millais, who said: "What! Mr. Whistler! I am very happy to know—I never flatter, but I will say that your picture is the finest piece of colour that has been on the walls of the Royal Academy for years." What do you think of that old lady? And Sir Charles Eastlake took the Duchess of Sutherland up to it and said "There Ma'am, that's the finest piece of painting in the Royal Academy."

But to hear Jemmy tell all about it beats anything I ever heard. A more enchanting vagabond cannot be conceived. He will introduce me to his brother-in-law etc. and I shall not lack nice houses to go to. O'Connor is a dear little fellow.

I am very happy and comfortable here—sorry to leave, they are so kind. Emma reading up reviews about pictures and I don't know what not—she *is* a darling, by jove. My eyes are all right. I intended to write you bits at night but what with running about all day etc. I cannot even think of home, except when I shave in the morning, and when I jump into bed, for the five minutes before I go to sleep tired out—then Dusseldorf comes like a shadow. It seems as if I had never left London. Met Jew Lewis, my old Landlord in Barge Yard, Kensey, and Ellen and Annie Levy, the

[1]Whistler.

latter a beauty. Je me suis payé le plaisir melancolique avant-hier d'aller à Wharton Street,[1] ça m'en a beaucoup coûté, à cause de cet aimable farceur Jackson, mais je n'ai rencontré personne. C'était à la nuit tombante et j'ai grimpé sur le mur; il y a maintenant un kiosque dans le jardin qui sent fort le gôut Pentonville. Un policeman m'a dit de descendre. Le brave homme n'appréciait pas mes sensations intimes. Mais je n'y retourne plus—devoir accompli.

What a dear old fellow Armstrong is but he's so beastly conservative, you know. Do you think Isabella likes him; tell the little puss to write to me—I hear all about her—how she is a beastly little flirt, d—— her. Her beau Douglas is a handsome fellow, mais d'un bête, vois-tu? He's got us tickets for Don Giovanni to-night; but I am too excited and anxious to enjoy it much. Best love to Isabel, and to that kindest and Dearest of cousins, *Miss* Isabella if she will not be offended at so familiar a message; if not, polite regards. Tell old Best all about me, avec réserve, bien entendu, and now, dear ould Mammy, adieu. Write soon—I will do so too.

Your ever affectionate baby
Kyckie

70 Newman Street,
Oxford Street, W.C.
[June, 1860]

My dear Mamma,

Ouf! Je commence à respirer. It is utterly impossible for me to give you an account of this last week, all the troubles, fatigues and vexations I have wiped (essuyés)—Clambering up the staircases and knocking at the doors of editors who are always busy and always in a bad temper. Sometimes treated rudely, sometimes put off with much politeness and slight hopes of future employment etc. etc. At last by

[1] 44, Wharton Street, Pentonville, where the du Mauriers lived for five years, from 1851-1856, and where Kicky's father died.

cabals and intrigues of which you can have no idea, a slight opening seems to offer itself in a weekly periodical, price two-pence, called the Welcome Guest, on the express condition stated by the editor that I am not to make it a stepping stone to Once a Week, his rival. If the man gives me a certainty, I shall spare his feelings in that quarter of course —To-morrow I go to see him—do not yet be too sanguine, however. Il n'y a jusqu'à present rien de fait—but I am a little quiet in my mind and I wanted it.

I was delighted to receive your last letter with all the Dusseldorf news. Hang it, what a thing it is to have a home to think of, and travel back to before going to sleep.

I must tell you that I am now in Jemmy's studio which he has left, and for which I pay 10/- a week, unfurnished—but Jemmy has left me his bed, his sister's sheets and towels, 2 chairs, a table and lots of wonderful etchings to adorn the walls, besides the use of a dress coat and waistcoat, quite new (when he doesn't happen to want it himself). I wore the articles at the Wightwicks' the other night when Jessie and Charlotte Blyth dined there. Lovely girls, but I am grown very cold to beauty, with the recollection of editors' faces haunting me; I like Emma better than any. The Ws. and Fisher and I went to some people called James, on Tuesday, at Clapham—such h-droppers, but in a most splendid house; 2 very beautiful girls there but very slow. Last night I dined with Poynter who is delighted to welcome his old Pal, at 64 Torrington Square, his brother-in-law's, where he is staying. His sister is very pretty and the most exquisite amateur singer I *ever* heard, though she has not an extraordinary voice. She and I sang all the evening till 12, Gordigiani, Stradella, Adelaide, etc. I enjoyed it altogether as my anxieties were beginning to cease. On Sunday I dine with old Ionides the Greek, who is beside himself with delight. They are great swells (Brixton), know all kinds of swell artists. I shall meet Mlle. Artot there, and M. and Me. Roche, née Moscheles. Je serai en pays de connaissance. I am degourdizing myself fast here—

shaking off the crust of abrutissement among these people, and intend to rival Whistler who is the pet of the set. I have two sets you see, the genuine kind-hearted unintellectual W. set, where I am cock of the walk, and the cultivated lot, where I shall be, if things go on smoothly. There are no friends like those one makes at 20, I feel that; the cordial and warmhearted reception of these old friends of my own making, and their families, is delightful. Mrs. W. cried when I left her house, she cannot do without me she says, and I shall never neglect them (D——d sight too fond of Emma for that). Poor Bill,[1] who arrived this morning, and who is now snoring dead beat on my bed, and who has already fraternised with 1 or 2 of the lot, is in sad want of being dégourdi—green, he seems, among all these wide awake fellows, where I take my place as naturally as an old habit. He is going to take lodgings near, and work here. He seems to think this a 'blasted apartment', and to buy a bed and sheets, it is not worth while. Tell Isabel I have heard Giuglini sing 'Il mio Tesoro', and don't care a fig for him, but did not dare to tell Emma so—she was most charming in her intense desire that he should be well appreciated by me. On the other hand I have heard Sims Reeves and have raved about him ever since. Emma is getting to care about pictures more than anything else, and to twig them too—I have hopes of rescuing her from the slough of unintellectuality, she listens to me as if I were a walking dictionary, never makes a silly remark, and doesn't at all dislike the charm of my conversation.

Living, after all, does not come to very much more than in Dusseldorf—I could get a rather cheaper and far more comfortable room, but I want a studio, and especially want it in Newman Street. My Breakfast is substantial, brought to me in bed, and costs sixpence. I can dine well for a shilling, and whenever I choose, sumptuously for nothing at all; but there are small expenses, such as buss-hire and postage (I have a large correspondence)—So do not just yet launch in to *reckless and imprudent expenditure* on the

[1]Bill Henley.

strength of the 'Welcome Guest'. Ma position n'est pas encore faite, je n'ai que des espérances, assez bien fondées, c'est vrai—mais qui sait? Luck hates me, you know, and I might require a pound or 2 from you—I have only spent 2 pounds out of the 10, and that has fee'd Mrs. W's. servants (9/) bought me collars, socks and 1 pocket-handkerchief (8/) etc etc. I need not tell you that I'm economical to a degree. And now, old lady, though I have much more to write, I have no time to write it; I wish you could see me in imagination as well as I see you. Love to Isabel and t'other. Do not yield to confidential impulses towards Best or the Lewises more than necessary. Write soon and as long as possible, as your letters are the jolliest pleasure I have, especially the larky ones—perhaps there is one waiting for me at Wightwicks, for I have seen my lucky number twice to-day. Eyes all right and health splendid.

Addio

Your ever most affectionate son,

Kicky.

When I came in from my déboires with infernal editors, how I longed to drink the cup of tea and smoke the cigarette of tranquillity with you—I should have such things to talk to you about, were I with you now. I have not time to write to Isabel for a while—she must make out this.

70 Newman Street,
Friday
[June, 1860]

My dear Mamma,

I was as usual delighted to get your letter with the Dusseldorf news, and as usual very much disgusted with Gyggy's.[1] Of course paying his debts through the Duke is utterly out of the question and he is an idiot not to know it. There is nothing to be done in *his* business just now, and he must of

[1]Eugène, Kicky's younger brother, a corporal in the French Army. The Duke of Palmella was his Godfather.

course take his chance. I don't believe a word about his prospects, and I should very much like to see the receipts he speaks of. How the deuce he can be a hundred pounds in debt I can't understand—Enfin, I cannot think of him just now.

As yet I have done nothing (except specimens). I am waiting for a letter from the editor of the Welcome Guest, one Capt. Wraxall, to make an appointment with me. If I do not get it by Monday I shall quite throw that periodical over. The beast has made me lose a week, by saying that he must monopolise me, and letting me hope to monopolise his paper, which would of itself be an income and a very pretty one. I find the first steps are the great difficulty, but once my footing is established I think I shall make money like dirt—The beast Gilbert makes 3,000£ a year and has saved 50,000£!!! All the other men make lots, though less than he, being more scrupulous. I have just done a finished sketch for the W. Guest which I should like to shew you. I find my eyes all right, they can stand work; but I have been very unwell this week from a bad cold and the beastly weather—it is better now. But anything like anxiety knocks me up as much as anything; I am always in such a hurry which I fear is a bad plan and this room of Jemmy's is so beastly uncomfortable. As soon as I get one drawing in anywhere I shall cut the place—not but what the old landlady is in a great state of mind lest my bed should be uncomfortable etc., and always wanting to make gruel for me. I always told you that only having one eye was a key to all people's hearts.

Last Sunday I went with Jimmie[1] to the Greek's, such a charming house and such charming people. Seem to have quite cut out Jemmy there in one séance. There were about 20 people, and after dinner, being in tremendous voice and spirits I quite delighted them; Jimmie behaved very well, trotted me out to perfection—Jemmy was adored, I appear to be *idolised* there, and they are very *useful acquaintances*.

[1] "Jimmie" has not been identified. "Jemmy" (usually spelt Jimmy in later letters) is J. M. Whistler.

Aleco, (the young one, whom you remember perhaps as 'ye audience' in some of my sketches) was constantly having spasms of affection and hugging me—his married sister, Madame Coronio, is one of the most charming women I have met—J. *in love* with her which he has no business to be. I was invited to spend to-morrow, Saturday, Sunday and Monday with them, to meet Mlle. Artot, but she is not coming so it is put off till next Saturday. Pity they live so far (Norwood). On Tuesday I went again to the Saines's with the W's. Mrs. W. is stopping there. On Wednesday to a dance at the Blythes, rather slow, though Jessie and her sister were very charming—such beastly men there, hate them. There is a big conceited squirt called Walton Hood, who appears the great gun there and flirted with Emma, but I made her twig that he posed in a most beastly manner, and that his posing was of the most beastly kind, by taking him off. Tell Isabel I saw Tom-Tom, (who's not bad) that James B. is a mixture of a snob and a cad, that Mrs. B. is a rotten old woman and that I shan't go there again. I thought I might get to know the Proctors through them, do you twig? but I find they've quarreled with them. You will infer that I spent a slow evening; I did—I hate to see a girl I have a slight regard for dancing with a lump of whiskers all down her neck.

Last night I went to the Bells (Poynter), dined there and spent the evening. They are really most charming people, and Poynter a stunner, something in the Bancroft line. His sister is so amiable and natural and reminds me forcibly of Mrs. Fortescue, only younger and handsomer; and her husband is a regular brick and a thorough gentleman. It is a godsend to me to have so many places to go to, as I cannot stop at home by candle light, and loafing about with Henley to casinos would be sickening; and when alone I devour myself—I took Jimmy Whistler to the Wightwicks, he delighted mother and daughter but the old fellow couldn't stand him, tried to shut him up, failed and went to bed sulky and sick with a cigarette Jimmy made him smoke. J. and I slept two nights here together and spent 48 hours during which he talked nearly the whole time. He is in my opinion the grandest genius I ever met, a giant—considered besides, as a 'wit', greater than either Hook or Sidney Smith, by those who have met those swells. To-night I am going with an old friend, Ormsby, to Munro's the sculptor's, where I may *perhaps* meet Hunt, Millais, Rossetti, Ruskin and the Deuce knows who; Ormsby is behaving like a thorough trump to me, though I know so very little of him. He was a friend of Wills's, who has now 3 children, his father dead, brother's wife dead etc.

I shall write to my uncle. No clothes yet. Men dress tremendously here.

Altogether when once I have my foot in the stirrup, and granting that I keep my sight, I shall have a comparatively brilliant existence—as I have so many things in my favour—You've no idea, for instance, of the use my singing is, and the more musical the people, the more my particular style seems to be twigged. Mrs. W's kindness is beyond anything. She wants to give me sheets, an umbrella, towels and the lord knows what not. You need not fear my becoming amoureux just yet—J'ai bien d'autres ânes à étriller. This alternate excitement and worry is so different to the calm comfortable abrutissement of Dusseldorf.

My weaker nature sometimes regrets that place and you and Isabel with a most painful intensity, but then I get strong again, 'nerve myself for the fight', you know and that sort of thing. I nearly always dream of Schadow Strasse, at night, Why Schadow Strasse? I don't know, except that it was so beastly comfortable. Your letters are capitally written—I can read them right off. Write anyhow to Tom, only do not be too confidential, and let Isabel write to him and illustrate her letters; you talk as you write, of course, and as he likes your talk he will like your letters. Isabel will give him the small news of the family. How does that little party sleep now, and is she looking better, and you? I hope *Isabella* will give Webb the sack—I hope you will have got well of your cough.

I shall now shut up this which I have written in an awful

hurry, Henley and two other men in the studio making a great row. Henley has invested in the most nobby knick-nacks. He's a good fellow, but his mind is an empty nutshell. Love to my two I's (no pun intended) and kind regards to Lewis, Best and everyone.

I get about 4 letters a day, write soon old lady and believe me,

Your ever affectionate cygnet,
Kicky

Remembrances to the Caughts whom Isabel must not neglect. If Isabel's en train she may as well write me a line when you do—If she doesn't I'll forgive, knowing what a bad correspondent she is.

[Summer, 1860]

My dear Mamma,

I am under the disagreeable necessity of troubling you for some tin. The landlady has just sent up her bill amounting to 3.1.6; the extras consisting of a spoon I have broken and a latch key I have lost—and when I have paid this and my washing bill, I shall not have sufficient to go on. So if you can conveniently send me 5£, that will carry me on well till October. Mark Lemon owes me 3£, but I *cannot* ask him for it, I must wait till he stumps up. Pour comble d'infortune, Jemmy was obliged to send for his linen-trunk. My drawers and socks have reached a state of decrepitude which *absolutely* requires them to be privately burnt.

I must now tell you my adventures. The news are on the whole very good. My block has not yet *appeared* in the British Lion, but I was agreeably surprised by receiving the sum of 1£.1.0 last Saturday—This was my first guinea; unfortunately the custom is to give a small treat to the friends through whose agency and introduction I earned it. I objected to this that as I could not drink, an exception should be made for me. Then it was suggested I must spend it in a present—There was nothing to say, but I claimed the right of giving the present to whom I pleased—agréé—so I bought the Illustrated Tennyson, which I was fortunate to get at the trade price 15/- and gave it to Emma. I have thus covered my little obligation there, and in future I can do as I like about going when I please, or staying away.

I then made a very stunning block for Punch (tracing enclosed) and took it to Mark Lemon (running after this Mark Lemon has worn out a pair of boots). He expressed himself delighted, but instead of putting it into Punch, gave me a commission to copy the drawing in a peculiar kind of ink which he gave me; it will be published from this transfer-ink drawing on Wednesday—where, I don't know. Besides which he gives me a pressing introduction to Once a Week. So at present my cards are uncommonly good—But these specimen drawings cost me money; I have to furnish the block, and pay for the models. I hope soon to do the drawings for Routledge's publication, and that will be a fortune.

I have no time to enter into further details about business at present.

The Wightwicks were at the Mosses last week. Emma was delighted with her present; I spent Sunday afternoon there with J. Whistler, who likes Emma very much, and made himself very agreeable. Emma and I are flirting a little.

I hope you are quite recovered from your cold, and Isabel jolly. Best love to her and everybody—I hope to get a long letter and that you received my last all right. Please send the tin directly. I have to be off sooner than I expected. My next will have more detailed news.

Your ever affectionate son

Kicky

70 Newman Street,
Oxford Street, W.

The above is the correct address—you had perhaps better register the cash letter.
Can't find tracing—send it next time.

70 Newman St.
[October, 1860]

My dear Mamma,

I received your very jolly letter yesterday which put me in great spirits. I hope you are not working your eyes too much at night; I should not be alarmed much at *outward* inflammation; the sparks are the most disagreeable—you do not say whether they are better or worse. You will sleep better and so will Isabel I hope in your separate buggies. On Wednesday last I sent you Punch with one of my sketches, which is so badly engraved that I hardly recognised my drawing, none of the likenesses are preserved; the scene happened exactly as it is represented; the Photographic hero is the great Herbert Watkins who must be in a very pleasant state of mind just now—beast! There is nothing of mine in this weeks O.A.W.; 5 more sketches of mine have yet to appear in it, and 2 in Punch; I sent in my bill to Bradbury and Evans for 16£.16s. which will probably be paid me next week, and which I am in considerable want of.

Last Monday I was suddenly and agreeably surprised in my den by the appearance of my uncle.[1] He is looking very well, and of a distinction which has edified my friends—but says that his heart disease may take him off any day. On Tuesday I dined with him at the East India. You would have thought we hardly would have found time to talk, what about Milford, and them and G., and ourselves etc. etc. Mais non, we discussed in fashionable voices on phrenology and the bringing up of little children; I then walked him all the way home to the Great Western hotel. I know nothing about them whatever, but fancy that he likes to forget his Milford and be young and gay for a moment when he can, poor old fellow; que cette vieillesse est triste, thought I as I raced back across London to the Haymarket where at about 12 I found the two Armstrongs, Poynter, Whistler and Aleco Ionides at supper. How you and Uncle can be brother and sister, I don't know, and

[1]George Clarke, his mother's brother.

give it up. I fancy that having such a clever son must have elevated your intelligence and appreciation of things.[1]

Tom was in town for 2 days with his brother—off to Paris for a week and back—shall try and get him to fin here for the winter. What a grand old fellow he is. Tom Jeckell is constantly writing to me, the little man *clings* to me, one would think. He, Aleco, and I are thinking of taking some small house somewhere and living together, as it would be cheaper and more comfortable than this desultory kind of thing. My blasted apartment is the very personification of discomfort and disorder—and I shall leave it as soon as I can. Tom Jeckell has set his heart on doing the Rhine with me this month, paying my expenses beyond Dusseldorf of course. Well, I am now beginning to consider about it. If I can get blocks to do on the way I shall go without anxiety; but as my position is only entamée just now I must be very careful and not leave the iron to grow cold; besides the trip will cost *me* not Jeckell a matter of five pounds I should say, and we should have to pay the Hofrath's[2] bill. Out of this 16 guineas I shall have to pay 10£ about for debts. The more I have to do the more I shall have to spend; you have no idea of the thing. Enfin nous verrons la semaine prochaine. I have got to illustrate a small poem. If I can afford it next week I shall run down to Ramsgate and draw Emma on the block with a sea background, as from a sketch I have made, she as a model would be admirable. If not I shall have to victimise Jessie Blyth. Tell Isabel that I met Matilda and Dolores, and shall call on them when I can. Bill is back again and is stretching his fat limbs on my bed which serves as a sofa to all who come. He is going back to D. in a week—perhaps with me.

I am very sorry to hear of your poor old snag coming out; indeed you *will* have to resign your attempts on the unmarried men of Dusseldorf. Si tu pouvais en avoir de fausses cela te rajeunirait de 10 ans; j'espère que cela

[1]Kicky may have been unaware of his grandmother's reputation. George and Ellen Clarke could have had different fathers.

[2] He evidently had not paid the oculist in Germany.

viendra bientôt. I should like to have my own jaw looked into one of these days. The front are all right.

I am going te see Johnny[1] as soon as he comes back. Le vieil oncle says I shall be received à bras ouverts. Guess I shall meet some very heavy people there, Tollemaches & Hallidays, and *our lot.* I lead a very dissipated life as far as going out in the evening to people and all that; I am beginning to be a little lion and the big lion Jemmy and I pull together capıtally dans le monde—no rivality whatever, both being so different. Jemmy's bons mots which are plentiful are the finest thing I ever heard; and nothing that I ever read of in Dickens or anywhere can equal his *amazing* power of anecdote. He *is* a wonder, and a darling—we are immense chums, though I see less of him now for he is working hard & in secret down in Rotherhithe, among a beastly set of cads and every possible annoyance and misery, doing one of the greatest chefs d'oeuvres—no difficulty discourages him. I think that I am more *liked* than he though, being d'une nature plus sympathique as the french novels say; and this 'Horgin' of mine, you know. He talks women over to him, and I sing them back again to me, and both are delighted at being cut out by the other—ah! this immoral world!

I of course answered Damask's letter immediately and got one back from her most flattering & affectionate—will send her letters when I go.[2]

My uncle brought me clothes which will not fit, so I will have a small sale here.

I shall have to write very carefully to Gyggy—this promotion is a small progress anyhow, and I hope it will settle him a little.

I will take care of the receipt and get the tin sent as soon as possible. I must now shut up, altho' there are lots of things I want to say which I can't recollect just now, my

[1]A Clarke relative.

[2]Damask may have been a nickname for a Mrs. Fortescue, who figures in subsequent letters and who had taken an interest in Kicky when in Duşseldorf.

head is always so full. I hope to tell them you soon. Best love to sister and cousin—why doesn't I. write to me, little pig. So now Dear Old Lady,

Your ever affectionate son,

K.

If you want to read the cleverest French book out buy and get Madame Bovary by Gustave Flaubert; it is of course pretty filthy being French, but its tendency is directly opposite to the french literature of the day and therefore, dans le fond, moral.

Michelet's 'L'Amour' which we read of in Malines and which made such a fuss is the most sickening, infamous revolting piece of bestiality of the century—

The reason of my only coming into 16 guineas is that I was advised to charge less than I intended, for prudence—2 guineas a block instead of three—faut pas être trop gourmand d'abord, il paraît.

About this time misfortune came upon the Wightwicks. The family business failed, after many years, and the Wightwicks were left very hard-up in consequence. The following note to Emma (at Ramsgate) refers to this misfortune. It would seem that a temporary coolness had grown up between the two of them—but only very temporary. Caution on the part of Kicky. Pride on the part of Emma.

Wednesday.
70 Newman Street
[October 3rd, 1860]

My dear Emma,

I send you Punch with my sketch, and the original drawing as I had promised. As you see the wretches have completely spoilt it in the engraving and I intend to make a great fuss.

I also send you the initial letter Q.

Tom Armstrong and Henley are both here. Henley

going with me to Dusseldorf, probably next week. Tom sends kind remembrances.

I saw your Mamma the day before yesterday and had a long chat with her. She is well, but of course very sad; I have not seen your father this week. My uncle, Captain Clarke, is in Town.

I suppose I must not write any more for fear it should be *highly improper*—I hope you will keep your courage up; your letters are a great consolation to your Mamma.

With kind remembrances to the Caughts and Levies believe me my dear Emma,

Yours very sincerely,

G. du Maurier

Friday
70 Newman Street
[October, 1860]

My dear Mamma,

I have just left your receipt in Melmoth's hands, he will send you a bank-post bill. The money is paid in to-morrow.

On Wednesday I sent you Punch with one of my sketches in it, this time splendidly engraved. You will see that I have put myself in it walking with Damask. I am now doing a block for Punch which will be very spif indeed, I can tell you. You do not say whether you like the Q which is very much admired here; I have since done another initial letter on zinc, little Penny riding on a cochin-china fowl which is very funny.

There was no sketch of mine in this week's Once a Week, nor will there be in next, as they are crammed full of drawings of Millais. The brutes have not taken the trouble to pay me, though, so you will have to send me a fiver; Once a Week and Punch owe me 16 guineas for last month's work, and have not sent me the cheque, the consequence is I am deuced hard up, and feeding on borrowed money.

I must now tell you, old lady, that I have decided not coming over this month to Dusseldorf for these reasons—Keene's going out of town and I wish to exploiter his absence as I have done that of Leech and Millais; such is everybody's advice. Besides this the journey will cost me 5£, and we shall have to pay the Hofrath; and as my eyes are all right the trip is not indispensable; indeed all along I have only thought of it for the fun of seeing you and Isabel, a wish that comes over me so strong sometimes that I feel like rushing off to the boat at once.

But everyone says that it would be *very unwise* of me to leave just now, as my position is only just making itself. It is a very beastly disappointment to me I can tell you, although (in this weather especially) it would have been a great bore to have done the Rhine with little Tom J. to whom I have just written—how he will take the disappointment I don't know.

I should so like a fortnight or 3 weeks rest with you out of all this tourbillon and discomfort; this abject apartment and all the draughts and clothes hanging everywhere—but I am soon going to leave it. I, Tom J., Aleco Ionides and Henley are going to take a house and furnish it by degrees, keeping a servant of our own. This will be much cheaper and far more comfortable than the way I am living now. Henley starts to-night or to-morrow for Hamburg, thence to Dusseldorf and back to London in a fortnight or so. He will tell you all about me and the fellows. You will be much amused, but do not make him a confidant, you know. If I had received my cheque I would send Isabel's boots by him, mais hélas! je n'ai pas de quoi les acheter aujourd'hui.

When we are settled, I shall live much more quietly, at home in a warm room with the comfortable Henley at night, and early to bed plus ou moins.

It is impossible for me who cannot draw or read by candle-light to sit after dinner by myself in this wretched cold room, for no fire will warm it. I hope to *settle* my position this winter; as it is I have been very quick and very lucky. But I am confident my talent is very great, and I am sure that if I keep my sight as good as it is my avenir will be brilliant.

You are mistaken when you think I want to flirt with Emma—it would be absurd now, and she gives me not the slightest encouragement. Funny thing rather, there is a certain beautiful Greek girl of great talent and really wonderful beauty, with a small fortune of *her own* of 80,000£. She is supposed to be attached by mere obstinacy to a Greek of low birth in Paris and is of that rudeness and indifference that she will not even answer those who speak to her; neither Poynter nor Whistler could get a word out of her; and about 2 months ago when I met her for the first and only time, she and I had quite a talk to everybody's astonishment. Shortly after at a dinner party at Tulse Hill I ran her down and abused as much as I possibly could abuse a lady, knowing every word would be carried back to her. Well, the other day as I was walking through Kensington Gardens I saw a group of ladies and little girls talking and in one glance recognised the beautiful Cazaretti, but pretended not to know her through her thick veil and walked on. What does Cazaretti do but leave her friends and with a little girl for a chaperone just follow me about the Gardens, I apparently very innocent of it all, but dodging about everywhere, and she still following and passing me. The thing was evident, and from a girl of her position and peculiar indifference the performance was rather significative. I did not say anything to anybody about seeing her, but when I meet her shall certainly do some little quiet manoeuvres, and abuse her more than ever.

I suppose you and Isabel find Dusseldorf rather slow; I would not fraternise too much with all the good people who wish to, it will become a bore. What does Isabel Lewis say about her sister? I fancy my getting on so well must have taken a good load of present anxiety off your mind.

My room commence à se remplir d'individus qui font tant de bruit qu'il n'y a pas moyen d'écrire; je vais donc te dire adieu—n'oublie pas de m'envoyer 5 livres. Love to Isabel, 2 Isabels. Best will see to getting your medicine; remember me kindly.

No fear of my making enemies; that is, I must make

enemies every step I take, impossible otherwise; even in this little beginning of mine I find a public artist's life as full of little worries and annoyances as it is of satisfied vanity.

Well adieu old lady, write soon you know, your letters after all are the jolliest sensations I have; I always make myself peculiarly comfortable when I read them, feet on the hob you know, and cigarette with a cup of tea. Make that impertinent puss Isabel to write also. Adieu, your ever affectionate son

K.

8 Berners Street, W.
[November, 1860]

My dear Mamma,

I just write a line to say that I have emigrated from the 'abject hole' to the above which is at least comfortable and nice and for which I pay only 1 bob more a week. The change was necessary—ouf! je respire.

Tell Henley that it will be useless to think of the *house* before Christmas, but there are rooms to let in this house, and he is welcome to use my *studio* (my bedroom is an alcove partitioned off). I am now going to meet the dear Fortescue at Buckners, who's painting her portrait. Tom Armstrong will be in town this afternoon. Nothing in this week's Punch (except perhaps Penny); I have been resting and déménageing—both occupations very fatiguing. Shall begin again to draw to-morrow. Just had a visit from Higginson, Bancroft's chum. Sunday and Monday last at Tulse Hill with Poynter—Paradise. Had to describe you and Isabel with prœraphaelite detail. It would be a home for Isabel if she were here. Hélas! quand serons nous donc réunis? L'été prochain j'espère.

Wightwicks got over their troubles; poor as rats but no longer anxious it seems. I have no time to write more now; please write soon. Love to everybody. Tell Henley he needn't bring the Richter. Be very jolly to him, for he's very nuts on me. Tell him I got his letter, and will write to him this week.

Your ever affectionate son,

Kick

8 Berners Street
[November, 1860]

My dear Mamma,

I have just received your letter about Louisa.[1] I will write immediately and call though God knows I have little time to do it in. (Would you believe Madam that I rise at 8 and work till 10 or 11 at night?) I will give Louisa also a O.A.W. with the Iris—I sent it you last week and Tom posted it for me, I wonder you did not get it. It is called 'Non satis' by Berni, illustrated by me. Had you not better inquire at the Post Office?

I am now illustrating a Christmas book for Dalziel, and making the Supplement page for Christmas Ill. Lond. News—a most complicated affair by jove, don't I sweat over it. I am limited to time for both of these people, so I work hard all day, have a chop cooked at home and a cup a tea, and then work on by candlelight. Strange to say I do not find it affects my poor old peeper beyond slight fatigue. Then I have many little intervals of rest when I smoke my cigarette, and I manage to go out for an hour at dusk; awfully hard work, but very satisfactory to jump into bed with a contented chuckle after ye day's work. You see it's altogether out of my line but I do it for tin of course, and have to force my nature.

I don't know what I'm to be paid for it. Anyhow I've been and gone and ordered that necessary article a dress suit (which I don't ever intend to pay for).

Do you recollect in the Cousine Bette about the artist—'Il se met au travail avec désespoir et le quitte avec regret'?

[1]Possibly Louisa Lewis, the eldest Miss Lewis, on a visit to London. Kicky had flirted with her, rather seriously, in Dusseldorf.

How I feel that in this case—When all this work is over, I shall rusticate a little for health—perhaps Norwich for a week with plenty of riding and driving—or else invite myself to go and live at Tulse Hill.

I will call on the Bests when I have time. Have not heard again from the Fortescues. You know it's all very well but my path is not among those people, who pet an artist, make him lose his time and spend the money he hasn't got, and never buy anything of him—besides thinking it a piece of condescension I've no doubt. I hope not to have the time to know people; as it is I hardly know which way to look—almost every post brings me in notes of invitation which I have hardly the time to refuse, even. The only condition of my ever doing anything *swell*, and I hope to, is to be very much alone and uninfluenced. One gets to think one's brush or one's pencil better company and more important than any pleasure or 'satisfaction d'amour propre' in any other line. I shall not require patronage or influential connection, or charlatanism of any kind so long as I keep my sight. Many little things which occur to me in social life etc., and which a year ago would have excited me and pleased me beyond everything in the world, seem now as commonplace as possible, and I am getting of a cheekiness and nonchalance which Isabel would think disgusting.

I am very delighted to hear of the improvement in that young lady's health and spirits and appearance. I'd give anything to go over at Christmas. I wish you could have Emma over for a month (Tu sais, c'est pour rire que je dis ça). I am getting very much attached to that 'ere young person, I can tell you, but of course shall not tell her so—yet.

If I got myself thoroughly independent, I fancy you and Isabel could exist on the income in these diggings. You can fancy what lots of eligible men I could introduce if we had a decent home. Mais tout ça, c'est des rêves, quoi, à present.

If I got as much work as I could do, I could make 800£ or 1,000£ a year. But I can't say which way it will turn.

This is a terribly hurried scrawl; you can guess why. Can't send you a sketch from utter incompetence; but if I could I should be *rather* inclined to make a caricature of Tom and myself gorging at the St. James's Hall dining rooms. Write soon, old lady, your letters delight this individual—so glad to hear that you have some faith in my talent. Went to the Levies and enjoyed it very much. Lawson and I got on very well—little Annie such a love of a beauty and so quiet—Angelina a darling. Sung one of my new crack songs with great success, though in beastly voice—'Svegliaté la mia mia' by Pergolese. But my real crack song now is 'il nome de mia madre' by Gordigiani, which I sing à faire pleurer—a great compliment to you old lady.

I will write again when I have time—with best love to I.

Your ever affectionate hopeful

Kicky

Tell Best I saw Pepys in the Burlington Arcade, but didn't speak as I was already late for a dinner party—should like to have known how his eyes are. I dreamt about Best last night, and that his eyes were better—are they? Love to Bill, and tell him I would write but haven't a minute—printer's devil waiting.

The following letters to Tom Armstrong, written in the late autumn of 1860, *show that Kicky did not spend all his time working; nor every evening with the Wightwicks.*

My dear Tom,

Your letter aroused me this morning from the arms of Somnus and dreams of the talented Angelina Levy with whom I spent the evening last night.

1st. the address is 16, Allée Strasse
Dusseldorf—

2dly. I will call today for your glasses and if there take them and send them to you when I can.

3rdly. Swain has *no proof* on rice paper, but one on *thick yellow* paper, which he won't part with, and which is hanging up now in his office between two Millais—rien que ça; mais puisque tu y tiens tant, ce que me flatte énormement, je te donnerai mon épreuve quand je l'aurai montrée à quelques personnes.

I have been working very hard and have done what I think some very good things in the chic line—among others the 'Pegasus', of which the original belongs to you. I am as proud of the copy I made from it in pen and ink on a stunning yellow block as a dog with 2. Dalziel wrote & sent me a block which I have just finished. M. Lemon wrote to give me an order for the Ill. London News supplement, to make a large ornamental page for Christmas—ça leur coutera cher.

I have managed the chinese story capitally, I think—Poynter delighted with it. Tom Jeckell is in Town & sends many kind remembrances. Polly[1] was here yesterday and spent the day, took her to dine in Leicester Square; after which I spent the Evening at the other Levies who had written to ask me. They twigged this individual's singing in a way which was full of artistic flattery—splendid Angelina! *Lovely* little Annie Levy, my old friend and playfellow! En v'là une, de beauté blonde! Tout ça sera pour Once a Week.

I think I'll get you to write a poem for that periodical in praise of female Jews, and illustrate it myself. Angelina at the piano would make a splendid picture.

You were a muff not to stay. Tom, nurse & foster thine aversion towards the Godforsaken city[2] in which thy lines are cast now.

I will go to O'Connor's straight and leave this envelope open to say about that & the eyeglass.

I must now shut up as I am awfully pressed for time, old fellow.

Yours ever Kick

[1]Polly. Obviously not a friend of Emma Wightwick.
[2]Manchester.

85 Newman Street
[November, 1860]

My dear Tom,

So you write at last—c'est pas malheureux. I shall begin to think that you only consider fellows worth writing to when they're going blind or otherwise auf-gebuggert. I will go to day and get the information you require in time for post. I believe I told you all about Mark Lemon in my last. The reason of his sacking me is probably that his staff is big enough and expensive enough as it is, besides which I do not think that I am very specially fitted for Punch—can't say—might be in time, I suppose. It never rains but it pours—I have had to do three things over again for O.A.W. J'y ai mis de la bonne volonté. But they are reducing the number of blocks to each paper, and as you know increasing the number of artists, which looks uncommonly blue. They have three blocks of mine, one coming out to-morrow. I have done one for them, the best I have done yet, of a bedside. Jimmy went on about it as he did about non satis, so you look out for it. I have no work on hand just at present—am going to etch and at the same time look out for some book illustrations. Met Reade who was very kind and blew me up—said I was to send my illustrations which I will. Of course I shall not be able to go over to D. & superintend the déménagement of the family.

What a damned grumpy cruxty old beast you are getting—you write as if you had a gout, or several . . .[1] don't tell us what you are doing or anything.

Jimmie was foolish enough to paint out Annie's head which you admired so much because Leighton told him it was out of harmony, and the last time I saw him he was in complete despair, couldn't put it in again—hope it's all right now. He's got deuced little time—Poynter painting his Dante Angel for the Acad., Bill doing little pictures to get some real tin—is very much in the blues about his prospects, but he needn't be as his talent is of an essentially saleable nature—of that I am quite sure.

[1]Word crossed out and illegible.

Serjeant Thomas has bought Jimmy's etchings for 7 years and is exhibiting them—does all the printing (Delattre) and advertising, and gives Jimmy half—but I think I told you all this in my last. He saw my bedside on the block and fell in love with it—wants me to etch for *him*. I am going to etch Emma in a beautiful evening landscape—ça sera rupin—lick non satis all to fits. That maiden & I more inseparable than ever—chains of adamant, gilt over by the illusions of vernal youth—*ain't* we chums, that's all! Oh for a small competency of 3 or 4 thousand a year, or even less—a cottage! a studio divided by a sheet! When you come you'll fraternise with Keene—he's *such* a stunning fellow, as stunning as Bancroft. Alecco has flown to Greece. We have very jolly little evenings in my room sometimes. Oh Damn it! Do come quick—such a damn lot to talk about, and plenty of fun.

I expect Polly here every minute—En v'là une qu'a l'air de tenir à moi depuis trois mois que j'ai pas l'sou, qu'elle vient m'épuiser avec une regularité. . . . Decidément j'ai le feu sacré pour taper dans l'oeil du sesque! un doux regard plein de feu, une voix enchanteresse, et un certain petit mouvement ondulé qui me fait regretter que je ne suis pas femme, afin de m'avoir pour ma que. . . .

Wednesday

Poynter's just been in, and says you can send your picture to him 28 Grafton St. and he will send it with his—you must send it to him by Saturday the sixth as Monday & Tuesday following are the days. Send it with a note to the Secretary of the Academy: Sir, I beg to send for your inspection my picture entitled 'the social evil' (or whatever its name is), the damage of which is 5000£, (naming its price)—besides which your name, and the name & price of the picture must be pasted at the back of the frame, giving Poynter's address for the picture.

Since I began this (yesterday morning) I have been with Bill to Rotherhithe, last night. Jimmy will have the picture done—all the background perfectly gorgeous.

Moscheles is coming to town—I am now going off to his sister Mm. Roche and must therefore end this.

Hoping to see you soon, old fellow

Yours ever—

K.

Expecting to hear from Dusseldorf every day.

[January, 1861]

My dear Mamma

I was delighted to get your account of Christmas doings, and to find that it went off pleasantly with you as it did with me. We've always a horror of Christmas, but I think that the two we spent in Malines were the lowest pitch and in future it's always to be excelsior. Christmas '59 was already an immense improvement as we had Isabel with us. Just see what *this* year has done—rendered me independent of you; il est vrai que vous avez perdu mon agréable société.

Your account of Isabel's flirtations with the handsome Ned and the interesting Sam is very jolly—y aura-t-il moyen?

I am beginning at last to know a little comfort; and having been through such squalid discomfort at the two other shops, I appreciate it. Bill and I have got the house pretty much to ourselves, and make uncommonly bon ménage. He has the 1st floor, I the second—I have two bedrooms, one of which Alecco pays 6 bob a week for—and a drawing room, or studio, 'faut voir.'—So far 2 luxurious armchairs, and a very first rate piano, a subscription affair, on which Bill is now strumming, for this is an evening at home, and by and by Keene and Jimmy and Co. will come in. I am going in for practising this worn out old organ of mine, and getting up new things to sing. It won't do to trot out the same old things every time at a place like Lewis's, and it won't do to fluke accompaniments either.

I spent my Christmas day at Mrs. Haden's—very jolly—New Year's Eve at the Majors where it was most uproarious fun and jollity I must say. As the clock struck 12 I paused in Sir Roger de Coverley, got a glass of wine and respectfully drank your health and I's.

The Theatricals went off splendidly. How Isabel would have enjoyed it. Such splendid embroidered costumes the Greeks had—national you know. I did my part stunningly, Bill also distinguished himself. Jimmy was magnificent, but unfortunately got awfully drunk at supper and misbehaved himself in many ways. What splendid people these Greeks are, I never met any people like them.

I have already gone to work again hard, and you know how I work when I'm at it—forget to wash, to eat, even to smoke, and the result amply repays me for to-day I sent to Once a Week a little bedside scene, which will make an effect. Everybody has brought out bedside scenes, Millais two within the last six months, and I make bold to say that mine if well engraved will smash them all. When it comes out I will send it with Millais and you shall compare. George Cruickshank I hear has been abusing me at the Once a Week office, saying I am a damned prœraphaelite. This can only do me good and him harm. The Once a Week people are as nuts on me as possible—I went in with a drawing a week ago on the block which I had kept them waiting for a long time and expected them to be very angry. Here's the style of thing—

Ed. (Lucas) Ah! du Maurier, it's you is it at last.
du M.—Yes! I've been very ill. . . .
Ed. Stuff—you're a lazy dog; now come and sit near the fire, and tell us what little good you've done—
Sub. Ed. Let him write it down on a piece of cigarette paper—etc. etc.

Whenever Editors treat one in that style, you know, one is all right. I had the cheek to say that it bored me to illustrate other men's poems, and that I could draw quite well enough if I chose, to have poems written to my illustrations, and Lucas said it was a very good idea, and I might do just as I liked,—After which they chaffed me about 'Non

Satis' and asked me if I was in love with her. In short I remained there in the big armchair with my feet in the fender for about 2 hours. I am now sulking Mark Lemon, who will have to fork out 21£ very soon, whether he likes it or not.

I wrote a long letter to Gyggy, very artfully and carefully combined; he hasn't answered yet. In future if he gets into debt he will write to me and I shall know how to answer him. I wish I could have sent him a fiver but I am too hard up. To-morrow I am going to do a large drawing for Punch which I have been neglecting lately.

On the 14th there is going to be a grand bal costumé at Tulse Hill—150 or 200 people—I wish Isabel could go there. We're all going—ça sera drôle. To-morrow evening I go to the Levy's—about 3 evenings a week at the Wightwicks'—Mrs. W. always making me presents. I think Mlle. is getting prettier every day.

I suppose Isabel has heard that that beautiful inanity Jessie Blyth is going to be married, in March. The lovely idiot thinks of nothing but her wreath and veil. Such an overdone vulgar flare-up the marriage will be. The bridegroom, James Franklyn, is a very nice gentlemanly fellow in the 14th Foot with his pay and about a hundred a year I believe to set off against Jessie's 000£ per annum. His brother wishes to marry her sister, on the same terms, and she's a still more magnificent nonentity than Jessie. Henley and I went to meet them at the Wightwicks. Henley's Mamma has been writing to me on the sly to know about her son—Henley and I concocted letter to Mamma satisfying all little maternal anxieties. I don't think I could live without Henley—he's as good as a wife; and makes 85 Newman Street feel like a home. The angel Alecco has gone to Athens with his brother, a sad loss; but that wonderful family of his at Tulse Hill is always open to us. His mother and sisters drive up to our studio, and bring us home-made jams and marmalade for breakfast. We go down on a Sunday about twice in the month to dine, Poynter, Henley and myself, and can never help feeling good and virtuous for at least one hour after. The women will sometimes take one's hands in talking to one, or put their arm round the back of one's chair at dinner, and with all this ease and tutoiement, or perhaps on account of it, they are I do believe the most thoroughly well bred and perfect gentlefolks in all England. They have come to the conclusion that they would adore you, but are not quite settled as to whether Isabel is not a little bit spoiled by favouritism. They saw Emma at the Chrystal Palace, read her character in her face in about 5 minutes, and in consequence like her—almost as much as I do—without ever having spoken to her. In short they are darlings and angels; I have an unerring instinct for twigging a really good woman when I meet her—there are certain lines of feature, tones of colour, texture of flesh and hair, indications which I don't mistake. You see Madam, that I have lived so long and in such close companionship with your honoured ladyship that I have become very weatherwise on the subject of women. You should hear me expatiate on the subject in public—and you should see the women that I draw before the engraver distorts them.

What a long separation this is; you and I have never been parted so long—although I think that it is right and good that we should be—However in another couple of months j'espère que nous nous reverrons.

Monday

I must now draw this scrawl to a conclusion. My Editor has just written to me to say he wants me to go and chat with him about my drawings—probably a blowing up—too elaborate for the engraver, or something of that sort, I suppose—nous verrons—Last night I dined at Poynter's sisters—to-night at the Wightwicks—to-morrow a party at Solomon's the painter, Wednesday at the Tennants and so on. J'exploite mon dress-coat, as you see. Pray write me one of your long letters. I am going to write a few words to Tom Armstrong. I do not think the latter party would be able to marry I. for a long time, whatever his intentions might be. I saw his picture at the British Institution, the old woman you know. It is very black, and although the intention is honest and good enough it is awkwardly carried out, and an unsaleable sort of thing. Best love to Isabel and yourself and believe me my dear Mamma

Your very affectionate son

Kicky

How did you like my two last and the Punch.

85 Newman St.
[February, 1851]

My dear ~~Emma~~ Miss Wightwick,

Although the ungenial coolness of your note was most unpleasant I was delighted at its contents, and will ~~shew up~~ make my appearance at $\frac{1}{2}$ past 7 in ~~full fig~~ evening dress.

I remain ~~my~~ dear ~~Emma~~ Miss Wightwick

~~Very sincerely~~ respectfully yours

~~Kicky~~ George du Maurier

To Miss Wightwick

[March, 1861]

My dear Isabel

I received your honoured epistle with Mamma's today, which I was as usual, delighted. But first I must blow you up for your great unkindness in not acknowledging Emma's little birthday present, a piece of neglect at which she is very much hurt indeed—all the more so that the great change which has taken place in their circumstances has made her more than usually sensitive to these little slights.

Having thus done the severe, I will proceed to give you the gratifying intelligence of Jessie's marriage which took place this morning, at Marylebone Church. Bill and I, inseparables, attended this melancholy performance (as spectators, nothing more). Such a getting upstairs in the way of Bridesmaids. Jessie looked lovely when the fatal noose was adjusted—un mouvement de tête! aie, pourquoi suis-je donc artiste! Charlotte and Emma very magnificent, in white muslin and blue velvet coronets—church full. All

Photographer: No smoking here, sir!
Dick Tinto: Oh! A thousand pardons! I was not aware that ——
Photographer (interrupting with severity, but tempered with dignity): Please to remember, gentlemen, that this is not a common artist's *studio!*
(Dick and his friends, who are common artists, feel considerably shut up by this little distinction.)

DU MAURIER'S FIRST CONTRIBUTION TO *Punch*

Original design for the wood engraving published October 6th, 1860. (Du Maurier, Whistler and T. R. Lamont entering the studio of the photographer Herbert Watkins.) *See p.* 14

(*a*)

(*b*)

(*c*)

THREE INITIAL LETTERS FOR *Punch*

(*a*) Q, (Whistler); from the wood engraving published October 27th, 1860. *See p.* 17

(*b*) T, (the tenor Tamberlik in *William Tell*); from the wood engraving published May 25th, 1861. *See p.* 41

(*c*) A, (Charles Keene and du Maurier caricaturing each other); from an unfinished drawing in pen and ink and pencil.

was nuts to me, even the faint recollection of having seen you christened there 2 and 20 years ago. What a nasty little red thing you were—I can recollect your frown and the absence of your eyebrows.

The whole affair seemed to me a rather vulgar overdone thing, in spite of much beauty and many carriages. A hasty match, and I shall be much suprised if it turns out a happy one.

I am writing to you from Jeckell's apartment in Pall Mall—1st floor, immense drawing room regardless of expense, open windows on balcony. Whistler, Keene, Henley etc. all very lively as usual. I have just finished a *beautiful* little work of art in the shape of a block. They are raving about it. You will see it in about a month. I think you will appreciate this—you did not 'non satis' which is with this the finest thing I have done—totally different from all the rest, which are clever and amusing illustrations, but this is a work of art.

Everything is going on as usual—leading a jolly life you know, hard work during which I forget to eat, wash and smoke. Periods of rest and intellectual dissipation. Sometimes of an evening in Poynter's room or mine, where there are pianos—and a dozen jolly fellows, l'élite—first rate pianist called Slinger and I do the musical part of the entertainment, sometimes when I'm in voice they will make me sing for two hours at a stretch. Mais aussi, faut voir comme je chante with those sort of fellows to listen.

Did I tell you I went to Solomon's conversazione where Miss Mansford, and some other professional, a baritone sang, before 200 people, and I cut them out altogether with my famous Pergolese? Cimabue[1] was there—I don't know whether you would like him, very blasé and finikin, and quite spoilt—one of the world's little darlings, who won't make themselves agreeable to anything under a duchess. You would like Lewis the Linendraper much better, ever so much more genuine. But you would require

[1] Frederic (later Lord) Leighton.

a year's training my dear, to get on with these fellows—perhaps less, as it's you. You should see how Henley is being trained, and what a stunner he is growing into—I tumbled into it in about 3 *months*, mais tu sais, moi!

I shall not have time to write you as long a letter as yours deserves—in fact it quite bores me to write when I've got such a lot to say that nothing but a whole fortnight's chat would do. I have just read your letter over again, and hope you will keep me au courant of your flirtations.

Tom A. hasn't written for an age. Samivel seems to be the right fellah. Who's Bromer? Douglas is in Alexandria—Belle tête mais de cervelle point. Je lui dis franchement qu'il est d'une bête désespérant. Il est vrai qu'il dit toujours tant de bien de toi qu'on lui pardonne la bêtise. What does Annie Levy mean by Emma's intentions not being honourable? Does she mean to tamper with my heart's young affections, and then blight me with a look like Clara Vere de Vere. . . .?

Henley is in the blues, as he is not getting on with his picture. He is also smitten with Charlotte Blyth. . . .

Monday
85 Newman Street
[April, 1861]

My dear Mamma

This is my first letter to you containing bad news (about Milford), and I am afraid my next will probably contain worse.

I received a letter from Georgie[1] this morning saying that my uncle is very ill indeed, and not expected to recover, and the symptoms are so like my father's were that I really fear the crisis will come very soon. I know how much this will affect you and can hardly say how much it pains me to write it, on that account. But it will not be altogether unexpected, for strangely enough your last letter contains 'pressentiments' on the subject.

[1]Georgina Clarke, uncle George's very young wife.

I got a Tel. message this morning from one Henry Edwards in Milford, to call on Greville[1] at the Great Western Hotel and drove there immediately, but he had just left for Milford. I was very sorry to have missed him for many reasons, but suppose I shall see him soon. I may perhaps have to go to Milford. I do not suppose that any change will happen to us personally from this sad event, any reconciliation with Greville for instance—I cannot say one way or the other.

The only thing I can think of now is that you will pass a very sad week, and I wish I were with you.

I have only the *best* news to tell you about myself, but will not write about that now; you will hear again from me to-morrow, and I feel very sure that the worst will have happened then. And so my dear Mamma, with best love to you and Isabel, I will not write any more at present, for I am hard pressed with important work which I *must* do in spite of everything.

Your ever most affectionate son, who loves you better than anything in the world

George

85 Newman Street
Thursday
[April, 1861]

My dear Mamma,

I write by return as you ask me, but not to answer the principal points in your letter—for strange to say, I have not had a line from Georgie since the note she enclosed to me to send to you, and am quite ignorant of her address. Why she conceals the latter I can't understand—you are quite right about her not living in the same house—such things are impossible. And as to her going to Dusseldorf,

[1]Colonel Greville, George Clarke's one-time commanding officer, who lived at Milford, and had shown great generosity to the Clarkes and the du Mauriers.

it is no use my talking about it with you till I have seen her—as soon as I do I will write.

You must not be uneasy about me when I don't write immediately, as if anything happened, I should let you know subito; and as writing home is one of the greatest pleasures I have (after receiving letters from home, of course) I like to have a little time to do it, and not write when I am so pressed that I have hardly a word to say.

O.A.W. left me a whole week without sending anything, but I went there yesterday and got a poem to illustrate—a filthy poem, but affording beautiful subject for a block—I could write better poetry with my left hand. I am very anxious to be kept on O.A.W. as it is the swellest thing out, and gets one known, and the more carefully I draw the better it will be for me in the end, as a day is coming when illustrating for the million (swinish multitude) à la Phiz and à la Gilbert will give place to real art, more expensive to print and engrave and therefore only within the means of more educated classes, who will appreciate more. During my semaine de chômage I made some abortive attempts to etch, just enough to see how delightful it is, and how well I shall do it. I made an etching of Keene, but Poynter spoilt it in the biting (with acid) and it has come out too faint. I have no doubt I shall tumble back into Punch again some day. F.B. is a man called Bellew, just over from America (and the handsomest man in London, Isabel) who is not regularly on the staff any more than myself. You are quite right about Millais' drawing of the Duke of Omnium—it is exquisite, but not of a nature to make me despair at all. I have no doubt I shall have many more difficulties to go through before my position is made, but it must come in the end. I wish you could see my drawings (some of them) on the block, before they are engraved.

Of course paying Gyggy's debts at present is not to be thought of, for every possible reason. I am afraid I shall not be able to come in May, faute de quoi.

I have not called on Johnny as he did not answer my letter—besides I am getting deuced shabby, as my toilette is always regulated by my means—ça viendra. I was getting to miss the feeling of pecuniary anxiety, one of the Busson characteristics, and I am in my element again, and think it is good for me. I can well understand you feeling dull at not ever seeing me, for I, in the midst of all this mouvement and excitement have desperate fits of home-sickness, and feel as if it would be a treat to *walk* all the way to Dusseldorf, and walk back to work next day. I think that when a man gets to be a certain age the society he likes the best is that of the women that belong to him, the Mammas and Isabels and Emmas etc, etc. Do not be uneasy about my love—ça ne presse pas. And I do not think after all that the fair Emma will have nothing, as she has a frightful Aunt called Fanny who has 200£ a year, and likes her and me, for she clutches me round the neck and kisses me. Then you must recollect that this 'ere love isn't the fruits of Idleness and Damask and L.L. (nor of petticoat-absence). Bah ma chère Maman, like *your pet*, I love all petticoats besides, but only where all petticoats are beautiful as in London. Do you recollect my explaining to you all about what I called 'Muslin-fever'?—But you've no idea what a noble fellow Emma is.

I say, it strikes me Isabel is very seriously smitten (in her way of course) with Sambo, and if I can trust I's account, he seems to be a very fine fellow—any chance? I will now scribble a few lines to her. What bricks you both are to write such jolly long letters. When my slavey brings them up at breakfast, how nobly I forgive her for the odious butter and milk and ask her how her tooth-ache is instead of throwing a boot at her (this metaphorical).

Adieu Maman.

[April, 1861]

My dear Mamma,

I received your two jolly letters, but have not had time to answer them till now, and now I must do it in a hurry, as I have so much to do.

I have not heard from Georgie, who is now in Hastings and I don't know her address—so that I am completely in the dark about her, and am expecting to hear every day. As soon as I do I will write to you. I think Germany and your society would be a pleasant change, but fancy that she must be already in a more healthy frame of mind.

This last month has been unlucky to me—you know it never rains but it pours. Immediately after my dismissal from Punch I did some blocks for O.A.W. and although I was pleased with them, they by some caprice were not, and I had to do them all over again. A sort of crisis I've passed through, in fact; fortunately I did last week a block which will be one of the most beautiful O.A.W. ever produced, and they were delighted with it. My name hasn't yet sufficient weight to force on them drawings which they don't like, like Keene or Tenniel, and I cannot illustrate all subjects with equal facility. This depending on one paper is certainly precarious, as you say. If I had barely an existence I should etch, as I feel sure my etchings would be wonders like Jimmy's. Fancy Jimmy's first set of etchings, a dozen (the whole set sold for 2 guineas), brought him in 200£ and he has just sold the 12 plates for another 100£, that makes each etching 25 guineas, and I for a drawing on wood, more elaborate, only get 3. And he doing anything he likes, while my subjects are cut out for me. If I could only work at etchings for 3 summer months I may perhaps be able to combine the two. Jimmy's latter etchings, those of the Thames, which are most *magnificent*, have not sold so well, but because he asks most exorbitant prices for them, 1 and 2 guineas a proof—but however, all will turn out well in the end I suppose. When you think how short a while I have been here, the way I have got on is simply marvellous, as I can judge from others—patienza—I have so many ideas one way or another, that they must fructify in the end. Do you recollect what Charles Reade says about great versatility—that it is dangerous? It is like a man beginning to drive 6 or 8 horses in hand. However good each individual horse may be they kick and plunge at each other, and are no use until the driver has got them to go well together, when they will soon gallop by the fellow with one horse. I think my real line will in the end be this, simply to write and illustrate myself. If I went blind I could make a handsome living by singing in oratorios and concerts. My voice has got so powerful since my health has improved that I could fill Exeter Hall—and when in voice and with an auditoire sympathique I can sing certain things in perfection, Schubert and Gordigiani, for instance, which it is true require a very educated audience. I sometimes sing for two hours at a stretch to a whole room full of fellows, who never tire of listening. Why talk of this I don't know, as my eyes are as well as ever. But if ever I go to an opera or concert, I always think how I could sing such or such a phrase which such or such popular singer seems to me to murder.

I am so delighted when Isabel writes with you—what a thing it is to have a home. Henley and I went to see Jessie married, a splendid sight, but I think it will be an unfortunate match, such utter apathy and stolid indifference on one side, with the dangerous gift of extraordinary beauty. Won't she be a garrison favourite! Her sister Charlotte was at the Wightwicks last night—a beauty à vous rendre fou—a magnificent Venus from head to foot, a great goodnatured devil without one spark of feeling or brain. I am very sorry and, confess, conscience-stricken about L.L. If she is as bad as you say—Elle devrait avoir plus de bon sens. Does she think that I am realising a rapid fortune to come back and carry her off? I wish to God Emma had 300£ a year—wouldn't I marry her just—such a genial and charming companion, like Henley you know, and so kind and warm, and a capacity for attachment that makes one feel rather funky. Tu conçois bien ma chère Maman qu'il n'y à pas d'autre femme au monde pour ton cher fils, aussi ne vas pas croire que je vais faire la cour aux héritières. Avec ça je crois que personne ne m'aimera comme elle le fera (si ce n'est déjà fait).

I am very glad to hear of Gyggy's being in good health. Mine is stunning—I am all shoulders and chest.

Thursday

Now to try and finish this letter. I posted a letter from Georgie to you yesterday, which I received with a few words saying that she had forgotten your address—that she was in London and would see me soon. Ainsi you know more of her than I do. I took a block to Once a Week yesterday which they liked—but things are looking blue, as they say they can't afford to publish so many drawings, and are going to reduce the number. Do not be uneasy about me however; I shall tumble on somehow, and a little anxiety and worry is good for the soul they say. I've got pluck for anything. I am expecting more work for OAW, and shall begin to etch et alors nous verrons.

Pray write soon, your letters and Isabel's are jollier than anything in the world. And now my dear Mamma, adieu—best love

Your ever most affectionate son
Kicky

Kicky preparing for coming struggles

I received a letter from Bobtail[1] full of absurd romantic bosh about Picciola—he is coming over here. There is a sketch of mine coming out next week I believe. I will send it.

[1]Felix Moscheles, the painter, with whom Kicky had lived in Antwerp and Malines.

[May, 1861]

My dear Mamma,

I have just received your very jolly letter and answer immediately to relieve your anxiety. Affairs are much more cheering pour le moment than when I last wrote, as I have been doing some very successful initial letters for Punch; something so much better than what is ever done there in that line (now that Tenniel has left off) that I hope to keep on and get enough for an existence. They are very little paid (15/- each) but do not take me more than a couple of hours. Keene (the finest and kindest fellow) brought one of the Punch writers, Silver, to me, and next day I received a note from him to make a caricature of Tamberlik as Arnold in William Tell, and send it in before 12 next day. I had to take Emma and Charlotte to a concert, and as soon as it was done I pelted off to the opera just in time to catch Tamberlik's ut de poitrine, sketched him doing it, got up early next morning, finished the thing in 2 hours and sent it in. I have several more to do. So the wolf is from the door for a while, and I shall not offer myself for America. Andrews has refused, and I am pretty sure they would like me to go.

All the fellows are here, and the meeting is most delightful. Bancroft and T.A. are such magnificent fellows—Moscheles is a poor little posing Frenchman among a lot of heroes here.

I am afraid they will not get on very well with him, as the grand thing among all my fellows is the complete and utter absence of all humbug of any kind. He is full of wretched little sentimentalities about that girl Picciola—which is absurd; but seems so d - - - d fond of me that I would forgive him anything.

I hope you will be able to go to Heidelberg—a village is out of the question, Isabel would die of ennui. I do not think I shall require another sou this summer. I am in a room at 4 sh. a week and quite as comfortable as if I paid 20.

Georgie called here for a minute yesterday but would not

come up—she says you have only written a few words and appears somehow hurt but will explain all to me on Tuesday, when I shall see her. I took her to the Academy with Emma, all went, Jeckell, Henley, Jimmy and Poynter. Jeckell likes her very much, the other fellows like Emma.

I read all your account of parties and gaieties with delight; the greatest pleasure I can have is hearing from you and Isabel. Isabel would be an immense pet with my fellows—she has the gift of pleasing to a great extent, and uses it. I use my little capacities in that line less and less every day.

T.A. to my great surprise said the other day after calling on the W's.: Kicky, you ought to be able to marry her in a year. He thinks very highly of my performances. Bancroft dines with Thackeray on Monday at the Reform Club.

I have passed a very very anxious month but am better now; and would give anything to go and have a fortnight's chat with you; such a lot to pour out that I have never written—accumulated family wealth including of course linge sale. I am in very good health but very thin; lost an inch and a half round the neck from rage and vexation.

Mark Lemon told me very kindly that as their artists, Leech, Tenniel and Keene, received a yearly income, he could only take large sketches from me when they were very much better than theirs, which is sensible enough—the O.A.W. people are shabby beasts. I shall and must get on, of course I shall have many struggles; but I am one of the brass pots, get dented in, and bumped out but will not split or break. How this rough life forms one's character; I feel so strong in purpose, and so confident of the end. Fancy the difference of this and Malines or even Dusseldorf!

I cannot write to you any more today but will send this off just as it is, for to-morrow's Sunday and there is no post. Pray let Isabel write to Emma as soon as possible and to me. Henley dreamt last night that he asked you for Isabel's hand and that you told him he was too poor; Isabel it appears waived this objection, but you were stedfast, so he informed Isabel that he would learn driving, riding, cricket and all the manly accomplishments of an Englishman in order to make himself worthy. Bancroft is staying in this house, and Armstrong close by—always together. I send you the rough sketches of some of my initials.

You must rub the black off with bread or indiarubber.

Adesso, vecchia, ma carissima madre, adieu. Do not be anxious about your son who is getting more bull-necked morally, every day. God tempers my skin to the tempestuous wind. Best love to I., and the others. Poor L.L. ought to be more sensible—I suppose it would be a bore if I went—I feel for her though, for if Emma were to drop me I should kick over the traces (and perhaps become a very great man, but a very seedy one).

Your ever affectionate son

Kicky

85 Newman St.
[May, 1861]

My dear Mamma,

Although you haven't written, I write again as I have several things to tell you. First, I am getting on better, so quiet the anxieties of your old maternal soul. My initials are much liked, and I have no doubt you recognise my touch in Punch.

First of all here's what Georgie says: She will if you permit go to Dusseldorf in a month, and I will take her, she paying my expenses; there she will study you and you her, and if you find you can exist in any way together with peace, she votes for you and she taking a small house together in London as she will have it appears about the same income as yourself, and has furniture. There would be enough money to live comfortably. I do not say that it is possible, or that it is not—it is but fair to see how you will get on together for should you be able to agree, such a plan would have very great advantages. Think of it and write me your thoughts on the subject. She is now going to Hastings to her parents, and I told her I would write you about it. She expresses herself very humbly about you and says she will try in every way to suit herself.

Secondly I have just received a letter from Gyggy, so affectionate in tone, and so different to what he has written for the last 3 or 5 years, that my heart warmeth towards the youth although he does not seem raisonnable yet, his letter seems to show some kind of a change which I shall work immediately by writing a long and equally affectionate letter back. He does not speak of either debts or discouragements, and although amusement while young is as usual the young man's 'profession de foi' he does not state it in the idiotic manner he has accustomed us to of late. So let Isabel write to him without saying I have heard from him, or shewing in any way that we wish to convert him to milk and water steadiness and that sort of thing.

Thirdly the mutual affection of the angelic Emma and talented Kick has grown to such an extent that it was absurd to go on any longer without speaking. Armstrong advised me to speak on the subject so I did; told her all about it as we were coming home from the opera, and came to the conclusion together that we had more or less liked each other for the last seven years and that now the affection having reached fever heat on both sides it was as well to calm it by a mutual explanation. Funny little scene of course with the Mamma, usual objections made; Emma and I however as engaged as engaged can be, ainsi il n'y a plus rien à dire. So you needn't grumble, dear old lady, for she is a perfect angel, in every thought and action. So you must immediately write her a long and kind letter, and Isabel too please. When we shall be married, God knows—but I am sure that in the end I shall make money enough and to spare for Isabel, Emma and myself (and Isabel's nephews and nieces—unless Isabel gives *me* nephews and nieces, when she will be the swell of the family).

I really can't tell you how enormously and preposterously I adore the fair Emma, and how her influence on me is wholesome; good in every way; had it not been for her I should have yielded to the seduction of society and other seductions very much more dangerous (in Society)— perfect ruin to an artist like me. You ought to see Emma as much as I have to know how *thoroughly* good she is—so warm-hearted and kind and sincere, and with so perfect a sense of duty and yet without the necessity of a sense of duty—and as I have been improved by her so she has by me in many things. Enfin c'est une charmante femme, quoi. I shall never, never change—for this is not a morbid passion born in idleness, like that at Malines.[1] So please write to her that you like her too so that she may not have any painful doubts as to whether you approve of it or not. Tell her that you know I have always liked her. She is more like you in disposition than any woman I know. I have not concealed from her that I have been a great vagabond and all that sort of thing. And make Isabel write to her too. Don't of course say anything to the Lewises. I am going for the sake of self discipline and to get once for all into unalterable habits of work, to leave her and London for a while. I am going to take a small room with T.A. (the noblest old buck, as you know) in Hampton Court. My work for Punch will go on as before, but I am going in for very serious work indeed during the summer. I shall come to town for the Sunday only. I am going to etch and paint in watercolours, and blunder down there in secret; we shall live like hermits, early rising etc. He has an order for a picture which he will paint there. I have no doubt I shall have to struggle and tumble, but more than ever I feel the strength of my own gifts and the security of success if I keep my sight (which is as usual all right). The happiness of another being entrusted to me, I feel as a great responsibility, and understand it in the deepest depths of my consciousness. Of all the inducements to work there is none like that—and I feel more keenly now than ever all that I owe you, even in many ways that you possibly do not see yourself. Enfin, ma chère Maman, je t'embrasse aussi

[1]Possibly a reference to Carry, the tobacconist's daughter, who lived at Malines. Both Kicky and Felix Moscheles had paid court to her.

qu'Isabelle de tout mon coeur; écrivez-moi de suite, et à Emma. At the same time give me all the little news about Dusseldorf. What is this offer Isabel seems to have had? C'est pour rire?

Your ever affectionate son

Kick

Bancroft gives us a farewell dinner today. He leaves to-morrow—and we are all triste, for he is *such a splendid fellow*, you've no idea. What a lucky beast I am in my friends. Great or little, they are each stunners—T.A., Poynter, Keene, Bancroft, Alecco, Henley.

Direct the same; I keep my 4/- bedroom, and my letters will be sent. I may see you for a couple of days in a month if Georgie goes.

Ellen du Maurier, Kicky's mother, and Isabel, his sister, wrote to Emma on her engagement to Kicky.

[5 June, 1861]

My dear Emma,

Kicky has written to me to tell me that you are both engaged—and I assure you that I am not at all surprised, as I have long known of his admiration and attachment for you.

Nothing could give me greater pleasure than to hear this, as I know no one so well calculated to make him happy as yourself, and who has such influence over him. He says he is sure of success—your happiness being entrusted to him, he will feel the responsibility, and of all the inducements to work, there is none like that.

During your short stay in Dusseldorf, I often thought to myself, how much I should like you for a daughter-in-law, but my son's position at the time made me doubt the possibility of his ever being able to marry. I think he may well consider you his guardian angel, for certainly his love for you must have made him more steady in London, than he would otherwise have been.

I think you are suited to each other in every way as you both take such a lively interest in everything. From what Isabel has said of you, and from what he writes about you, I think you must be too good for him—though of course, being his mother, I think there is nothing like him.

I suppose Isabel has told you, that we have some thoughts of going to London next Winter, to live with my sister-in-law. This plan would offer many advantages, without speaking of the immense pleasure it would give Isabel and myself of seeing you and your Mamma continually.

I will not write any more at present, for nothing that I can say will express my happiness at my son's good fortune, at having you for a wife. So now, my dearest Emma, give my kindest love to your father and mother, and tell them how proud I shall be to have such a charming daughter—hoping to hear from you very soon

Believe me
Yours ever affectionately
Ellen du Maurier

Sunday Evening
Dusseldorf
[5 June, 1861]

My dearest SISTER,

I really feel quite puzzled for words to express how very happy I was to hear from Kicky that you are, no that he is, no, in fact, why how am I to say it—that I can call you by the above name. I never had a letter to write on such an occasion, so that if there is any particular form of speech to be made, I am ignorant of it. Of course I must not make use of the word 'congratulation' to you, as it is my own brother who is the other party. The moment I received Kicky's letter, I drank health and long life to George and Emma du Maurier.

I need not speak of the love, affection, esteem, respect etc. I have for the future bride, for she *must* know that already, though she is perverse enough to pretend to doubt it. To think of that dear little girl whom I saw so many years ago, for the first time, walking near the Foundling with Helen and Annie—a straw bonnet with green silk crown—being my sister-in-law. I wish I were in London to tease you both. Pray give me an account of yourselves, how many times a week you tiff and make it up. Whenever I want to get anything out of Kicky I see I must ask his verlobte to ask him, and from the state of his heart, I should say he would do it par express, whatever the request. So to begin with, dear Emma, do lecture your bräutigam about not writing often enough to his unfortunate and forgotten sister. Does it make them taller, or shorter, or fatter, or thinner? I expect a very long letter from you, by return of post in the form of 'Consequences'—Who the gentleman was? Who the lady was? Where did they see each other? What he said to her? What she said to him? What the consequence was? and what the world said?

It would be very pleasant if Mamma and I went to live in London next winter. I hope indeed we shall do so, tho' barring the idea of being with you oftener, and seeing Kicky, no place could suit me more than Dusseldorf.

I never was so attached to a place. Every street, every avenue, every tree I am fond of, tho' I should be very puzzled to give a reason, not having found one yet. The Lewis's leave for Heidelberg in five weeks. Edwin starts for England on Tuesday—he meant to go to-morrow but there's a grand party at the Perrotts, and he cannot be spared. Tell Kicky that Edwin will go and see him and Tom Armstrong at Hampton Court, consequently he (K) must send me his address in his next letter.

I will not write a longer letter now, as I told you the news (none) in my last letter. Please give my kindest love to your Papa and Mamma, and tell her I try to persuade myself that she will be my mother too, since my brother will be her son (in law). So as I am his sister, of course I must be her daughter a little bit.

Pray write very soon, and do not be so sparing of your

"NON SATIS"

Illustration to a poem so entitled by Berni. *See p.* 22 *et al.*

From the wood engraving published in October 1860 in *Once a Week*

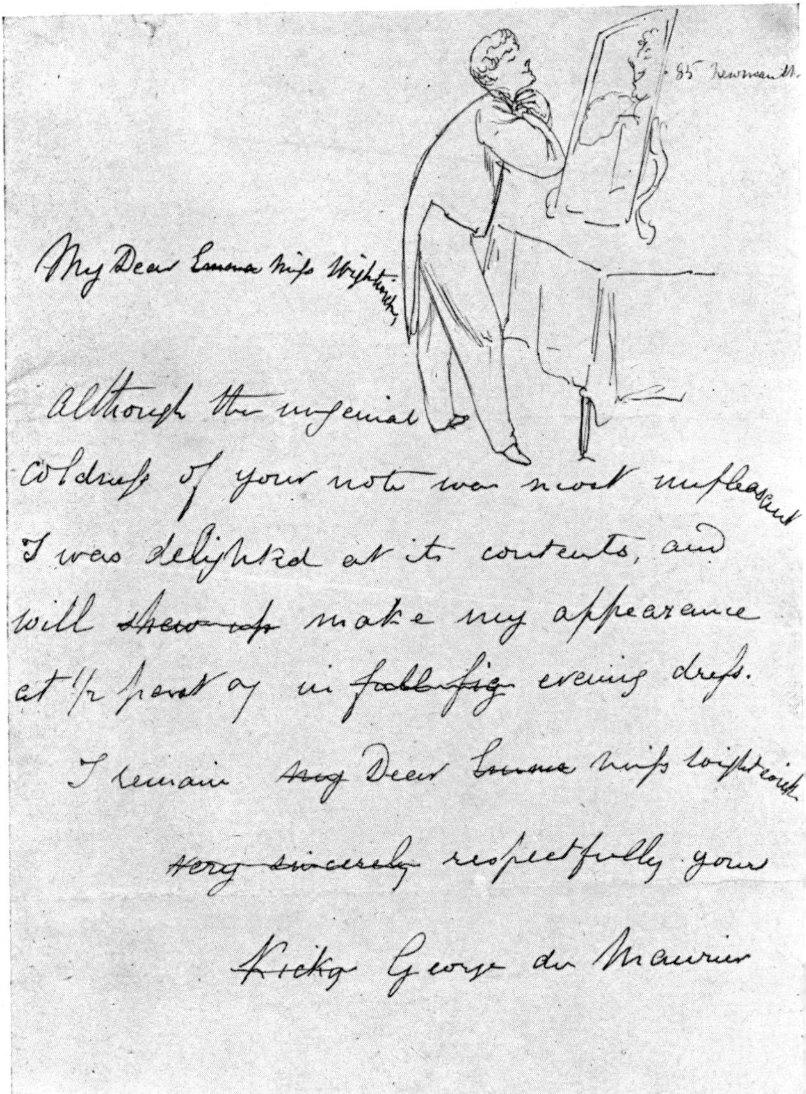
85 Newman St.

My Dear ~~Emma~~ Miss Wightwick,

Although the ungenial coldness of your note was most unpleasant I was delighted at its contents, and will ~~show up~~ make my appearance at ½ past 8 in ~~full fig~~ evening dress.

I remain ~~my~~ Dear ~~Emma~~ Miss Wightwick

~~very sincerely~~ respectfully your

~~Kicky~~ George du Maurier

To Miss Wightwick

A LETTER TO EMMA WIGHTWICK

time, or words. Meanwhile God bless you, my dearest Emma, and believe me

Your ever affectionate sister
Isabel du Maurier

P.S. I would not write on black-edged paper this time, as the occasion is too jolly for such sombre paper.[1]

85 Newman St.
[June, 1861]

My dear Mamma,

You will see by the address that I am not yet gone to H. Court. The fact is the weather has been wretched for the last week and is now—added to which Master Tom is very unwell. We are thinking of going on Wednesday or Thursday D.V., if there is any change in the weather. Bancroft and his friend are gone back, and tout est rentré dans l'ordre accoutumé.

Emma was delighted with the very jolly letters you and Isabel wrote her, and has answered them she tells me.

First about business. Yesterday I saw my Aunt who leaves today for Hastings, and told her all you said. She will go over with me to Dusseldorf in a month and I shall accompany her, which will be very jolly. I don't know how you will get on together, but I hope and think it will be all right. After 3 months trial you will know whether the London notion is possible. She clings to us with all her might evidently, for she hates all her own relations, and I understand it. As for her mother, she's simply a beast—and her father not much better. Her brother a downright idiot and 'guts'—thinks of nothing in the world but eating. Little Bobbie[2] is not a nice child but something may be made out of him. He is as cold-blooded as a fish, utterly without affection of any kind,

[1]Uncle George Clarke had died shortly before the date of this letter.

[2]Bobbie Clarke, small son of Uncle George and Georgina.

very cunning, and full of amour propre. Le fait est qu'il n'est pas trop bien né, cet enfant. I tell you what little I know about the lot to prepare you. It would be such an immense advantage to live over here. Enfin tu verras et tu pourras juger par toi-même.

My own affairs are just now precarious enough although on the whole better. I am doing initial letters for Punch which just suffices to keep me. I am trying to make a dead set at that paper, so as to be one of the regular staff someday. Leech is beastly idle, so Mark Lemon tells me, and gets his 1,000£ a year salary. Tenniel gets 500£ a year for doing the large political block. The other man is Keene who makes a very good thing out of it too. I do not see any others in the field against me. Little Walker who had the first start in Once a Week has cut me out there, his style is very much appreciated by the public and he has the knack of making his work easy to the engraver. But he is utterly without fun or humour of any kind, and so is Lawless, and therefore Punch is not for them. Once a regular member of the Punch staff there is a certainty as there are many other things besides. This damned up-hill work which I thought I had all done at Christmas time is most harassing—mais tu conçois cela viendra, il le faut. I read the papers and am always on the look out for my chance.

Thursday night I was at a conversazione where Mark Lemon had invited me, and I must say he was deuced civil—"Hullo Du Maurier, mong ami, how are you?" which looks healthy. Tenniel also was devilish jolly, and Keene as you know is a very firm friend. Enfin voilà.

Shan't think of marrying till I have 1,000£ in the bank, then all will be safe.

I shall not write any more about the goodness and delightfulness of the fair Emma since you appreciate all those qualities in her, as your letter to me which made me happy for a week shows very plainly. Isabel would be much amused if she were with us. I have been so much accustomed to rather clandestine spoonifications that this legitimate kind of thing is quite a new emotion; fancy going 3 miles off to Church to hear Bellew and that sort of thing, eh! Isabel!

As I am going to see you soon, I will not write a very long letter now. I have written a long letter to Gyggy. Write to me soon. I am so beastly jolly at the notion of seeing you. I have been dawdling over these sketches so now I have hardly time to finish. Tom sends his love so does Billy. You don't say anything of my last Once a Week—the Death bed—I sent it you a fortnight ago.

And now my Dear Mamma I shut up with best love—to you and Isabel. I was much amused at Isabel's account of the sudden German suite—pas moyen de nous délivrer de cette sacrée Isabelle, hein? Edwin has not yet made his appearance. Will L.L. have left by the time we go over? Don't say anything about my being engaged to Emma.

Your ever affectionate son

K

I *shall* have a lot to tell you.

Observe! . . . 91 Newman St.
Oxford St.
[June, 1861]

Angiolo mio Pem,

I am afraid I forgot to tell you my new number last night, in case you should happen to write. Dear Pem, I am very much in the blues at my exile—besides which I have got into rooms where years ago my pal Peter Jeckyll, and my cousin Charlie Bowles, both long dead, used to live, and though the rooms are not very full of furniture they are full of very blue recollections.

I have just written to my Aunt who had sent her love "to her pretty and amiable niece", a detail I forgot last night.

If you have an hour to waste on me in the course of the next few days, let me know. Adieu mon bien cher trésor—I kiss your dear hands

Kicky

Best love to Papa and Mamma-in-lor.

91 Newman Street.
[June, 1861]

My dearest Pemme,

I was very much pleased to get your letter this morning. I also got one from Home. Edwin Lewis is *not* coming over after all. Isabel says she won't write to either you or me until we write a long letter to her. She sends a cheeky caricature which I think very improper—but I send it to you nevertheless. I went to the Lyceum with Silver last night and like the "Ballo" better than anything I ever saw or heard of Verdi's. Your pet Giuglini hasn't got very much to do, but the barytone Delle Sedia sang most exquisitely, and would have excited you to the utmost pitch. I did not miss you at all of course—in fact was quite delighted you were not there, and my features wore the following look of contentment:

Alboni was in one box, Tibernini and his wife in another (she's not at all pretty) and Mario and Grisi in another, so you see it was rather an interesting evening.

Darling, I am wretchedly bored at the news your letter contains about Barney stopping till Tuesday—perhaps she'll be tuk ill, and remain a long time—and then recover—or die, or something. There is a chance of my being able to look in tonight, if I can get away from Thornbury—Anyhow tomorrow night is sacred to you—Can't you go out in the daytime?

I have been working very hard yesterday & today—doing two large sketches for Punch (which will not be accepted of course for it never rains but it pours). I am going to take them now to M.L.

Did you read about the fight for the championship in the Times, and how the littler slender Brahmin whopped the giant into paste? That's the way it would be if I were to have a pugilistic encounter with your gigantic Uncle John.

Dear Pemme, I do not think your letter spooney at all.

I've not got the blues so much as yesterday, for I've been working, but I can smell Peter and Charley Bowles all over the house—I am not able to write longer than this, as I have to go off to Mark Lemon. Love to Mammy & the governor —I suppose Douglas hasn't shewn up.

Goodbye my Dear Dear Darling,
à demain,
Kicky.

Kicky writes to Georgie Clarke, his uncle's young widow, and so that she should make no mistake about his attachment to Emma and his engagement, he heads his letter with a sketch of them both and a little fable recording their mutual devotion. A reproduction will be found on another page.

Georgie Clarke was an incorrigible flirt, and only a few years before had encouraged a calf-love infatuation on the part of Kicky.

91 Newman St.
Wednesday
[July, 1861]

My dear Aunt,

I have received your two epistles and will hold myself in readiness to be your escort at the appointed time; I hope we shall have fine weather so that you may enjoy the trip and not become a victim to sea sickness. I am sorry to say I shall not be able to go to the Wilkinsons with you much as I should like it for two reasons, want of time and want of tin.

Your niece sends her love—she has been in great trouble. The poor mater was operated on last Saturday for tumour in the breast and is still in bed. The tumour was very large, and the operation painful and severe. I have just heard a report that Jimmy Whistler is *dying*, and although I do not believe it I am terribly perturbed in my mind, and am going to seek him.

I hope you will prize the enclosed sketch which has not passed through the engraver's hands, and is worth on that account at least ½ dozen initial letters. How did you like my things in Punch?

My affairs are still very shaky. There is an amusing report among the artistic world that I was seen with my sister who 'is pretty although strikingly like myself' at the Academy. She was in deep mourning—I hope you feel flattered.

Last Tuesday I dined at the Solomons (Painter) and it was very amusing. As usual at all great artist spreads, Millais *was* to have been there, and *wasn't*.

On Saturday, I believe, the fair Pem and myself are to go to the Rose show at the Crystal Palace—no chance of your being there, is there?

Write to me and let me know your movements, and believe me, my dear Aunt

Your ever affectionate nephew
Kicky

[July, 1861]

My dear Isabel,

Many thanks for your most jolly and amusing letter and the dear old lady's. I confess I don't deserve it, but when I said I had no time I was no humbug—and as we only had one Kew excursion I couldn't take half an hour out of each.

First, Mrs. Wightwick was operated on last Saturday week for tumour in the breast, it was very large and she had chloroform. Emma was in a most frightful state about it, but it went off very well, and on Sunday last she got up and sat in a chair for the first time. She was in dreadful pain from the wound for the 1st 3 or 4 days, but now she looks 10 years younger and so pretty you have no idea. She will soon come down. I wouldn't mind going through an operation myself just for the sake of being nursed by Pem, who's got the gift of God for that sort of thing. Your notion of coming over for a fortnight makes my mouth water as you may fancy, but it is of course a question of money; I haven't got the sou my dear Isabel, and am not by any means so fat as my sketches. If this month should be very profitable we might manage it. It is such a damned question of luck; I should wish it for many reasons which I will tell you in a fortnight—nous verrons. Your account of the

Princekins is most amusing, but I should prefer Sam to any prince in Christendom. Il parait que ça ne marche qu'à moitié, hein? If I were married, and you and Mamma could come over here, on te trouverait des maris en veux-tu, et voilà! But that lucky event can't happen for a year or two. You say that engaged time must be pleasant —I believe you, but I should like t'other better. The affection I have for Pem is something totally different to anything I ever felt before, because besides being in love with her, I feel towards her as an old chum, and as a brother besides; she's so deuced sensible and all that you know; and when people one thinks cold and undemonstrative, suddenly turn up everything that's caressant and spooney, it doubles the charm of that sort of thing.

I have seen a good deal of the Moscheles people lately—the old ones have left for France. Tom of course doesn't like him, the others do pretty well, but he's quite different to our very genuine set. I took some fellows to a grand musical party there, given I suppose for Clara, who has pupils in a singing class. She sang and played, the latter very well; I don't care a damn about her singing much as she and her people do. She's a conceited girl I think, but very clever. They all beg for sketches so, et quand on les vend on n'aime pas à les donner. I like sending sketches to you, or my Aunt or Emma, but that keeps them in the family, you know.

Mrs. Wightwick has written a history book for children, and wants her publisher to get me to illustrate it. Moscheles' painting is not much, but he will get on by charlatanism at first and that's just what we fellows don't sympathise with.

I have not heard from Tom who is painting hard, in H. C. I couldn't afford to go with him, and then he occasionally rather bores me about Emma. It's very foolish to tell a fellow to propose and then say you wouldn't be in his shoes for something. We had an awful discussion at a dinner party at Bell's one Sunday, in which I got so bitter that he (Tom) sulked me for 3 days; I was wrong but he had aggravated me most damnably in the day; and he has the most foolish prejudices. He riles me by running down *Jews* like a stupid school boy.[1] The *very kindest* people of my acquaintance are Jews, the Levyes and Solomons for instance. I dined at the Solomons, tremendously rich people, I believe, and holding a very swell place in the artistic world (though I don't go in for S's painting). They were delightfully kind, and on Saturday at the Crystal Palace Rose Show Miss Solomon came up and introduced herself to Emma in a way that was charming.

I get tickets to go everywhere—it is a sort of stock in trade. If I get on the Punch staff half of my business will be to amuse myself by going to every possible gaiety, which I find a bore, except that they give me ideas; all my last things have been inspired by the crystal palace—the 'suggestion' in last week's Punch has been a good deal liked, but beastly engraved. If I could *only* get on the staff, chose qui peut arriver demain, ou qui peut aussi ne pas arriver du tout! On starting I could make 300 a year out of Punch, if I had but the carte blanche. But I am always nervous now.

Jimmy Whistler is dreadfully ill with Rheumatic fever. Tom J. in Jersey nursing the High Sheriff. Tom J. is rather a little tuft-hunter, and will probably cut me for marrying a linen draper's daughter, unless I make a great name like Leech, in which case il me léchera les pieds. I think he would lend me a hundred pounds if I read your letter about the Princekins to him. Je commence à le bien connaître.

If we could have managed the house plan that would have been jolly. Henley's parents have just taken a most charming house in Regent's Park for 60£ a year. He is going to live with them. He soon forgot Charlotte and is now smitten with a Miss Durham, an engineer's daughter, a perfect beauty he says and 300£ a year. Puisse-t-il se faire agréer! for he is a nice fellow—and would make an excellent husband.

[1]Emma had an uncle Reuben, which is perhaps significant.

How delightful to see you again, damn it. I must not remain long unless I can get some blocks to do with me. Now my time will be coming. In August the Punch artists will be going out of town and I shall be very necessary, I fancy, and will try and do my very best in the light comical line. Leech *gets* 2,000£ *a year* and perquisites! from Punch alone.

I have not heard from Eugene, although I wrote him a long and affectionate letter—I hope nothing serious is the matter with him.

Alecco is come back, and I dine with the Tulse Hill darlings today. I want to get Emma there, but have been rather hard on the rope performances at the C. Palace in Punch, and old Ionides is one of the directors. He takes it very well though, I must say. (Perhaps he'll bribe me to be quiet, eh?) I called on the Solomons yesterday, they want to know Emma very much. Great fun going about to swell artist swarries and dinner parties with her, if we can manage it.

For the last fortnight or so, I've been living on such a very heconomical plan that I'm rather shaky. Perhaps I shall have to ask the old lady for a fiver this month; I hope not; but the W's are so poor now that I cannot dine with them very well, and the last 3 months have been so disastrous to me that I am always in arrear, and have to be dooced close.

I send you the tracing of the sketch I have just done for 'P'.—Tu conçois that I *must* go down in the end if my peeper remains alright, and it is certainly all right now. Let them once get me to one of the Punch dinners, that's all! I live the quietest and most wholesome life, no racketing whatever; leave the W's at 11, straight to bed, and breakfast at 8. In spite of my great anxiety, and little pecuniary deficiencies, I am happy as I have never been before, so full of hope and conscious of the power of fulfilling it in the end.

I am very glad L. L. has given up all notions, but hope they will be gone when I get to Dusseldorf, as I suppose it will be rather awkward. I shall have to return by Antwerp and take Damask her letters.

You ask me when you think I shall be in a position to marry. I've no idea. If I got on the staff, in 6 months—perhaps not for 2 or 3 years. Wouldn't it be fun all living together with heaps of money, and plenty of fame?

I have now, I think, told you all the writeable news I can think of, and as I have this time honoured *you* to such an extent, I shall not honour Mamma. Write to Emma directly on account of the Mater's illness and operation, and write to me too.

Very best love to the old lady
Your ever affectionate brother
Kicky

Newman St.
[July, 1861]

My dearest Pem,

I'm off—I've taken the photographs (and kissed them) so your mind may be at ease about my not forgetting the one with the bonnet. I shall miss you every inch of the journey, *my darling*—you will get a letter either Wednesday or Thursday.

Addio—your ever, ever loving Kicky

Pray think of your absent fellow in Church this evening.

16 Allée Strausse
Dusseldorf
Tuesday
[August, 1861]

My dearest Pem,

We arrived here last night safe, and you can fancy how very jolly it was to meet again, and how everybody rushed into anybody's arms. Isabel is looking very well but my Mother seems to have fallen off rather, and to get shaky on account of the great heat. We sat up talking till 1 or 2 o'clock.

They thought my Aunt looking very nice and young and pretty, and Bobbie 'higeous-ugly my dear'. My Mother was delighted to have the photographs but did not think they did us justice, especially Mrs. Wightwick's.

The Lewises had left last Thursday. Dusseldorf is looking lovely, and I don't know what I would give for you to be here.

We had a most beautiful passage, with a splendid sunset and no end of a swell moon. My Aunt who had been very nice and jolly all day was took ill as soon as it got dark; and I remained on deck stretched out on a tiger-skin, smoking many 'Pemmish' cigarettes as I looked at the stars and things. I regretted your absence so much, as it was just the sort of thing you like, and that I can only enjoy when we are together. Many of the people had their beds up on board in the most charmingly Bohemian fashion, and it was a very pretty sight. We would have done so, and wouldn't we have had a delightful chat before going to sleep. I hope we shall have many trips and journeys some day. We arrived at Dusseldorf at 7 on Monday morning and left at 9. The journey by rail was very tedious and slow and dirty.

Little Bobbie is such a strange little ruffian, neither fears God nor his mother and nobody can have the slightest influence on him. I don't know how they'll all agree when I'm gone—doocid problematic I should say.

Isabel was very much delighted with the wreath and looks very well in it. She has been playing so exquisitely, things of Chopin you know; just the sort I like. She has completely divorced from the Tapage School and improved wonderfully.

I am sure your ears must have been tingling last night and this morning; old mater frightfully nuts on you.

I suppose you are coming home from Noel Fitch, I hope you have posed nicely. My Aunt will tell you when she sees you again that whenever anything of interest occurred on the journey I made your photograph look at it in the most gallant and attentive manner.

Isabel will not be able to return with me. On Thursday we shall all go to the concert at the Geislers.

How about the engraving? I shall be back in London on Tuesday night, but will write again before I leave. If you write by return I shall get it, not otherwise. I hope you did not neglect the performance with the locket. My Mother sends her dearest love—and I must now hurry off to post this. There is another photograph of you here that you had given Isabel; I don't like it although it is very handsome, for it looks doocid melancholy and you seem in it as if you were thinking of quel nome ch'io detesto.[1]

Adieu—My dear, dear love

Kicky

Best love to your unnatural parents.

Dusseldorf
[August, 1861]

My very dear Pem,

I got your jolly letter this morning and it imparted quite a delicious flavour to a very cabbagey German citizen. Since you *do* condescend (although in the coldest and most unspooney fashion) to say you miss me, I don't mind telling you that it seems quite unnatural to me to be without you, and that I've a regular demnition longing to see you every hour of the day.

The delight of seeing the maternal and fraternal birds is very intense, we are always together; and my Aunt who is looking wonderfully pretty and helegant gets on with us very well. On Thursday we went to Geislers, and it seemed very strange and yet quite natural. My mother and Isabel blew me up for not making myself agreeable to a lot of Perrots and people, but you see, my dear, I couldn't.

I have not seen Best yet. He is coming to town to-night I believe to see me. Yesterday evening we all sat at the Ananasbergs while the band was playing—and I must say it was a very lovely scene. Every time they played a waltz

[1]Some former flame of Emma's; identity unknown.

I shut my eyes and performed the new step with you in imagination (but not knowing the figure well you were always tripping me up).

I am very glad about the Solomonses, and hope you got on well there, as they are all disposed to admire you very much, and seem to be doocid fond of me. As for Angy in the velvet dress, I shall not be able to do that yet as I shall be overwhelmed with work when I return, for I have not drawn a stroke here, as you may fancy.

We sit up till two or three, and can never wear out our tongues. When you are the theme, Miss, my tongue wags ever so much faster, and the old lady prizes you even as the apple of the eye.

We will talk about the engraving as you say. I fear there are many difficulties, enfin nous verrons, ma chère amie.

I shall (as far as I can see) be in town by 5 o'clock on Wednesday morning, as I go by Rotterdam for the sake of cheapness. Please think of me on Monday evening in Rotterdam where we were so happy—also on Tuesday night think of your lover exposing his life on the wild and stormy ocean (miserere domine!) and if you are able to sleep all night you will be a heartless woman.

I have not succeeded in getting many Punchy ideas yet. Dusseldorf is certainly a delightful sort of a village and I think if you were here you would enjoy it immensely; I have seen some of Isabel's green and blue silver-mounted beaux. Fancy my mother's feelings of dismay at the whole officers' table rising at Geislers as she and Isabel walked in—such a nervous little old party as she is!

I suppose there are no initials of mine in Punch?

I am afraid you don't miss me very much, do you? Much less than you used to miss Isabel, I am sure, by the way you write. But as you are really not a bad sort of a creature and my *friendship* for you is *sensible* and *unselfish*, I suppose I must put up with it.

I must now shut up this and post it. Everybody sends their love to everybody, and it's all so complicated I will not enter into details. Expect me on Wednesday at about 12 or so unless you hear to the contrary; I may come and breakfast with you at 8, if I have a quick passage. And now my dear Lady Kick, who art not only in Grosvenor Street, but also in my heart and soul and every thought, à mercredi.

Your ever deeply attached

Kicky

Pem, my darling, you are everything to me, so love me well and think of me often and miss me.

Sunday

5th [August, 1861]

My darlingest Pem,

Just a hurried line to say that it is Thursday morning, not Wednesday that I shall be with you again, as I must go by Antwerp and the baron after all.

I leave here on Tuesday morning sleep in Malines and go on board the Baron Osy on Wednesday at 1—probably reaching London at 5 on Thursday morning—so I will breakfast with you, dear, on that morning—if you will permit.

Longing to kiss your dear hands again

Your ever loving

If I went by Rotterdam I should have to pass two nights there.

Saturday
Hampton Court
[August, 1861]

My dear old Lady,

I got your very jolly letter, and didn't answer it immediately as I had just written to you and wanted to wait till I had something more to tell; I only got down here yesterday, having been so pressed with this serial, which was published sooner than I thought. I came down here for the Sunday, and when I got back to London next day had to suddenly set to work tooth and nail; finished one drawing on that very Monday, began the next on Tuesday, and did not get it done till Friday; had to go about after nun's costume and Catholic oratories—j'étais rendu, quoi, and needed this change awfully. Today has been a complete holiday; I stop till Thursday, but in the interval have to do another Once a Week and two small blocks for London Society. But as I shall be very much in the open air, and get some rowing, I shall get on capitally; so you mustn't be in the slightest degree anxious about me; indeed I feel ever so much better already.

I will send you the Once a Week directly I get back to London; the two first of the serial will have been out by that time and also my famous drawing of the kettledrum which is splendidly engraved.

And now my dear Mamma I must blow you up for being so anxious and worrying yourself so much. Do not fancy that I did not thoroughly enjoy my stay in Dusseldorf, I was only very sad because I had to leave you so soon, and because you didn't seem as happy as I wished you to be—and as for the notion of my overworking myself to get you over to England, why my dear old Lady, I should have worked just as hard without. Tu vois donc que tu as tort de te tracasser là-dessus; and I want you over here quite as much for my own happiness as yours, and always shall.

Pem and I hope to be married in the middle of the winter, and to come and live 3 or 4 months down here on account of the cheapness and other advantages; health not the smallest. We get out of the window right into Bushy Park; and we could have most comfortable lodgings for a guinea a week; only 5 shillings more than I pay for myself in London for only 2 rooms, and shan't we take care of our health; 2 poor halp'orth of cheese as we are.

Both yesterday evening and today we have been on the water.

Maman bellemère in a frightful state of funk the whole while.

I look forward to doing landscapes in watercolours—anyhow etchings.

Who do you think turned up in my rooms the other day?—Schenck, who has just returned from China where he spent three years in brutifying himself as a clerk in a tea office. His father and mother are both dead; and his appearance and manners not much refined; indeed he seems more like a coarse rough sailor than anything else.

Maman bellemère has quite recovered from her illness and looks very well. Pem still looks a little bit delicate. They have been over walking themselves. I am very glad that Isabel has taken to the piano a little; I hope she will go on. *Damn* that fellow Sammy, not liking music, and making her neglect it.

Tuesday

I have delayed this a couple of days hoping to tell you more. I can only tell you that my health is improving every day, although I've been working as hard as in London, but fancy the difference of working when half your body isn't in your work—the drawing I've done is one of the best I ever did. In the evening we have a hard pull on the water, and go to bed early after a hearty supper and lots of beer.

I hope to remain till next Sunday—I will send you some drawings then.

How does my Aunt get on with her blocks? Give her my love and also to Isabel, and accept the same for your old self. I will always write even when I have no news, to prevent you from being uneasy—and this shall be the last unstamped letter as there are no stamps to be had at this hour, and I do not wish to delay this another day.

So adieu

Your ever most affectionate son
Kicky

91 Newman St.
[September, 1861]

My dear Mamma,

I have been a long time answering your last; for the last fortnight I've been all day long without a holiday, stooping over my blocks till my neck is so stiff I can scarcely look round. On Saturday I shall go out to Kew the whole day with Emma.

To-morrow morning I take in 2 large blocks for Punch and one large one for Good Words; the latter I'm afraid not very good, but I spent a week on it sweating like a nigger. Next week I have a drawing to do for O.A.W., and one for the Greek book. My tale and illustrations didn't appear yesterday or I should have sent them to you. You got last week's O.A.W. safe I suppose. My sketch of the artists and jew was immensely liked. On Wednesday last a Catholic priest called on me. They (the Catholics I mean) are getting up a tremendous historical periodical to be translated in 3 languages and appear in France, Belgium, Germany and England—full of small and large illustrations. He said the large illustrations (10 and 15 guineas a piece) would be chiefly intrusted to me and Lawless—I am to get one I believe to do next month. It is only in the germ yet, but if it succeeds, it will be a tremendous affair. He was on his way to Paris to negotiate with publishers there; he had lots of the small cuts already by German, English and French artists. O.A.W. is apparently quite fond of me once more; so you see my star is at present in the ascendant, but I'm not going to be over confident again.

Wasn't Fred Sandys's drawing exquisite? That was the poem that I illustrated, and which they refused on account of its being so elaborate—(Don't you recollect my writing to you about the muslin dress?) the source of my quarrel with O.A.W.

In the winter I shall write during the long evenings. T. A. was very much pleased with what I wrote for O.A.W., and advises me to stick hard at it, since he says I can do it—and this uniting of the two has never been done before except by Thackeray, who can't draw a damn, and Toppfer in Switzerland qui ne dessinait pas comme moi. I want to write about artists for I have met them and see them in a way different to anything that has been written before. But they all tell me to reserve that (it being a sort of pièce de resistance) for a book of my own publishing; being too good a subject to scatter in a periodical.

T. A. is gone back to Manchester, very unwell; so mind and write directly, Ardwick Place you know. He is all right again and wrote a sulky note; he was charmant the last few days; had made a wretched mull of his stay here, spent lots of money and did no good.

Tom Jeckell has just arrived; what a little lying snob he is! As soon as I can pay him I shall see much less of him.

Jimmy Whistler gone to Paris—bon débarras; j'en devenais las; nothing is more fatiguing than an egotistical wit. I told him about my Aunt's friend Campbell saying he was a scamp—"Campbell? don't recollect the fellow, I'm sure; I suppose he had some damned sisters or wives or something. . . ."

I must tell you a very funny thing he said to Rosa Major; at their theatrical, he wore her pork-pie hat (that was the evening that he got so drunk); afterwards it appears, Rosa M. found that somebody had spat in the hat and didn't wear it any more; and the other day she gave it to him, saying that he might have it as it had been spit in, and thinking that he would be much ashamed, but he took the hat quite delighted, and said:—"By jove, Miss Rosa, if that's the way things are to be obtained in your family I only regret I didn't spit in your hand!" (If Miss Rosa knew whose head her hat adorns at present, she would have kept it in spite of the spit).

Next Tuesday the W's go to Ramsgate; c'est moi qui va s'embêter alors; I shall work hard for a fortnight and then go there for a week and bring them back. They are kinder than ever; if I leave their home with a headache or stiff neck they come next day and bring one biscuits and things for lunch.

Mrs. Wightwick insists on rubbing my neck with eau de vie camphrée for the torticolo; I've a good mind to knock up and go there for the fun of being nursed. Barring a little fatigue however I am as well as possible.

91 Newman Street
19th century
[September, 1861]

My dearlie beloved Pem,

Your letter and my breakfast came in this morning—food for the body and food for the soul. I am very glad you are at a nice place and like it. I wish you were going to stay there instead of going to Ramsgate—and that I were coming to Ashford.

I will now tell you the news. When 'the gates of heaven were closed and you were gone' (Maud) I went straight to Pamphilon's on a yellow bus. The sunset was as you say splendid, but my sunset, darling, had taken place already, when your dear jolly fat face was nodding goodbyes out of the carriage window as the train went away. Poynter and Keene were there, and a friend of Poynter's, called Chapman; after dinner we all went to Poynter's who had just received 6 bottles of Macon one of which I finished to my own cheek, and got wery tipsy, wery—Nothing else could cure me of the fidgets. I sang the whole of my repertoire, and did the parting and goodbye songs so feelingly that I was encored—didn't get home till one. Next day Wednesday I worked at my OAW block but didn't get on very well with it—I can't work with spirit when you are such a deuce of a long way off. I was agreeably surprised by receiving a very civil note from my friends in Edinburgh enclosing a cheque for 4 guineas, and promising more work (they haven't even seen the drawing yet, but being a religious periodical you see my dear, they believe without seeing.) Bradbury and Evans haven't paid me yet but I shall go next Monday. I also received a hand proof of my sketch for the mining story which is to appear next week I believe. I went very late to dinner and spent a curious evening—Poynter, Chapman and I went to the Alhambra, and after hearing a lot of beastly music saw Léotard; what a splendid animal he is. On walking home after, just as we got to Newman St. we descried a terrific glare in the Eastern heaven, miss; so they left their money and watches in my room and we started off towards Waterloo Bridge. Crowds of cabs and people running in the direction; splendid night and about 1 o'clock. When we got on the bridge, the finest sight we *had ever* seen—the bridge was crowded; and the fire seemed in Ludgate Hill. (I hoped it was Holdrich). Fancy a jet black mass of old houses and wharves on the river, and behind a furious lot of flames, with red clouds above, a dark blue starlit sky beyond, against which St. Paul's stood out blazing in red light so that one could see every little detail of architecture quite sharp—and the whole reflected in the perfectly still water beneath, which was covered with sleeping black barges and things, dammit! Just like some of the opium-eater's dreams—Poynter and I almost mad. One wants an arm to squeeze with such a sight as that. Well, Miss, when we had feasted our eyes from W. Bridge we made a start for the city; and the view of the fire, when we got into Fleet St., was beyond anything in this world or out of it, and left an impression on me which I shall not forget till I cease to love you, darling.

There were all the houses up Ludgate Hill, seeming perfectly black for the fire was just beyond in Paternoster Row, St. Paul's lighted up in a haze which made it look 10 times its real size, and that pointy steeple at the top of

Ludgate Hill coming out quite black against the Cathedral. Mountains over mountains of black and blazing red architecture till one was nearly maddened with a sort of notion of eternity, for it seemed never to end, and playing over the whole a perfect orgy of bright gold dust and sparks and lighted steam from the engines—crowd swarming about like black weeds, ankle-deep in water, and a frightful looking fire engine worked by steam and making a terrific noise. We stayed there nearly an hour right in St. Paul's Churchyard. Sometimes the steam fire-engine would stop and the fire immediately gained a frightful ascendancy, then a fearful spluttering and hissing which made all the crowd heave to and fro (and tread on your Kicky's feet) announced that the hose was turned in a new direction and the engine at work again. I don't think it will have done very enormous damage, but the Insurance Companies may console themselves with the idea that London was treated to a rare sight. We walked homewards saturated with emotion (and with water and mud from the main plugs). That enthusiastic devil, Poynter, will be laid up from it, I reckon. We went and supped in the Haymarket, and drove home, dead beat—Don't you wish we had been together, O milk and wine and honey?

You want to know if I miss you? I am perfectly dépaysé without you; when you are away the wish comes to turn night into day, and tumble into old familiar habits (but I won't). This morning from last night's fatigue and late supper, I awoke with seedy eyes and weary back and parched mouth; doocid familiar sensation, yet seems quite forgotten; brought back all sorts of recollections which I hate with the whole strength of my affection for you, recollections of so many nights with Whistler and Tom A, and Tom J. and lots of fellows, years ago and even lately; and in which a great deal too much wine and smoke have been taken in, and too much wild talk let out, for happiness. So Miss Salvation (as T. J's friend, Watson, said) you had better *not* lose your nose or your life in a collision.

(Pem says: "What a *brute* he is!")

I have not heard from home yet, but expect a letter before the week is out. I am writing this today instead of tonight as at 3 o'clock Keene and I are going to Chiswick together, to his friend Stewart, who is newly married, and with whom he went to Devonshire.

Lawless has just been in; he has received an order for 10 small drawings from the Catholic priest, and I have quite demoralised the poor fellow by telling him that the Reverend old 19-inch-round-the-calf wasn't considered good pay.

I think I have now told you all the news I have; (except that I have dreamt of you two nights running, and all night). I think I am pretty sure to come down to Ramsgate; if they pay me for the MS (and they must) why, I'll come next week—end of next week, you know.

Write to me again directly, as your letters, although they are *not* spooney, are a great happiness to me. So write long ones to me, do you hear—deliver me from evil  and kiss my photograph as I kiss hers who left her photograph with me, for yours, darling is the power.... There, I'm getting very wicked again, and you will frown.

Give my very best love to Maman Bellemere, and kiss for me her aged venerable cheeks. Do you think you will stop till Tuesday? To see the chaw bacons guzzle in the High-street? (What part of the town are they to be sick in, after)? If you do you must describe to me the scene. Why don't you write longer letters to me, Tesoro? and write directly; why don't you write as much as you talk, you chattering Rahat-Lakoum?

Adieu my darling of darlings, I kiss you many times with all my heart.

Your ever deeply affectionate

Kicky

Doocid sight better fun writing you than drawing for O.A.W.! Heigho—à l'ouvrage!—but first of all, a cigarette and a little more folding of the hands to think of you, Pemmina.

Wednesday morning
[September, 1861]

My dearest Pemina,

The beloved envelope with my name in your jolly old fist outside made its appearance at the usual time. I am very sorry to hear that you have been suffering from toothache, and hope that it is over now; I trust it is not so bad as it has been sometimes, and that the decay in the tooth is not making any progress.

I shall not be able to come to Ramsgate on Tuesday as I have engagements up to that day; indeed I have not received my money yet. I am to get some of it today I believe and perhaps the rest next week early; if so I will come on Wednesday, and will call on Douglas beforehand.

I have no very particular news to write; not heard from home yet. On Sunday I went to Kew; got there at 3; all the men had gone out; found Mrs. Bell and Miss Poynter at home and took them a long walk to Richmond and back in time for dinner, which passed off very jollily. I got very tipsy on Beaujolais which is an insidious Burgundy; there was no music, and we left early (George Bell and I) to catch the 10 o'clock train in which I fell fast asleep. When I got home I read Vanity Fair for two hours (as I have been doing every night in fact) and finished it last night. Every time I shut the book and put out the light I have a frightfully spooney fit on you, and love you with all my heart and soul, thinking what a trump you are. You may flatter yourself that you *are* appreciated, young lady; and although I haven't seen you for six months at least (so it seems to me) every day binds me closer and closer to you. Your absence teaches me how necessary you are to me, you Pem.

I should like you to read that Book of Books over again, as carefully as I have just done, and if you don't finish it a wiser woman than you began, I'll be demnitioned.

I spent Monday evening at Poynter's chatting. Yesterday

we all sat at Pamphilon's with Marks who is come back; I spend the evening with him on Tuesday. Saturday I am going to a supper party at a fellow called Leigh, in Furnival's Inn, to meet Morten, Thornbury, Dutton Cook and some others. I'm sure I don't know where I shall spend next Sunday.

Morten and I are getting very thick; he is a very stunning fellow; he has just lost his favourite sister, poor fellow, and is very blue about it; so should I be I suppose.

This fellow Leigh, where I went with Morten last night, seems to me rather a demned cad, but he knows lots of very nice fellows, it appears.

My tale does not come out today, so you will be disappointed; en revanche I believe there is a large drawing in Punch by me, a proof of which I saw (very badly engraved) at Swain's on Monday. I took in my last OAW block and have not had it sent back to me as yet.

I am going to do two more; that one of the coachman saying "Wo-ho" to the blanc-mange; and do you recollect at Robin's party that charming little mistake you made about your invitation card? I shall do that, but think it very likely that old Mark won't have it.

I daresay T. J. will be up by the end of the week—quel régal; I suppose we shall see lots of each other.

Je t'ai maintenant tout dit, ma grande-et-belle-et-bonne. I shall now write a few words home as I am anxious about them; I suppose you have not heard either; what the deuce can it be?

Shall I have a letter on Friday morning? And tell me how long you will remain in Ramsgate. I might be there now for the good I am doing here; but am pretty sure about Wednesday; will write about the room you are to take for me. Give my kindest love to Maman Bellemère, and make civil speeches for me to the C's and B's; I hope Clarke is not going with you to Dover. I don't think you miss me *very* much, do you darling?

How do you like the sketch? ain't it spiff? Lucky LUCKY girl!

With many affectionate kisses, and hoping to see you, soon, my dearest Pem,

Your every dutiful

Kicky

Je t'aime un peu, passionément et encore plus. (In the sketch it's a *hat* I've got on my head; not a *halo*).

Friday
[September, 1861]

My darling Pem,

I am very much distressed to hear that you have been suffering so much from your teeth, and that you have had to go through such a painful operation. Thank God it is a back tooth; pray have your back teeth stopped in spite of the pain; of course gold is the proper thing; if you don't I fear the decay would make rapid progress in such delicate little fangs as yours. Deuced glad to hear about the front ones, but do you think the dentist is a clever and trustworthy sort of fellow? I want those beautiful little jewels (my property) to last as long as my fondness for the mouth that holds them; (which it's not in the nature of phosphate of lime and enamel to do).

I have not received my wages for the tale; but as I have swindled my old landlady for a while I shall be able to come on Wednesday. If I can get Marks to make it Monday evening, I will come Tuesday, but won't promise. We'll have a jolly week together; as for the evenings I will make myself so fascinating to snowy Susannah that you shall suffer pangs of the bitterest jealousy, and her gentle bosom shall thrill with hopes never to be fulfilled (unless you run away with the dentist opposite).

I wish I could say that my time has been well employed, but I *really* can't work when I'm not going to spend the evening with you; everything I do is out of drawing and stupid and the tale I have been trying to write won't do at all. How can you ask if I miss you, you beloved old stoopid? I loaf about with the fellows talking shop till ten or 11 and then read Thackeray nearly all night and smoke like a factory flue. I'm now reading Pendennis over again and wonder at the end of every chapter which I'm most in love with, Thackeray or you (of course the affection for T. is rather more Platonic).

On Wednesday I went to Mark Lemon but he was not to be found; I go again today; and hope he will let me do the things.

No news from home yet—very fidgetty about it—I wrote on Wednesday; my Mother was never so remiss before.

I wonder if she and Georgie Clarke have had a fight. If it comes to blows I'll back the maternal.

I've positively no news to tell you, except that Morten, Keene and Poynter are doocid fine fellows, an observation which Susannah would probably censure as being tautological. Last night for a little fresh air I went and roamed about the Old Places; Torrington Square and company, like a sentimental young poet who has lost his guiding star and loves to haunt the places sacred to her memory (singing willow, willow, willow) which is wery spooney and ridiculous; but see, my dear, I am of a speculative turn of mind, and an incorrigible fondness for old associations is the characteristic of my illustrious family. I began again in memory all our little innocent school flirtation, and lived through seven years between the smoke of two cigarettes; what lots to write about, and how I *will* write about it someday![1] The result of which hunting after shadows is the fit of deep and passionate spoonification for my beloved

[1]And he did. In his third novel, *The Martian*.

old Pem, which I felt on returning home—and the wery stunning sketches with which I have adorned this letter. If I could only draw for Punch as well as I can for you! hein ma chère? J'espère que tu apprécies.

I have nothing more to say, except the *tautological* thing; that you seem to get on pretty well without me etc. and that your affection for me is of the quiet and sensible order etc. and that I wish it wasn't—so in another 5 days darling; will they appear long to you?

It is quite unprecedented, and altogether improper and against the received order of things, that the male should suffer the most from absence; but I am very much inclined to think it is so with us.

Give my best love to Maman Bellemère and the compliments of the season to 'mong cousang'.

Adieu chérie; your too much attached and ever affectionate

Kick

I must have a letter on Monday morning, do you hear, Pem.

[September, 1861]

My dearest Pem,

I have just received your dear letter—you paint a most discouraging picture—in spite of which I am so overjoyed to think that I shall see you to-morrow that I don't know what to do with myself. I *can't* exist any longer without you, *my love*.

I've been perfectly miserable, and if it were only to see you once a day, and if Ramsgate were 10 times worse than it is, I think I would rather *walk* there, in dress boots, or à quatre pattes than be another day without seeing you. I am going to Mark's tonight and shall take the boat to-morrow morning (Tuesday); shall I see your fat face waiting for me, you big and bony object of K's adoration and worship?

Any room will do for me, if possible near you; 7 bob is capital; where can I grub? Get me a room to-morrow, unless darling, your poor teeth were giving you pain, and then don't trouble yourself, as I should find a room in 20 minutes.

I hope for the sake of appearances I shall be able to restrain myself from going down on my knees to you on the pier, or performing a war dance.

I hope I shall get a letter from home today, or else I really shan't know what to make of it.

I went to Leigh's supper party on Saturday and stayed till 4 o'clock; it was pretty jolly until they all got very drunk; Marks would insist on putting the gloves on with me, and I was victimised by my own heroic kindness in not hitting an unscientific man, for he made a most terrific onslaught on me when my head was jammed in the corner, and reduced my nose to such a jelly that I daren't blow it. I didn't get drunk for a wonder.

Yesterday Jeckell came to town and fetched me off to dinner. He was quite nice yesterday and we really spent rather a pleasant evening.

On Saturday after dinner I went to Grosvenor St. (having also called on Douglas who wasn't at home). The Governor and D were dining together; D won't come to Ramsgate. He has given me cigars, and came yesterday and spent a couple of hours chatting. They went to Mellons after. I shall bring down a block or two. I've done the girl with the invitation card and will send it in today. Will it really make you happy to see me? O my dear, *dear* Pem, this separation has shewn me how impossible it is to live without you; I am sometimes really quite in a funk when I think how thoroughly I have made myself dependent on you for happiness and everything.

Who do you think I fraternised with the other day? the *trident*, such an odd little fellow—M. Lemon introduced us and he was very civil, as indeed he ought to be. They gave me a cheque for seven guineas on Saturday; exactly what I thought, you see. I wonder if there are any sketches I shall pick up at Ramsgate. Old M. L. was very jolly, took me in a cab to Whitefriars.

I shall not bring you your slippers darling as I should rather choose them with you when we come back together.

Now my pet I shall go and post this; à demain; I feel so jolly. In fact you must forgive me for saying that I feel d—— glad, for really no other expression conveys satisfactorily to my mind what I feel. Kiss Madre for me, and believe me my darling, my love of loves

Your deeply attached

Kicky

I don't care about a shilling or two for the room but would like it near you. Anything from 7 to 12 bob. Don't care how small. Can leave my legs outside, you know.

[September, 1861]

My dear Mamma,

I have just returned from Ramsgate where I spent a week; your letter came the day before I left—I was getting very anxious indeed—Tu me racontes des horreurs à propos de notre gentilissima vedova, et je regrette tout autant que toi . . . mais enfin il est trop tard.

I am dreadfully sorry about poor old L.[1] I suppose that by this time it is quite settled one way or the other. If it is the bad way, of course it is a horrid thing for the girls, except that they will stand a much better chance of marrying among their own people in England—at least I should fancy so.

I am writing this today as I shall have lots of work to begin to-morrow and I shan't have a minute, otherwise I would rather have written to you Monday. I suppose you got the OAW with my story (which I find is very much admired) and the Spectator which I sent because it mentioned my name. I have just got the next number, about which I was very anxious, fearing they might pitch into me, but

[1]Mr. Lewis, father of Louisa and Isabella Lewis.

they have paid me such a handsome compliment, considering the severe nature of the article, and the very short time I have been drawing for Punch, that my interests with that periodical will receive a great push forward. Nobody but myself out of the *staff* is mentioned except Julian Portch who has been drawing for years for them, et tu vois qu'on n'a pas dit grand chose; as for Bellew, Haden, Lawless e tutti quanti not even a mention. I will send you the paper to-morrow after I have shown it about a little.

I shall soon be able to send you a little money, I hope; I have paid about 10 or 12£ of very pressing debts; the Ramsgate trip cost barely anything, or I should not have been able to go. 10sh. for my room and fed by the Caughts who were very kind in their peculiar way—went by the boat, 5 bob. I got very seedy before going, and would have liked to spend a month in the splendid sea-air. It was too much for me in such a short time and brought on inflammation of the bowels from which I have almost recovered.

That naughty Isabel hasn't written to Emma, to whom I am getting more and more attached every day; we were together walking about all day, wet or fine, in Ramsgate, and I was dooced happy in spite of gripes in the stomach, anxiety, two Caughts and many cares. The last night I spent in Ramsgate I slept with one of Emma's flannel petticoats on my stomach. Oh maternal, whose youth was fed on the rhymes of Byron and the romances of Walter Scott, see how the world is improving, and take me, my passionate love, and the flannel petticoat as a combined type of the practical spirit of the age. Would you have lent your under-raiment to my father before you were Madame la Comtesse, or advised your admirer Graham, who read Rob Roy to you, to take some tincture of rhubarb before going to bed? May Isabel soon have occasion to lend one of her flannel petticoats (if she happens to have two) to a man who will love her as much as I love Emma!—and may his means permit him to reward her by always keeping her underclothed in flannel of the best quality, since you say flannel is necessary to the moistness of her constitution.

The reason why I should have wished to write Monday is that I am going to try and humbug Lucas to give me the illustrating of a serial which is coming out in OAW, and shall not know till then. I have to begin one illustration for him to-morrow; two for Punch, two for a Greek book and so on. Tu vois que ça marche—J'espère bien t'envoyer du pécus bientôt; Comptes-y, à moins qu'il ne m'arrive malheur. If nothing wrong happens to me, there is every probability that by this time next year you and Isabel will be over here, and I shall be married.

I hope you have written to T. A. Never be so long without writing to me again, as I always fancy that you have tumbled down those dangerous stairs at No. 16 and in your present state that is not exactly to be desired; and if anything happens to you, I would much rather you should let me know—and always long letters please; your last was delightful.

This winter I intend to write very hard in the evenings (Emma amanuensis) having several subjects—and they must be well and carefully done. The last tale with the two illustrations was eleven guineas; if it had been the Cornhill, I should have got 5 and twenty for it; and I intend to aim at the Cornhill soon. My mind is always absorbed in these things now, and I should be writing a great deal but that I wish every thing to be perfect in its way. Best love to Isabel, and my Aunt and Bobbie, and now my dear Mamma take care of your old but beloved carcase, and write soon to your ever affectionate son,

K

Tuesday
[September, 1861]

My dear Tom,

I am very much delighted to get your jolly letter—je ne m'attendais pas à pareille bonne fortune, for I thought that you thought that I thought that because I was virtuous there should be no more pastry & beer—Nay damn it, ginger shall be hot i' the mouth. I am very sorry to hear of these relapses which must be a wretched bore—alas that ill-fated Sunday, that underhung devil!

First the bad news; you will be very much shocked to hear that poor old Lewis is dead; his daughters are probably here by this time at their uncle's in Chester Square; the General & his wife & old L's lawyer were in Heidelberg when he died. It seems a dreadful thing for the girls, and I can hardly realise his death, he was so healthy & sound-looking for his age. The girls I fancy will stand a much better chance of marrying at their uncle's in England. I cannot call very well, for they have never mentioned my name in their letters to my sister, always pointedly enquiring after you to mark the difference. I'm damned sorry for dear old L with whom we used to be so intimate; and would much like to write or call & express my sympathy—and I think it a very childish idea in them to make a mountain out of a molehill & cook up nothing at all into a case of Oh no we never mention him, as if I were a scoundrel & what not. Do you think *you* might write? (I swear I never said a word to L. beyond what I told my mother & you at the time).

No particular news from Dusseldorf. I should think that great politeness & forbearance were the order of the day between my aunt & mother & sister, the cause of difference being chronic & their barely possessing an idea in common. Very glad to hear you are working hard; it must be a very important order which would bind you for a year. Is there any chance of your coming up in the winter—I suppose not.

Much pleased you liked my last Punch; there were two articles on 'Punch art' in the Spectator (2 numbers) about 3 weeks ago, splendidly understood I think as far as Leech, Keene & Tenniel go—by a fellow calling himself Dry-point—on dirait que la parole lui a été donnée pour exprimer notre pensée. The second article (on Tenniel & Keene) winds up with a regular shut up for the trident (Howard) and a very pretty compliment to me, speaking of my rapid progress & 'gentlemanly feeling' and saying Punch will find a great acquisition in Mr. du Maurier—I fancy this will do me much good, and have Punch ideas by the dozen. There are several things coming out of mine in O A W, the next one (M. the Governor) is very bad—but I have just done one for a serial in three numbers, the best I have done yet; Keene quite delighted with it. The other day the illutrated Times sent me a block & a sketch from Japan to make a picture out of; I did it in a day; if they like it it will be a regular fund and leave me time to do more serious work. Once a Week is very nuts on me just now—pourvu que ça dure. They complimented me very highly on my literary labours the other day, stating that I was the fortunate possessor of genuine humour—pourvu que ça dure. Not that I intend to write for some time.

I enjoyed my trip to Ramsgate immensely. Tout entier au bonheur d'être probablement père dans cinq ou six ans d'ici, I didn't do a single sketch—en revanche, been working like a nigger ever since I've been back. The Caughts were of a hospitality, fallait voir! Poor chaste little Suzannah whom you used very irreverentially, & with more feeling for form than colour, to call an earwig, has risen in my estimation to the rank of a mammal (or rather of one who was once a mammal). I also regret that you did not congratulate Emma, for truly that maiden reverenceth my friends (with a few restrictions towards Jimmy & a slight exception in favour of T. Jeckell). Shall I inform thee, O sarcastic one, that my attachment is even as the snowball, increasing & increasing, and that I wonder daily at anything so pure, honest, conscientious & affectionate, & so much 'Beyond mine old belief in womanhood—'

Kick

[October, 1861]

My dear Matera,

Je profite de quelques instants which the printer's devil gives me to have a chat with you; and it is so long since I have that it seems quite a rare treat to me to do so. You mustn't think it's from neglect, for very often while I am stewing over a block which ought to engross every thought, my hands and pipe are at No. 91 here, and my immortal soul is keeping you and Isabel company, and making itself deuced entertaining.

I must now tell you that my affairs are just now in the most flourishing condition. This month's work will enable me to pay all my debts, I guess, over my month's expenses (my debts amount to about 20£). I only hope next month will be equally profitable, and the proceeds will be honourably handed over to your ladyship.

Il ne faut jurer de rien, but I must say that prospects at present look most healthy. The civility I meet with at the OAW office is almost painful. I was there yesterday; took them in a most stunning drawing; the day before they had written to me to do them a drawing in a hurry about French sea-bathing. I went there, as I said, yesterday, and asked if I might do it on a page block, which was granted; quel honneur, hein! Besides which they said that there was plenty more work for me when it was done; they complimented me very much on my tale and said I possessed the peculiarity of genuine humour. This bathing scene for which I expect the block now (Thursday) will be done on Saturday; 5£. This month I shall have made from 30 to 35£. The other day the Illustrated Times sent me a large block to do in a hurry, giving me 2 days. I did it in 6 hours; only three pounds, but that pays for it is coarse, rapid work done anyhow; I will send it you.

Ainsi tu vois, old lady, that if I have only the decent luck I seem entitled to, there will be enough and to spare to fetch your dry old carcase and Isabel's moist young ditto over here before next April, and to marry Emma in the Summer. Mais comme j'ai dit il ne faut jurer de rien; the better I get on now, the more nervous I get about my luck. But I work hard and let no chances slip. I think of nothing but work, Emma, and my most unworthy mother and sister; and can find not the slightest pleasure or excitement beyond this limited circle of cogitation. As for that already mentioned young person, Emma, my affection for her is getting beyond all bounds; I'm always in a funk lest anything should happen to her. The other night they had a gas explosion, and Emma was so frightened that she was ill after, but their escape was what is called providential. Mrs. W. and I sometimes have little tiffs in which she is always in the wrong and next day she writes me a humble apology which is great fun; she is very proud of the beaufils, but gets into the most awful rages against him, being jealous of her daughter, of course.

Mrs. W. "There, Kicky, you know very well that if your lordship chose to wash your feet here in the breakfast room, Emma would say you did right, and go down on her knees with the towel; I'm nobody, now, nobody, nobod-bo-boooo . . . ! !"

The other day I had a letter from my friend Capt. Aidé, complimenting me on my literary production, and telling me that he'd been stopping at Warnford Park, with the Tunnos, that Mrs. Tunno had been speaking most tenderly of me and intends to ask me down there soon. Zut! I met the Tunnos in Grafsrath; Best introduced me. Some great author says (either Goethe or Balzac, or Shakespeare, or the Bible); an artist ought to be *able to go* in the very best society; but he oughtn't to *go* into any society at all.

I had also a most charming letter from my Lord of Ardwick Place, all smiles and good humour again; I hope you and Isabel don't neglect him. I am much interested in the little flirtation between the nobby Sam and Is. Is Is. really smitten? but I suppose there is no chance on account of Sam's rather slender prospects and unconscionable Mamma; otherwise je serais fier de mon beaufrère (comme je le suis de sa femme); of course I should like Isabel to marry; but am quite selfish enough to console myself with the idea that if she doesn't the future home of Sir K du M. R.A. will receive a desired pleasant addition to the fun, ornament and comfort thereof—and marriage without deep affection is the most questionable of all institutions, as I perceive every day and everywhere.

I am so delighted to hear about Best's eyes; he's such a good fellow, and has been so patient. I wrote to Tom about poor old L; he will be very pleased at Isabel's sending the photo. It certainly is very foolish of the girls not to mention me; makes it awkward if I should meet them, and so forth; one would think I was quite a tragedy villain.

The tracing of my Aunt's sketch was most delightful; she is a foolish little lady not to cultivate so great a gift of God, which properly trained would make her plenty of money and a stunning name; look at Mrs. Blackburn, who has monopolized the large page of Good Words, and is deucedly well paid for it too and courted much more for her talent than she ever could be for the title she possesses in common with some 2 or 500 other ladies. My Aunt has quite as good a chance as I have, she is only less advanced.

I must now finish this scrawl, for the block has been here (so large and inviting) for nearly half an hour, and the days are short and I have only three. There's nothing like a week's work to make one appreciate a Holiday. Last Saturday I went with Emma to the Chrystal Palace concert (old Lourdes gave me a season ticket you know). Tell Isabel, to make her miserable, that her pets Giuglini and Tietjens sang the gems of Don Giovanni and then the gems of Martha—and that E. and I were in a blessed state of crackedom the whole while. Do you recollect in Malines Isabel writing to us that the two finest things in the world were Giuglini's voice and Jessy's shoulders? I guess Jessie's shoulders have deteriorated now, she writes most miserable letters from Fattygycabalabad, or wherever she is. What dreadful things hasty matches are; Charlotte is in Edinburgh breaking her heart, at least what she has of it, for the brother is going to make some odd sort of a marriage it appears, and has sent Charlotte and his dying mother to winter in Edinburgh, a nice warm place for an old invalid. What a peerless beauty this big good-natured Charlotte is, a goddess, a Venus of Milo, as Henley says. Henley is in Yorkshire, Jimmy in the côtes du nord; and now old lady, addio for the present.

I hope we shall soon be all reunited, and your dutiful son hopes to surround the white-haired period of your existence with all the charms of good English fare, good books and reviews, no end of newspapers, clever society of nice men, and as much of his own amiable and facetious society as his arduous avocations will permit. He also promises you, (which seems rather premature), a blessed immunity from all babies bearing his name, as the same shall be confined to the nursery, and only exhibited in their best clothes and best behaviour, he having wisely reflected that you have had enough of that sort of thing. He mentions the white-haired period of your existence as it is his particular wish that you should overcome your prejudices to that style of coiffure and allow nature to have its own way; being ambitious to have a stunning white-haired old mother like Aidé, and all artists being fond of white hair etc.

To speak in a less facetious style, you must know, old lady, that the thought of your being made jolly at last after such a lot of trouble, comes before everything else, as soon as I get into a prosperous vein like this. We'll forget Malines, damn it, and all that came before and after.

So write me a jolly long letter, and give my love to Aunt and Bobbie. Don't fret yourself about Eugène; I shall soon be able to send him something I hope—tell Isabel to write also, and believe me

Your very affectionate son

Kicky

Thursday

[October, 1861]

My dear Mamma,

I have been preventing Emma from writing from day to day, intending always to write next day myself, but have constantly been prevented by heavy pressure of work upon me just now. For a whole week I have been concocting one drawing for OAW, and it is not finished yet.

I was very sorry to hear of poor Bob's attack of smallpox, and can well fancy the state of alarm you must all have been in about it. I hope none of you have knocked up from the fatigue and worry. Will he be marked at all?

All is going on well here; I have plenty of work just now, but am taking such pains that I do not get through it quickly. Have recourse to nature for everything, and spend 4 or 5 days over a drawing which a year ago I should have done in 8 or 10 hours. Indeed I seem to be in a great vein of progress, and hope soon to get a place in front of the first rank; you can have no idea of the passion and anxiety with which I work and the labour I bestow; and now I am settling down into an ardent plodding and patient drawing machine so that I must soon become first rate. In so doing I follow the advice of Sandys who told me never to let a block go out of my hands unless I was well satisfied that all that patience, time and model could do for it had been done. It does not pay one so well at first as quick drawing from chic but in the end one can command any amount of work and any price one likes. I have hopes of getting on to the Cornhill. I have not sent you Once a Week and Punch as you see them there. I will send you my kettle-drum which has been much praised both by artist critics and newspapers. I am also taking very great care of my health; Hampton Court did me wonderful good, and I hope soon to be living there with Pem. I used to have a good couple of hours row every day and was soon quite a new man, and besides the quality of my work was better.

Such a difference between working with one's face out in the glorious park and stewing away at 91 Newman Street!

I have no very particular news to tell you, having seen you so lately; Tom has just written enclosing a letter to the Miss Lewises, about their father, which he sends me not knowing their address. I shall forward to the general. I took the liberty to open it and read it—it is a very nice letter—he does not speak of my marriage, but states that you must be much pleased and elated at having a son who has so nobly breasted difficulty after difficulty and is on a fair way of soon sailing serenely. There, Madam, I hope you appreciate that son properly.

Gyggy has written, I will try and find his letter. He is going to exchange and join his former regiment in the south of France; he had a little before written for a 100 francs, saying that he could not make up his mind to part with his swell habit bourgeois, which he prefers leaving with Aunt Louisa. I wrote back that he had better sell them immediately for the 100 francs, as I should have to sell mine which were not worth fifty to send that sum. You see his answer—the sketches are very clever, so much so that I believe them not original; the fellow picking up a cigar shows a certain knowledge of effect that he never exhibited in any sketch before. If they are his he might certainly hope someday to prevent himself from starving by his pencil.

I am very anxious to hear from you, so please write soon; in your letter to Pem you said you were going to write me directly. I do hope Isabel will go on with her piano, and that she will try to occupy herself and improve the shining hour a little more than she does; when the taste for work *does* come to the idle after long and wearying efforts, there is no passion so absorbing or that repays so fully for the struggle to be gone through. Does my Aunt continue to draw?

So now my dear Mamma, with very best love

Your ever affectionate Son

[October, 1861]

My dear Tom,

Got your letter, sent enclosed to 74 Chester Square, General Lewis's, to be forwarded. Thanks for the phot. which has gone to enrich our album in Grosvenor St. It is very nice and elegant, but don't you think the top light, leaving dark shadows under the eyebrow, is hardly becoming to a female face; for instance I think it adds nearly 5 years to your sister's apparent age; otherwise I think it is charming. I send you one of Emma, the best I think which has been taken—although a little bit amenable to the same criticism as your sister's. I am very glad to hear your troubles & anxieties are clearing up, and would like to know what has come of them—no hurry about the tin.

I have been working awfully hard for OAW; have got a Sandys subject in hand; Norse ballad; c'est bigrement difficile, and I never appreciated till now the full extent of Sandys' marvellous power of execution, but think it a thing to be acquired. Oh for the physical strength to work 10 or 12 hours a day like Sandys and not suffer; I have been rather overdoing it, and feel queerish. How do you like my serial in Once a Week; the last 2 were done in Hampton Court, every bit from nature, and have been pretty well liked; Walker said the last, yesterday's, was the best I had ever done. I have also just finished a dozen initials for Punch, and hope soon to have something to do for the Cornhill. There seems no lack of work just now, but I seem to be spending almost too much time over it; however, as Sandys says, that will all pay in the end; and I find myself when I have just finished a careful block, and it is too late to alter, that I just then understand the way it *ought* to have been done, and that is autant d'acquis for the future.

Poynter has been working for Once a Week, and the next serial in two numbers is illustrated by him; he is too elaborate for social subjects I think; tu verras; I have only seen the first.

There seems to be a splendid opportunity now of carrying out your idea of a club, et voici comment. At 14 Berners St. (Morgan's) there is a school of cookery, and the result is at six o'clock the most marvellous dinner for 2 shillings that anybody ever heard of; soup, several entrees, roast, and dessert that I am sure could not be had anywhere under 15/. So that all the fellows have deserted Pamphilon's and dine there; and after dinner, coffee, pipes & piano in Morgan's studio. I am still faithful to Pamphilon's which is beastly lonely now, but the fact is that 2 bob however cheap for the food is more than I care to give every day for grub, so I dine there once or twice a week; and press the club question hard. It is awfully jolly there I must say; too good to last I am afraid.

I am going today to call on Mason the American, on behalf of poor Turner who has been and is still in a most awful way, from the supplies having been cut off by the war. He is going to send some pictures to Morgan's which reopens on the first of December; can you fancy a fellow without the sou in Dusseldorf, et le malheureux avec une maîtresse et un enfant par-dessus le marché! (this latter fact must not be communicated to Mason).

Poor little Bobbie Clarke has had the smallpox and they have been in an awful way; all the anxiety & responsibility seems in some way or other to have fallen on the maternal, who wrote to Emma that she had been thoroughly upset. I have just written.

Had a letter with some very funny sketches from quel cochon d'enfant, who is going to exchange into his old regiment the 8me. Chasseurs, and whose whereabouts whether Algiers, Mexico or the south of France seems undecided. I should scarcely have dared to tell this to my mother a year ago, but providence tempers the wind etc. and she has got not to believe a word he writes; I think he will tout bonnement remain in France.

I was very sorry not to find your other sister & brother-in-law when I called, and am grieved to hear of the sad misfortune that has befallen them; I suppose they are regularly upset by it. I was in Hampton Court and had no opportunity of thanking your brother-in-law for Darwin.

Now old fellow, hoping you will get on all right, and do good work, and with kind regards to Miss A.

Ever yours

K.

[December, 1861]

My very dear Mamma,

I think you are beginning to treat me shamefully; you know how I am always thinking of and wishing to hear from home, and you don't write. However fortunately Emma read me Isabel's letter.

As you see I send you a fiver; I've been deliberating whether I'd wait a day or two longer till my Punch account is paid, and send you two fivers; but I am afraid of Xmas bills, and will D.V. send you a tenner in January. I was much disgusted at Isabel not being able to go to the ball for want of a tarlatan (is that correctly spelt?) and do hope that henceforward she shall never want such a small luxury as that, only of course look out for squalls and contingencies as this may be only a temporary brightening up of the horizon. I am going to work hard and save, for I have bent my mind on having you over here before April, and marrying as soon as possible. I am mad to have you here and mad to be united to the fair Pem—Le jour de nos fiancailles, je fis un certain voeu intérieur que j'ai réligieusement observé; mais ce voeu me pèse. (This letter is for your private perusal.)

I hope you will not stint yourself in food; I *really* think you need have no more money anxieties. You must make up and send me a *correct estimate of what your debts would be about the beginning of April*, and what balance you will have in hand (*o*, I suppose) and Isabel must check your estimate, as I fear your spirit of nervousness and exaggeration of future evils—for all my efforts now until the spring will be to pay your debts, and journey, so that you will be able to start here without a penny less than the April dividend; tu comprends? And acknowledge the receipt of this by return, for although I shall register it, I funk the German postal authorities.

Now for the news. I have just had a letter from Gyggy which I enclose—and which I shall answer this week. I may be able to pay his debts some day but cannot think of saddling myself with such a task before my marriage. I had written to him about my marriage long ago; whether he is humbugging or whether the letter never reached him I can't tell—you will see that his letter does not seem redolent with veraciousness. I am working very hard and improving rapidly; I have done some famous things for Punch which I will send when they come out; have just returned from an early visit to London Bridge which I am to draw for a new Periodical (Britons going to business, 9 a.m.). I have done the cover for this Periodical which will appear every month from the 1st February under the name of London Society, and I shall probably have to bring out a series of these sketches for which I get 6 guineas a piece, but shall charge more if they are twigged. I am well with Once a Week, and also with two or 3 minor periodicals. Very well with Punch just now, but must recollect that Leech is hard at work on the almanack until the end of the year, when perhaps my drawings will not be quite so much wanted.

Lewis's evenings began on last Saturday night. I got there at 11 and was most stunningly received I must say; evidently my position has made great strides since last year. Leech to whom I was introduced treated me with marked civility, I thought, and the great Sandys and I did at last meet in the midst of celestial harmonies. I spent all Sunday morning with him and Prinsep, and he is going to give a dinner this week, the object of which is to unite artists and writers so as to have some influence on that ill-managed periodical, keep out weak and inefficient men and try and get the whole thing into the hands of a clique. Walker and I very thick; charming little fellow. I was in splendemious voice and sang a lot.

Emma will write all the minor news, as I have so little time to spare—I am getting to love Emma more dearly every day.

I've had no news from the Cornhill mag: and fear that no news is bad news. I'm now going to set hard at work for the rest of the day. Give my love to Aunt G and Bobbie and believe me

Your ever most affectionate son

Kicky

Tell Isabel she will not be so spoilt by my friends when she knows them, but the *quality* of the spoiling will be so exquisite if she gets any that it will make up for the wholesale offerings of the poor little German Princekins; and she will laugh as heartily at the young personage of royal blood 'hated by everybody for his haughtiness', as heartily as I did.

I am taking great care of my health and am just now so

fat about the gills and chin that Emma wants me to get photographed so as to send you a copy.

Unfortunately there seems to be no record of the MS. Kicky describes in the following letter to Tom Armstrong. There is no doubt that it was an embryo Trilby, *that was never published. Possibly it was put away, and forgotten, and thirty years later came to light again, to be turned into the novel that made him famous.*

[December, 1861]

My dear Tom,

I have just received your unkimmon jolly letter, which came however too late for the Destiny of my MS. to be influenced, for I took it yesterday to the Cornhill—24 pages of closely written foolscap, and yet I had eliminated lots. I had laid it by for 8 or 10 days, that the little crudities might suggest themselves to me on re-reading; by this process I cooked a lot of them into ripeness. Lamont is there as the wise and facetious Jerry, you as the bullnecked & sagacious Tim; the street is our Lady of the Bohemians. I shall idealise in the illustrations (if I get them to do), make us all bigger, and develop you into strong muscularity; having insisted on our physical prowess & muscular development—the natural antidotes to morbid Quartier-latin Romance—I shall be much surprised if it gets into the Cornhill. I took it there on Keene's and the other fellows' advice. OAW have told me *distinctly* that they are not jealous of their artists working for other periodicals since the number of OAW cuts has been reduced to 2. If this does succeed, I shall write lots more on the same theme, and try and embody the rather peculiar opinions of our set on art itself, and artists; and which I feel very strongly. I was yesterday at the OAW office where they were deuced kind and complimentary; gave me some subjects, and a serial of 3 or 4 numbers; so two short serials of mine will appear after Walker's. I was introduced to little Walker there; we fraternised most extensively, and took a long walk together

—a devilish charming natty and gentlemanly little swell—I had expected just the contrary from what fellows say. (Alas! a terrible rival!)

Strange you should mention London Society, the new monthly which according to its programme is to move & interest

The RANK, WEALTH, WIT AND BEAUTY
of the Capital!

The Dalziels sent to me to ask if I would do the cover, and bring out a series of sketches of London life—'course I will, what a question. The Frontispiece or cover is to be Rotten Row, and I begin it now, as well as the first London life scene, London Bridge at ½ past 9 A M—large block, to charge 6 guineas. They told me I should get lots more besides for Good Words who liked my last. Last Saturday had a call from M. Lemon, quel honneur (it is true I hailed him as he was passing my window in a Hansom cab, but that's neither here nor there). He took away the two blocks in yesterday's Punch and gave me carte blanche to do what I liked for Punch, if he might rub out on the block what didn't suit—hinting that if I would put the kicking straps on my *youthful* & *generally aggressive tendency*, I should be fit for the Punch staff before 20 years—Tu vois que je suis en veine of luck. I am also on a small monthly called Entertaining Things, and might get work from the Illustrated Times—Pourvu qu'ça dure, quoi!

My sister is not coming after all; for as I intended to do all in my power to bring them over before April, it would hardly be worth while for her to leave the old lady, who does *not* adore my aunt, with no other society; and the having her over here and fitting her out for 'London Society' at present would cost quite a small fortune. I am thinking that if you write to the Ls. it will give great & undue relief to the fact of my *not* writing, and write I can't—Enfin fais comme tu crois propre.

You are getting awfully desponding, old fellow; si tu étais amoureux, you would take quite a moral view of the 'dirt' you do not like to eat. I think your notion of writing capital, as the anti-dirt principles you stick to so strongly in practice are very much wanted in theory. I would second you bravely with my pen of light & humorous adventure; why not try a good virulent bullnecked article for one of the reviews, taking Frith's Derby Day for a text, and the 9000£ as an awful example? Isn't it beastly, brutal? I must say at the same time, that you seem to me to act rather too exclusively up to the other standard; some of the subjects you have mentioned to me as intending to paint would be decidedly popular, if you would only condescend to paint a pretty face, et je n'y vois pas de déshonneur, if it is well painted, and its beauty does not consist in a Solomonsy lie. I really believe that *mere female beauty* would actually make a well painted picture go down the swinish public throat, in spite of its artistic merit; indeed Millais is a very good instance. You don't seem to me somehow to get through enough work; I am afraid that the comforts of home . . . deliciae Capuae . . . eh? Your health I suppose is all right as you do not mention it. God save thee, old ram (battered, not battering), of the earth earthy, of the mud of the earth, muddy; and believe me thy virtuous & sincere

Kick

Bordel story very good; won't do for Punch as it pitches into bordel keepers, a large class of the community. Hope you will show up at Xmas old fellow; the after dinner pipe at Pamphilon's very jolly; Morten, Marks e tutti quanti, very stunning fellows. Bill come back handsome & jolly as ever.

Tuesday
91 Newman St.
[December, 1861]

My dear Mamma,

I received your letter last Saturday, you certainly do not spoil me; do Mammas leave off caring for their sons when somebody else takes an interest in them? besides which you seem to write out of spirits, I hope you are not ill or seedy

Isabel doesn't even send a message, I hope she did not take a wrong view of my objections to her coming; if she came she would I know be deuced glad to get back again.

There are several of my things in hand but none have yet come out and I doubt whether they will before Walker's serial is finished—I may then perchance get a long serial myself. I am just now a little bit en froid with OAW, they chose to take a dislike to my last drawing which was beautiful, but I trust that will soon blow over. Yesterday I finished a long MSS, the copying out of which alone took two days, such a good job finished and off my mind; tomorrow I intend invading the sacred precincts of the Cornhill Magazine with it—confronting the giant William Makespeare Thackeray—of course I am not very sanguine of success, and it is a mere spec; but *nothing venture*, etc. But if I succeed in getting it in, the good it will do me will be incalculable, and, with the illustrations it will bring me some 25£, a good fortnight's work. If they don't take it I don't suppose I shall have much trouble in disposing of it elsewhere, but it won't be the same thing either for money or reputation. Should the Cornhill take it, I have things of the same sort to write for a long time to come.

M. Lemon came to my room the other day; told me I was cruel and slightly improper in the nature of my wit, but hinted that I should be fit for the regular staff in time. I have lots of anxieties, being so desperate about getting on quick and well for all our sakes. Owing to the little contretemps with OAW, I don't think I shall be able to send you more than a fiver at the beginning of next month (unless the Cornhill, etc.) I might almost send you the 5£ now; but that I daren't leave myself with only a pound till the end of the month. I really do not think you need now be so anxious about money for I shall be indeed unlucky if I can't soon send plenty, but you are perhaps right not to be sanguine (I have had to buy shirts and unterkleide), and I can't conceive but what there will be quite enough for you and I. to come over before April, and assist Eugène into the bargain. Enfin nous verrons; I have no thought but work, and am always at it one way or another, but Rome wasn't built in a day.

I entertain fond hopes of being able to marry in the course of the summer or autumn, and that will make an immense difference in the quantity of work I shall be able to do, on account of the evenings; I can't work at the W's. and pass the evenings dictating to Emma, the father and mother wouldn't stand it, naturally enough, and my own eyes after a hard day's work require rest.

I am now always in bed before 12 and breakfast at 8 or half past; and it is gradually making an improvement in my health; besides which I take quinine; do you think quinine would suit Isabel? I think you might manage, 3 of you together, to get better food, if you were to try; for no real health is possible in the way you live. I eat devilish little but it is of the best—only one real meal a day, cost one shilling, the very best joint, and a glass of stout. Eyes all right; strange to say the veil on the left eye hasn't increased for a year; it used to take a jump every 3 months—not however that I have the slightest hope of ever recovering it.

About E's engraving. She and I went about enquiring. We saw a she engraver at Islington, and I saw several engravings; it is impracticable and I thought she had better give it up; I shall want her eyes for something else, and to make her so good an engraver that she should engrave my things in preference to Swain or Dalziel would require some 6 or 7 years, at it all day.

She is improving every day, and I could not now do without her at all; I'm a lucky fellow. The maman belle-mère is occasionally rather a bore; last night for instance she riled me so that I went away without saying goodnight, but she made it up by kindness a day or two after. I suppose it *is* disagreeable to see one's daughter care for somebody else more than one's self.

Henley has returned, with his accustomed jolliness; it is quite a club every evening at the smoking room after dinner, Morten, Marks, Keene, Smallfield, Poynter etc. This sort of society spoils one for any other. I have got to loathe swells

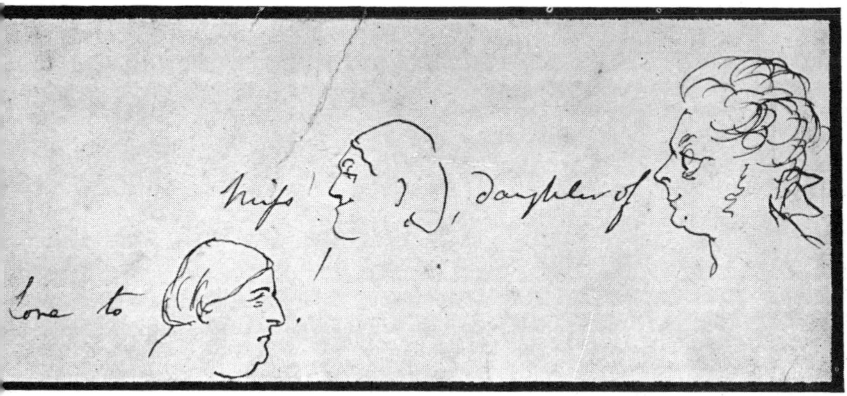

MISS WIGHTWICK AND HER PARENTS

From an envelope

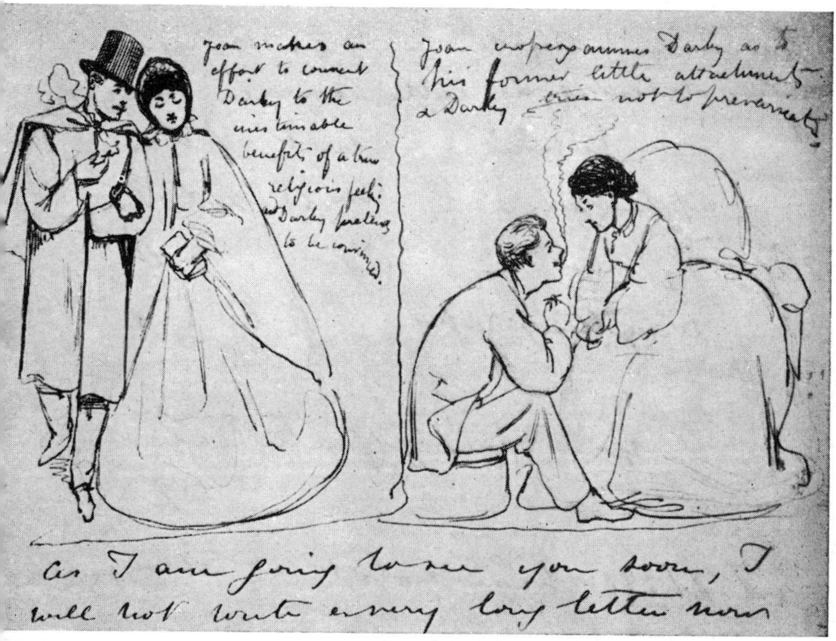

"DARBY & JOAN" (KICKY AND EMMA)

From the letter to Ellen du Maurier, p. 51

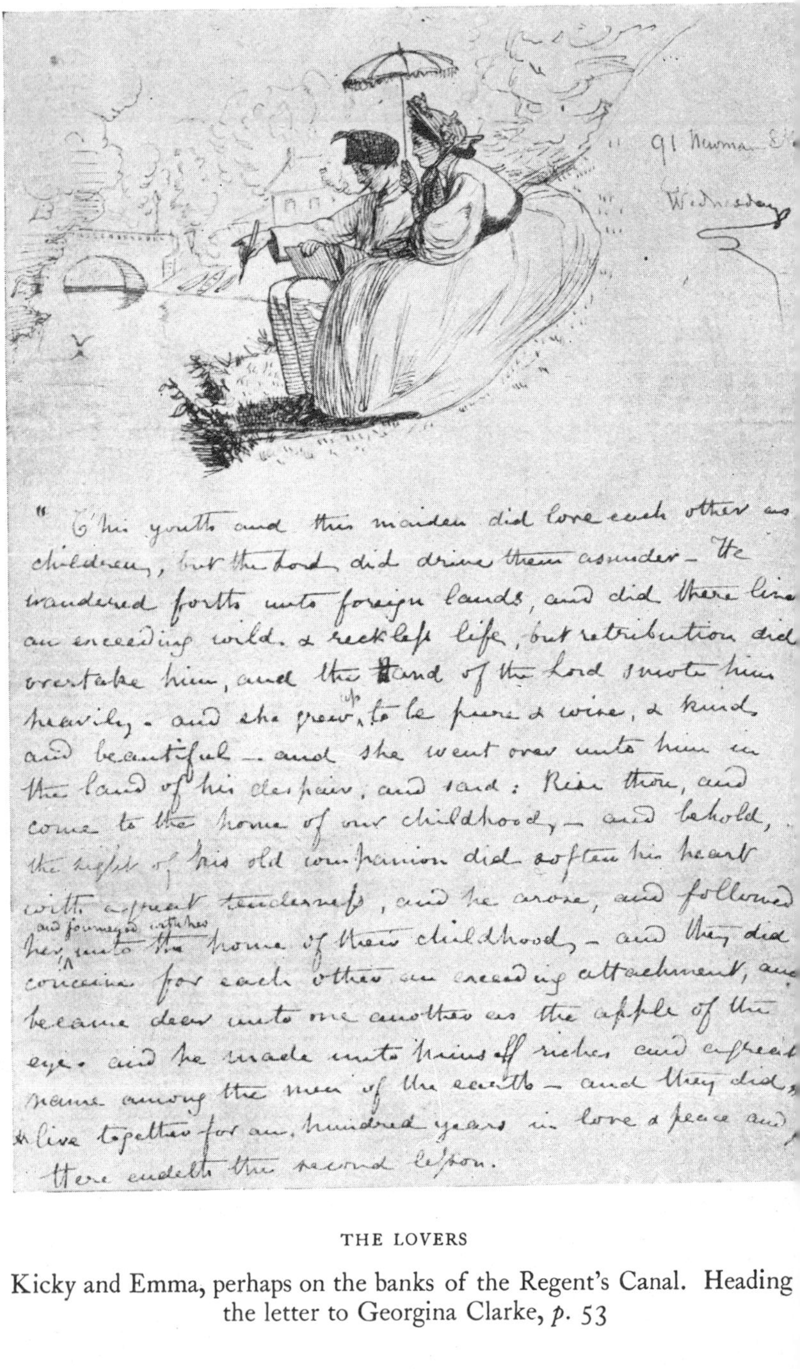

91 Newman St
Wednesday

"This youth and this maiden did love each other as children, but the Lord did drive them asunder — He wandered forth unto foreign lands, and did there live an exceeding wild & reckless life, but retribution did overtake him, and the Hand of the Lord smote him heavily — and she grew up to be pure & wise, & kind and beautiful — and she went over unto him in the land of his despair, and said: Rise thou, and come to the home of our childhood, — and behold, the sight of his old companion did soften his heart with a great tenderness, and he arose, and followed her, and journeyed with her unto the home of their childhood — and they did conceive for each other an exceeding attachment, and became dear unto one another as the apple of the eye. and he made unto himself riches and a great name among the men of the earth — and they did live together for an hundred years in love & peace and
Here endeth the second lesson.

THE LOVERS

Kicky and Emma, perhaps on the banks of the Regent's Canal. Heading the letter to Georgina Clarke, *p.* 53

almost as much as tradespeople. I had some very pressing invitations from the Tunnos (friends of Best) to go and meet the Fortescues; they wrote 3 times. How one changes; Mrs. F's Mayfair prattle about lady this etc. would almost revolt me. If I go anywhere else but among artists and their families or that sort of thing, I can't keep my good behaviour for more than an hour; the other morning at Jeckell's rooms I met a swell Hussar breakfasting with him, they almost made me spue, and I am going to put him in Punch. I shall try for the London News for Xmas; and send things to Punch regularly on the block, as I have given carte blanche to M. Lemon simply to rub out the drawing and send back the block if he dislikes them. He says to me: "A young fellow like you is always for pitching into somebody or something, but if you want to get on you must put the kicking straps on your dander and offend nobody"—Just like Beaumarchais's Figaro. *When* I am in the saddle won't I just offend a lot of people, that's all. That is if I ever do get in the saddle. I've now told you all the news. Don't leave me so long without writing; best love to all and believe me your ever thinking of you and affectionate son

K.

Just this instant got a note from Mr. Dalziel to go about some drawings, and must consequently cut in a hurry. I hope it will be a downright good expensive order.

[14 January, 1862]

My dearest Pem,

I've been painting hard all day and succeeding better than I expected—but terrible hard work and scratching out over and over again. Once a Week have sent me the poem, I'll bring it to-morrow—but what do you think, that pig of a fellow, Hogg, Jim, has written to say that he considers the London Bridge scene such a "shocking failure" that he is not going to publish it. You know it won't do for Editors to go about with such sentiments as this, and I think I shall make a fuss. Mad. Coronio has written to say that I'm to go—and I am now going. My darling, it is a wretched bore not to spend the evening with you as usual, for you are my habit, my hobby, my treasure more than ever.

Henley has just been and caught me painting—but won't mention it. Likes what I've done—

I'm afraid you've had a very bad day to go to London Bridge, (if you went).

I'm now going to dress and be off. Love to Susie. Think of me a great deal, and miss me—

I will come early to-morrow.

Your ever most affectionate and loving

K.

No news from home—cheque from OAW. 9£ 9.

I hope you've thought of me as much as I have of you.

[January, 1862]

My dear Tom,

Many thanks for your jolly letter and kind wishes, both from me & the future partner of my prosperity who doth also feel truly grateful at ye kynd remembrance. I had intended to write to you, but had been so hard worked up to the very last of the old year that I could neither write to you nor Düsseldorf—but do hereby wish a happy new year to yourself & all your circle. You do not say much about what you are doing, but I hope you are not idle. I wish you had been able to come here for a week, fancying sometimes you must feel the want of artistic entourage, which keeps the pot of enthusiasm boiling. I think you would much like to come to one of Lewis's[1] evenings & meet all the fellows; there have been already two, and Lewis has given me carte blanche to bring my friends. I must first tell you about them. The first Saturday was wonderfully jolly; and I fraternised with Leech & Sandys who were both deuced jolly; Sandys has just gone back to Norfolk but I saw a great deal of him, and never met a fellow who

[1]Arthur Lewis (no relation to the Lewis sisters of Dusseldorf) whose musical evenings were the talk of London.

took art in a better spirit. He showed me two crayon portraits he is doing, the finest things of the sort I ever saw, and as for his studies they are wonderful. If he has a patch of grass to do in a cut, an inch square, he makes a large and highly finished study from nature for it first; tu conçois qu'un gaillard pareil ira loin; he has work on hand for 2 years, after which he will go abroad. His painting tickles me not quite so much. Gave me lots of very good advice which I intend to follow. Walker too is always there, such a nice little fellow. Last time Millais was there, beautiful as a young God—Et verus incessu patuit, by jove. He went away directly after I got there so was not introduced. I have been fraternising extensively with Val Prinsep who next Sunday is going to take me off to little Holland house to see Watts. You can't fancy anything jollier than Lewises; as Marks says, the artists make a noble appearance there, & so they do; lots of professional glee singing & comic ditto (need I say that my Schuberts & Gordigianis meet with due appreciation?) The want of Jimmy is much felt.

Your opinion of my success is deuced flattering but I am afraid a little exaggerated. I don't feel somehow as if I had quite turned the corner yet; hélas! in the estimation of all here, I am nothing to little Walker, and by Jove I don't wonder at it for his execution is discouragingly perfect. Yet I feel somehow that if I could ever get to that perfection of pencilling, and exquisite rendering of texture, I have more go in me than he has, and a larger field of fancy. I needn't say that I work very hard, and do as much from nature as I can. Now and then I get an encouraging hint; for Madam Levain told me last week that Rossetti had been there and expressed himself to the effect that I was a "deuced clever fellow with lots of the right stuff etc." As far as the money making goes, I've been pretty lucky; on New Year's eve I sent in accounts for December 36£, 14; but am afraid I cannot always calculate on so much. You will chaff me about yesterday's drawing in O A W; more like than ever; but the fact is Walford came here on Xmas eve saying that whatever party I might be going to I must give it up &

work the whole night for them to do an extra cut for the Admiral's Daughter, to be ready next morning for engraving, and I made Emma & her mother sit and did it right off that evening. I will send you a proof in a week or two; have given the one you want to Emma, and can't induce her to part with it; but I've one coming soon of a girl playing the harp and will either send one or the other. Girl playing the harp for London Society (5£, 5); Poynter says best thing I've done. People seem to like my Punch drawings very much; did one the day before yesterday which I think the best I've done; don't know when it will be out, or if it's accepted yet.

The more I do, the more I want to do, and am looking forward to a life of the hardest and most devoted work, an endless succession of careful & improving blocks, I hope; I dream of creamy whites & silks & satins expressed with the 6 H point etc.

I've not heard *very* lately from home, and owe a letter; my mother in great spirits of course at my getting on so well, and my generous & dutiful donations. I want to get them over here before April if possible. Maternal always complains of the food; will take her twice a day for a month to St. James's Hall when she comes.

"Well done, Mar! it do my heart good to see yer feed so beautiful."
"Thank yer, Kick—I'm doing lovely!—"

Poynter is in Dover; he's been most frightfully hard up, but will come into some tin this month for his Eurydice. He & Morten great pals now. Marks comes a great deal to Pamphilon's, he is a very stunning fellow. Old Keene always there of course as usual, with his regular joint, College pudding, two pats of butter, glass of porter, coffee & 3 pipes; after which bonsoir la compagnie, nothing shall prevent him from going to his work at the Langham. Not seen much of the Greeks lately; Bill was there a little while ago, Madame Coronio and the fair Major as jolly as ever. Dined at the Bells'; Mrs. B. so fresh & pretty from the Pyrenees & in most splendacious voice.

I hope I shall be married this year; 200£ in bank is the amount fixed by ye stern parents before they dare to part with the light & joy of their whatshisname. It would be nugatory to observe, O cynic, that this woman groweth dearer & indespensabler to me every day, and that I must indeed be infatuated if she be not a most rare and delightful specimen for home-consumption.

They sent me back my MS from the Cornhill and I've offered it to OAW but fear it will be too long, not being divisible in two parts from the nature of the thing.

And now old fellow I have hurried together all the news I can think of, I will write the same home. I hope you will be up here in the Spring; meanwhile let us know what you're up to and don't be very long without writing again; I will send your proof soon.

Yours ever old fellow

K.

Had a visit from Polly quite innocent.

[January, 1862]

My dear Mamma,

I've not been able to find a minute to write or I should have answered sooner. Emma has probably explained in her letter to Isabel all about the way I have been pressed into work by OAW etc. I hope you liked the last specimens both Punch and OAW, which I sent you; I will send you the London Society drawings as soon as they come out, as they are very careful and form an important part of the last month's work.

In a week or two I will send you a 10£ note. None of my accounts have come in yet; altogether the last month has been the luckiest since I've been here; naturally very hard work and sticking at it. I find I can work much more than formerly, but hope soon to be able to do the same amount in much less time. Of course I pay very great attention to my health to enable my eye to bear the fatigue; it does its work nobly.

You seem not sanguine about coming over here in the Spring; I am afraid you are not fond of London, but am sure you would like it very much, and I think that with what you have and enough added to make 200£ a year (starting clear of course) you and Isabel would get on splendidly. If every month is as lucky as the last, there is no difficulty whatever, but I suppose I shall have ups and downs before I am quite in the saddle; sois tranquille carissima vecchia. My first thoughts will be to get you out of your fix as you call it, and I earnestly hope it will be done soon. I am going to try and get work for the London News which pays well and hope I shall succeed; I need not say that I don't spare myself and am never idle; I look forward to a life of very hard work, progress and quiet etc. and hope in time to make a very stunning name.

I think my position with Punch is improving and it certainly has much with Once a Week; but I do wish Editors knew something of art and were not capricious. The most important thing for me when once you are over here and all right is to get married. Your advice, Madam, won't do, I simply can't follow it. It is in the nature and constitution of your firstborn to be passionate and exclusive, and every woman but one is a gorilla; besides there are many other reasons too long to write about, but which you would very readily see the force of. I hope it will be in the Autumn; the sooner I found a home the better for Isabel as well as Emma and myself.

Do not any longer stint yourself and Isabel for grub and wine, as anyhow I think there will be no more necessity for such desperate pinching as that—and health before everything else.

Yesterday morning I received a very jolly letter from T. A. who seems to think I am all right now for ever; but I have a desperate rival of the name of Walker (who by the bye is a very charming little fellow with whom I am great chums). Isabel will be delighted with my friends when she comes over; je ne sais pas lequel lui servira de mari, par exemple, mais nous verrons.

My MS was refused by the Cornhill; embêtant, mais nous y serons un jour.[1]

The accounts I sent in for last month's work amounted to 36£ 14; If I could look upon that as an average I should be making 435£ a year, but daren't—I have many more expenses than I had, but am deuced economical I can tell you. Little bit in debt but not much.

The account you give of my Aunt is not conciliatory. Have you said anything about coming over in the Spring to her; and does she entertain notions of living together with you and Isabel, or what? and is Bobbie to be left behind?

I suppose Isabel will grieve at parting with her Sam. If by any chance there should not be quite enough for a regular and complete migration of the House of Busson to settle in London by April, you might perhaps make a move in the direction as far as Brussels there to await the fortunate shower of 5£ notes which would enable us all to get fixed here on the largest and most comfortable principles. My notion for myself and Emma is to go at first into lodgings and save together till we can furnish a house properly.

I have not time yet to write to Gyggy but will do so in about a week; meanwhile send me his address which I have lost, and if you write tell him. I can't write you a very entertaining letter as my facetious brain is quite exhausted by the constant draughts lately made upon it, but pray write me a long letter and let Isabel write to Emma, and

[1]Et comment !

say whether she has received the buckle which Emma sent for Xmas day.

As for Pem, I love her better every day; can't get on without her a bit, nor she without me. I never knew till now, or realised what marriage is for a fellow like myself or what a very peculiar sort of woman I required; car je ne suis pas fichu comme les autres. I dare say Isabel requires just such a peculiar husband. When I'm depressed and overworked and out of spirits, 10 minutes of Pem makes me lively and happy; nobody else can do that; when I'm cracked and over excited, she cools me down into wonderful reason and patience. In fact I've got at last to look to her for *everything* and am never disappointed; she must have been specially designed by providence for an overwrought unequal crackbrained artist like myself, to mesmerise him into constant calm and happiness, and be loved by him in return as I swear I don't think any other woman ever was.

And now my Dear Mamma with very best love to you and Isabel, I remain your ever affectionate son

Kicky

[February, 1862]

My dear Tom,

I've been so hard at work that I've not been able to write till today although I have had plenty to write about. In the first place the day before your letter came, Jimmy made his appearance early on the Sunday morning and sat recounting his experiences for about three hours on my bed. He only staid four days in London (avec accompagnement de Joe)[1] and came about his business with Thomas, who is dead—for as Jimmy expressed it: "I wrote to the old scoundrel, and he died in answer by return of post—the very best thing he could do"!—and J. considers himself well out of that business, the Thomasses junior being easy to manage. He described his picture to me; it's called 'Alone'.

[1]Joanna Heffernan, Whistler's mistress.

RR. Rocks of every kind of bright & varied colour. O. Sea line—of the very deepest blue. S. Greyish yellow sand. W. breaking wave with foam at top & of a transparence which is simply magnificent. G. little breton girl asleep on the rock.

(The sand was not laid on with a palette knife.) And there is not one part of the picture with which he is not thoroughly satisfied he says, and its open air freshness nothing can stand against; that's what struck Bancroft. Picture about the size of a small mantel-piece. Besides this he is painting the woman in white—Red-haired party, life size, in a beautiful white cambric dress, standing against a window which filters the light through a transparent white muslin curtain—but the figure receives a strong light from the right and therefore the picture barring the red hair is one gorgeous mass of brilliant white. My notion is that it must be a marvellously brilliant thing—you can fancy how he described it. His other adventures as described to a lot of fellows at T. Jeckell's in the evening were as amusing as usual. Joe came with him to me on the Monday afternoon, got up like a duchess, without crinoline—the mere *making up* of her bonnet by Madame somebody or other in Paris had cost 50 fr. And Jimmy describes all the Parisians on the boulevard as aghast at 'la belle Anglaise'!—They have both gone back to Paris.

Ridley has got a large picture of O'Connor's which I saw by gaslight, and a most splendid thing it appeared if one can judge by such a light—Sea port near Durham, with ships, mais vois-tu, ça!—a beautiful background of cottages & yellow sandhills covered with patches of green—& 3 splendacious figures quite large in the foreground, boy fishing, smashing any boy of Hook's I ever saw, & pretty girl reading letter to old man, all *beautifully drawn* & painted in a magnificent manner; must see it again by daylight. Jimmy owned that there were here & there some bits which he would not have been ashamed of himself. *I* confess that my opinion of the picture was that I would sooner have painted it than the Rotherhithe one; for it appears to have almost Jimmy's freshness & splendid painting, and qualities of drawing composition and *prettiness* which Jimmy's Thames picture doesn't possess. You should have heard Marks tackling Jimmy at Jeckell's the other night about Turner, it was so funny. Jimmy owned he couldn't see much in Turner, and expressed great disgust about the fuss Haden has lately been making about mounting one of Turner's watercolours which he had. Hence a long discussion in which Jimmy pitched into Turner for being so particular about being mounted, instead of Haden for mounting him. Marks with great indignation: "Particular! why he'd leave his pictures in his court yard, to be pissed against!"—Jimmy: "Well, that accounts for some of the damned peculiarities we're obliged to swallow!"

Fancy Marks getting into a serious discussion with Jim. Marks is a devilish clever fellow. One evening at Lewises (where by the bye he is the life of the party—preaches a yankee sermon which would make you crow again) he gave me a piece of information which rather destroyed some sweet little illusions of mine—namely, that he was the 'Dry Point' of the Spectator; but he assured me so solemnly that what he said about me was totally unbiassed by any private feeling of 'steem & 'gard, etc, that I tried to console myself & fancy so. He told me to be very chary about letting this about, & I've only mentioned to Henley, who is the soul of discretion, & yourself. He tells me he wants to write about Walker whom he does most enthusiastically rave about; I'm afraid I shall get it then. Did you see Walker's two last OAW? weren't they *lovely*? Hélas! Hélas!

My mother writes to me that you express yourself in

very encouraging terms about my late performances in Once a Week; you are about the only fellow I know who does. And as for O A W themselves they write to me to say that the admiral's daughter cuts have been disapproved of by the author of the tale, to whom they have made *apologies* for me—Est-ce flatteur assez? Sandys sends messages to wonder how the devil it is I don't *draw* better than I do. London Society says that my London Bridge scene is such a "*shocking failure*" they can't make use of it. Now I swear it's quite up to my average work & just see *what* they've got for their first number (barring Watson drawing which is charming). My Girl playing the harp, about the best thing I have done has not come out this number. O.A.W. have refused my MS. saying that it wants βωπασις, or some such damned thing out of Plato; why can't they take the story & put the Bwpasis in themselves? Punch however seems pretty much all right; they have two things of mine besides one which came out this week & was much liked. I have just been spending a whole week over a double drawing for O A W; so they have two of mine coming out also. Tu vois mon cher that I'm not yet in the saddle, & some months have yet to pass before I espouse ye kindest & most beloved of women.

Bancroft's letter interested me very much; how he does theorise & theorise; devilish sight too much logic for an artist. I'm getting more & more convinced every day that the less you think & speculate & the more you set your instincts to work, the better; fancy a fellow wanting to get into the good graces & something else of some woman, & remaining at home to study her peculiarities in this bancrofty manner. Our friend Jimmy would be down on his knees directly he saw her & pulling up her petticoat etc.

Feb. 7

I've kept this a whole week (for which I feel ashamed) intending to go & see Ridley's picture by daylight, but have not once been able. However Poynter has, and says it's magnificent & that he would devilish sooner have painted it than Jimmy's. Poynter has sent in his picture of the Eurydice but has not yet received the tin.

Thanks for the very jolly letter you sent Emma for the the proof, & with which I need not say she was very much pleased indeed.

Moscheles has just returned. I've been doing such a lot for Punch this week, 7 initials, and 2 socials, all among the best I've done. I wonder whether I could *ask* M. Lemon to cut out for me a certain amount of work to do, say a social & 2 initials a week—200 a year? in which case I could marry in the spring, and would spend the summer in the country near London, where I want to do some things qui me trottent dans la boule depuis 3 mois.

How do you like Sandys' last? best he's done I think. You never told me how you like Poynter's drawing which had a great success, all but the figures which were not quite up to the mark. I think you'll like my double drawing —cochon en diable. And now mon cher I think I've told you all the news—not heard from home for an age—Gyggy going to exchange into another arm. I hope you are working, and that you'll be up in May, with 14 inches round the arm. Write soon, and I'll keep you au courant of all the news.

Yours ever

icky

[February, 1862]

My dear Isabel,

I open Emma's letter to put in a few words. I shall take the 'at to the Tavistocks (first birthday present I ever made you by the bye) and also Emma's locket for S. P. to take with him to Dusseldorf. I shall also trouble him with this letter—should I not see him, I will leave the hat and locket and send the letter by post.

I think Pem's choice of the hat will please you, and I will answer for the colour of it becoming your hair and complexion.

Pray this time don't neglect writing to her as soon as you have received her little keepsake as you know how she cuts up at any neglect of that sort; and if you do me the honour to send a few lines to me that I may receive them before the sixth[1] I shall be highly gratified.

Yesterday I received a letter from G. asking me to pay his debts and saying that otherwise he will be broke; whether that is true or not I don't know, but I wrote him 8 pages by return of post, saying it was out of my power and blowing him up but in a very kind manner.

I also send you a letter from Miss Lumley. I will not presume to dictate to you, but if I were you, my dear, I should certainly drop that acquaintance. O'Connor's papa forbade her further acquaintance with one of his daughters on account of some peculiar indelicacy of conversation in which she was pleased to indulge. Enfin fais comme tu veux. If I'm ever married or in a house of my own, she'll not be a welcome guest.

Pem had a charming letter from T. A. in acknowledgment of a 'proof before letters' of one of my important performances, which she made him a present of—The hotel by the Rhine. I hope you do not neglect him. I understand you see Punch at Malines, in that case I'll not send them; otherwise I will; let me know. Nothing else of mine has come out; OAW next week, I believe, and London Society only next month. I've been working very hard but have made a bad month of it, as it's nearly all been initial letters.

Did I tell you in my last that my old friend Wills made his appearance here; very handsome, happy and prosperous, but with a droll countrified narrow mind and a northern accent. Talked of nothing but his great love for old friends and his exceeding affection for and felicity with, his wife.

I've been unwell rather this last week—East winds knock

[1]The 6th of March was Kicky's twenty-eighth birthday.

me up. The other night at Grosvenor St. I had a horrid attack of spasms in the stomach. Mrs. Wightwick laid me on the sofa and fomented the romantic seat of my sufferings with boiling water and flannels in the kindliest manner. Pem's agony in the other room was something wonderful—blue black under the eyes. I also the very same day operated as dentist on one of my own teeth which I extracted by means of a penknife and latchkey. How do your teeth wear? Pem has scarcely a back tooth in her head. Otherwise my health is good; I do dumbbells, take cold baths in the morning and eat oatmeal porridge for breakfast.

Last Wednesday week I received a hurried note from F. Leighton (Cimabue Leighton) to say that ye famed Mrs. Sartoris desired the honour of my acquaintance and requested the pleasure of my company that day to dinner at 9 Park Place, St. James's. I was so mad I couldn't go, but was already bespoke for that evening; however that's one of the few acquaintances I shall endeavour to stick to. She was Adelaide Kemble, you know, the best English Norma there ever was, of unimpeachable character and has one of the most agreeable houses in London.

I have it appears an enemy at the Punch staff, Shirley Brooks, who at the last dinner stated that Howard (you know) should do more, and that I should do less; but I hope I shall get over that little opposition, though Mr. Brooks is next in influence to Mark Lemon.

You cannot imagine, not being here, all the little alternations of triumph and anxiety through which Pem and I are continually passing, or the states we both work ourselves into, expecially she who is most unphilosophic; her despair at Walker's success is something comical, or would be if it did not make me despair a little also.

Tomorrow evening is Lewises. I took Moscheles to the last, and he was beside himself with delight; he did not do anything there in his usual line; for once lost his cheek and was dumb; but is coming out with me in a duet by his father for voice and cornet, in which he does the cornet with his lips. He has got a nice studio, and twice a week gives a painting class there to the daughters of the aristocracy. Leech was very jolly last time, but I do hate singing when he's in the room, and always look out next week for some frightful caricature of myself as a French count at the pianoforte, or something. Tell Mamma to write me a long letter (to send with yours); tell her also to give me an exact and statistical financial epitome of her present debts and assets (she neglects me as you neglect your future sister-in-law). I should so like to get you here in April; you could have lodgings in Hampstead all through the summer for one pound a week, small of course, but respectable. If the W's let their house Mrs. W. and P will go and live there, and of course so will I. If we marry this year we shall take lodgings there. Adieu ma chère amie—many happy returns and make hay while the sun shines, that is, dance away as long as you care for that style of amusement. Love to Mamma, Aunt G., Bobbie, everyone.

Your ever affectionate brother

Kicky

[February, 1862]

My dear Mamma,

I received Isabel's note and yours yesterday and also your jolly long letter of the other day which was full of interest to me, as I always like to hear exactly the life you are all leading and am delighted with the smallest details. You seem to write in pretty good spirits and cheerfully, and I am glad to see that Isabel is in good condition to enjoy her young existence—with a zest that reminds me of my bachelor days.

Sam P. has not yet arrived—I called three times and then left word for him to come for me (by the bye, what must that youth's infatuation be, to extend his admiration for Isabel to her brother! First compliment on my looks that I've received since I've been in England!).

I must now tell you some of the news, I suppose. Last Saturday was Lewis's—and young Prinsep, for the third and last time, as he said, invited me to dinner on the morrow

—so I was obliged to forsake Grosvenor Street for the first time on Sunday since I've been engaged and go off to Little Holland House to dine. I must tell you about the Prinseps. There were three beautiful women, sisters, who married 1. Col. Dalrymple, 2. Lord Somers, 3. Mr. Prinsep, a great East Indian of immense wealth I'm told. These 3 women stick together, and have formed a sort of nucleus, round which gather all that there is of swell; the nobilitee, the gentree, the litherathure, polithics and art of the counthree, by jasus! It is a nest of prœraphaelites, where Hunt, Millais, Rossetti, Watts, Leighton etc., Tennyson, the Brownings and Thackeray etc. and tutti quanti receive dinners and incense, and cups of tea handed to them by these women almost kneeling. Watts, who is a grand fellow, is their painter in ordinary; the best part of the house has been turned into his studio, and he lives there and is worshipped till his manliness hath almost departed, I should fancy. Well, I went there with young Prinsep the son, who is one of my heroes; I must describe the young athlete and Isabel will admire. He is 23; 6 foot 2; hasn't an ounce of fat on his body, being as hard as I am, and yet weighs the fabulous weight of 16 stone 6; 14 inches round the arm like Heenan. All that is manly, honest, clever and jolly, a painter, Watts' pupil; fair woolly hair, and an eastern face of a splendid ugliness which women love better than Ciabati's beauty. In short Thackeray's Philip with 20 times the brain, and none of the beastly egotism and bullying. N'est-il pas soigné, ce gaillard.

Well, we went to Little Holland House, a strange old-fashioned ramshackle lot of buildings in large grounds, and found them doing kettle-drum, i.e. tea at 4 o'clock, there being some visitors (among others Lord Elcho, of whom you may have heard). After departure of the visitors we dined; without dress coats—anyhow, and it was jolly enough—Watts in velvet coat and slippers. After dinner, up in the music room Watts stretched himself at full length on the sofa, which none of the women take when he's there. People formed circle, and I being in good voice sang to them

JAMES MCNEILL WHISTLER

Reduced by about one-half from an unfinished pen and ink and pencil drawing by du Maurier, dating from the 'sixties

Wednesday Morng.

advice to young men in love.

fill yourself your second cup of coffee; put in 6 lumps of sugar; make your cigarette, light it; open her letter, in which she tells you she misses you; try & believe it; kiss her photograph by la Bianchini; — and you will manage to pass a few very happy moments —

My Dearest Pamina,

The beloved envelope with my name

"ADVICE TO YOUNG MEN IN LOVE"

Heading to the letter to Emma Wightwick, *p.* 71

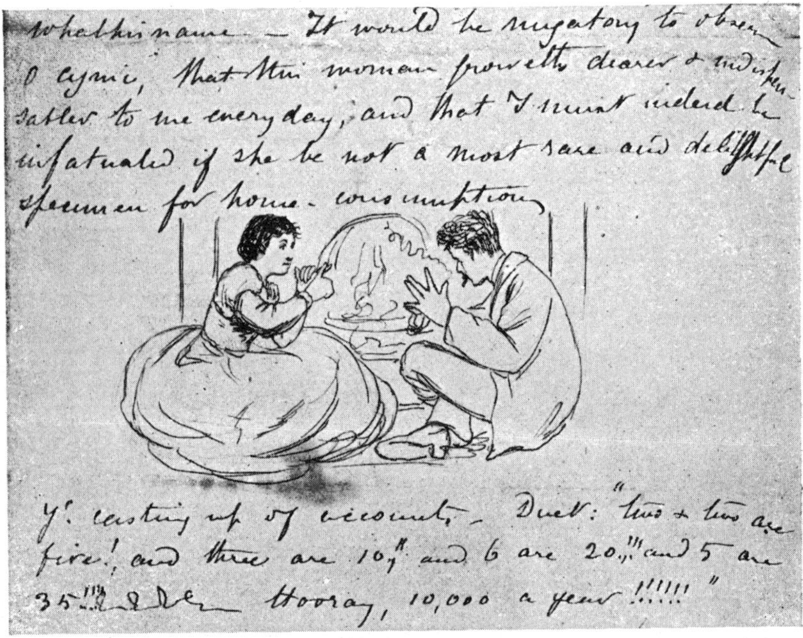
whatshisname — It would be nugatory to observe O cynic, that this woman proveth dearer & indispensable to me everyday; and that I must indeed be infatuated if she be not a most rare and delightful specimen for home-consumption

Ye casting up of accounts — Duet: "two & two are five! and three are 10!! and 6 are 20!!! and 5 are 35!!!! &c &c — Hooray, 10,000 a year!!!!!!"

"YE CASTING UP OF ACCOUNTS"

Wishful thinking by Kicky and Emma; from the letter to Tom Armstrong, *p.* 101

the whole evening, the cream of Schubert and Gordigiani—c'était très drôle, the worship I got. I wonder if they are sincere. At eleven we left, and Mrs. Prinsep almost embraced me. Drove back to Val Prinsep's studio in Charlotte Street, lit a fire and remained there chatting till nearly 5 o'clock. The fascination of this tender rollicking Hercules is indescribable; we fascinate each other I think. He read me such stunning poems of Browning's. In short very jolly people for Isabel and Pem and me to know when we are getting on, *if they are all right*—for there seems an atmosphere of looseness about this aristocratic lot—people say that Mrs. Dalrymple and Lady Somers are all sorts of things, et tu conçois, les mœurs avant tout. (As for me, I confess that after the first half hour, women's society bores me pas mal, and the jolliest part of the evening was with Val. P in Charlotte St.) But they are very nice people to know, and I am glad I went there, and will go again when I've time. I confess that nothing bores me so much as having to spend the Sunday away from Pem, who has got to be an indispensable condition of existence to me. I do believe that it is by an interposition of Providence that we were kept for each other, as no other woman would have suited me like her, such a peculiar fellow I find myself to be. In fact we are complementary counterparts of each other; what one lacks, the other possesses you know; but both have in common a passion each for each, of an intensity I never dreamt of before, my dear, and that very few people in a million have ever realised, I should think. Consequently I look forward to unusual happiness in my married life; but if I were to lose her, I should be done for.

Business is going on so so; I send you some Punches (2) and a OAW which has been much liked. I do hope I shall come to some arrangement soon about Punch. If M. Lemon would only guarantee me work for 200 a year! From your statement of finances I rather despair of getting you over here by April, unless this month proves unusually lucky. How does Isabel relish the notion of leaving her Sammy? and the flattering Prince? I begin to think it would take some time before she would get to like my people, who have more brains than pretty manners, and are more accustomed to get flattery than give it. I am glad to see however that she has fixed her fancy in the proper quarter. Is there any chance of that coming to anything? I must say, that though S. P. is a very first rate young fellow, if he were to marry I. it would be quite taking her away from me, unless he came and lived over here—by jove shouldn't I like her to marry my athlete, Val Prinsep!

Thursday

It is quite a week since I began this letter and I've not found time to finish it, but I must now by hook or by crook. I send you another Punch and OAW. Yesterday I had one of my Punch drawings refused, great pity for it was a little gem. I have now to do a french story for OAW—that is illustration—and hope it will be good. To-night I am going to a dinner party at the Prinseps, to meet his just-married sister, Mrs. Gurney; I was regularly hooked into it—and he is such a jolly fellow.

The other day I happened to mention to him that Pem had thought of engraving, and he went to Burne Jones, the prœraphaelite, whose wife is an amateur engraver. Yesterday he took me there, such a stunning fellow Burne Jones—what *dear* fellows artists are. He insisted on my bringing Pem to his wife to see all about it, and if she likes it begin with her. So I'm going to take Pem there this afternoon. It's so jolly this help-each-other hand-in-glove with brother artist feeling among them. There was Jones with four or five fellows in his studio (Ruskin had just left), fellows calling his little prœraphaelite-looking wife Georgie (I only caught a glimpse of her). Large studio with such marvellously coloured paintings—plain piano in wood on which he in his leisure moments paints designs which will make it very valuable some day. Kicky sits down to the same, and singeth for just about an hour to the intense delight of the lot. The wonderful extent to which my peculiar sort of music goes down with artists, especially the prœraphs! I see myself some day after the first little struggles are over, in a jolly studio with Pem—time 5 o'clock—the kettle-drum on the fire, half a dozen stunning fellows chatting with you and Pem and drinking the hospitable afternoon tea; Isabel playing Chopin on a pianoforte rendered of untold value by my important designs—Bobbie we'll say in the corner, eating the oxgall with which I paint, and his mamma flirting with Ruskin, etc. etc.

Espérons que çela viendra—I am going to paint in water-colours as soon as I can find time.

I am afraid there will be no coming over here by April though; affairs have not gone on quite as I have wished, although I can hardly complain. I have many ennuis and anxieties in the midst of my great happiness, and sharing them with Pem has made her as thin as a dear old skeleton.

I am very glad you have made such a jolly acquaintance in the Baronne. I hope you will know the Hightowers (hohen *XXXXX*) and that they will come and take tea with you, but I suppose that would not be etiquette. You talk of Holstein's brother; there is a prince Holstein who is a great scoundrel, Henley tells me, and whose presence in a house is almost sufficient to compromise the women thereof. I hope this ain't the fellow.

How are all your healths? Mine very good—oatmeal porridge in the morning. Hamilton Aidé was here the day before yesterday and wants to introduce me to his publisher, Smith and Elder, who is also Thackeray's. And funnily enough Walter Thornbury came just after and gave me a letter to the same—besides which I shall try and get Mrs. Prinsep to praise the article to Thackeray for me. Will tell her the romantic tale of my love, the want of money, etc. and tell her she must get me and Pem on in the world.

Moscheles is regularly settled over here now. He is always boring me with a duet for voice and cornet written by his father for him and me to sing at Lewises, and the damned thing is so difficult I can never get it right. He is a jolly little fellow, but with such a lot of unenglish pose and charlatanism.

I think I've now hurried together all the news I can think of in this 'busy whirl'. Isabel hasn't kept her promise of writing to Pem. Sam P. not having called yet, I send the locket; I hope Isabel will write directly *this* time.

Love to all, and kiss the tip of your old nose for me yourself—and believe me your ever most affectionate

son,

[March, 1862]

My dear Mamma,

I have just received your letter which is disgustingly short and disappointing after I've been waiting day after day—as if *you* didn't owe *me* a letter—fact is, you don't care half so much for your firstborn as you used, and I'm not going to stand it Madam. I must have you over here to remind you by the fascination of my manner and the charm of my conversation that you ought to have quite a peculiar pride and affection for me. I shall not be able to write you a long letter now as I have two initials to do for to-morrow. I've sent no OAW because there are no DM's in them, but will send you Punches next week. Young Swain, the engraver, has just called to say that M. Lemon had said I was henceforth to do the Essence of Parliament initials as well as the Dramatic correspondent—so I seem to be pas mal with Punch. Indeed, I hope there's no mistake about young Swain's information as it is rather important—looks like leading to a regular appointment. My last things in Punch have been a good deal liked. That one you mention is quite a little beauty, if you will excuse me for saying so. I've had one deuced unpleasant thing to do, namely to draw my London Bridge scene for London Society over again gratis. It will be done in a day or two, but has taken time. However I hope and trust it will be so good that it will lead to much more work of the same kind. Altogether these 2 months have been nothing like December.

Sam Perrot, who is certainly a very handsome gentlemanly young fellow, brought me the lotion; unfortunately, and to my great horror, he came when I was drawing myself as a roman warrior for Once a Week, and I had to hurry out to him in the most elementary state of hurried get-up. We had a long chat. He's worth half a dozen German Princekins, but wants knocking about a little and (if he's ever going to propose to I.) a little rubbing up for a year or so against some of my dear fellows. Doth I. really feel the "thrilling pangs"?

Let me tell her that nice as these little first distant symptoms of mutual romance are, they are nothing to the jolly feeling of being 2 parties in one which comes after a year's engagement or so, a compound of brother and sister, two inseparable pals, and something a great deal too warm to write about. As for Pem and me, you know, we are simply getting to love each other in such a desperate fashion, that the loss of one would be the total smashing up and destruction of the other and if we don't get married soon, we shall have brain fever or something.

You don't tell me anything about what kind of food you have now or if you are well etc. I must now leave off writing this letter which you don't deserve, as I have to be hard at work all the afternoon, and only send this to quiet your anxieties—but depend upon it unless you write me a really long nice letter full of chat and your own ideas on everything as you always do, divil another letter will you get from me.

Love to Aunt G. and Bob, and believe me

Your injured but very affectionate son

K. du Maurier

I've got into 2 rooms, as people were beginning to chaff.

Carissimo vecchio gallo,[1] Saturday Morning

I've been a very long time before answering you because

[1] *I.e.*, Dearest old cock (to Tom Armstrong).

something has always interfered to prevent me from writing; not I beg leave to say, from laziness. Very many things have been constantly occurring which if properly remembered and noted down would edify & instruct you, ô provincial abruti!! But I will try and give you what news I can remember.

In the first place let me tell you that I like the subject of your picture as per sketch very much, and hope you have by this time done justice to it in the painting; recollect you have very little time now.

Jimmy came to town just for a day; one of his pictures, the Bancroft one, is over here at Haden's; I've not yet had time to go and see it, but am going this week with Keene. The reason of his hurried visit was the death of his *Mother-in-law*: about which he was quite sentimental, and very much afraid that the bereaved widower, Joe's Papa, who is an impulsive & passionate Irishman, will do something to *disgrace* Joe's sisters (who are at present I believe here in Newman St, No. 69).

Jimmy's quite as amusing when he doesn't intend to be as when he does. The woman in white is nearly finished—Jim working at it all the winter from 8 in the morning; got painter's colic very severely, but worked pluckily through it all. His Parisian experiences, no longer bohemian, and the quarrels of Joe with Ernest who lives with them & on them, & who is still a bohème incorrigible are very droll; finished up with a fight between Jimmy & a Hackney coachman, 1 round, all three events for Jim, which was impayable. Poynter painting a girl doing her hair in a looking glass which is devilish well painted in some parts; also doing etchings from engravings of old Masters for Lady Eastlake; gradually getting out of his troubles I think (and will soon pay your doctor's bill) but has been miserably hard up, ill, all sorts of things.

Went with him last Wednesday to dine at Coronios with the old people who have returned; *very* jolly. P & I walked home and had a stunning long confidential chat.

I've been fraternising most extensively with Val Prinsep

who is such a stunning fellow—six foot 1, 23 of age, not an ounce of fat but weighs 16 stone 6! such a murderous looking arm of more than 14 inches! and a very jolly fellow, awful prœraphaelite—pupil of Watts, who lives at his paternal home in Kensington, Little Holland house; I've dined there 2 or 3 times and am going to dine there this evening to meet Tom Taylor & his wife. They are tremendous hero-worshippers; heroes are Watts, Millais, Rossetti, Hunt, Leighton, Tennyson, Thackeray etc. etc. Joachim, Halley etc. and last that very delightful amateur singer & composer G. du M. whose composition Op. I you have the good taste to ask for, and which you shall have as soon as it's written out. Instead of dressing for dinner there, you undress; Watts without a shirt collar, and in long velvet painting jacket & list slippers; dines frugally on toast & butter; handsome romantic fellow, said to have been desperately in love with Mrs. Prinsep's beautiful sister Countess Somers (probably does private soda waters besides his toast & butter). Old Prinsep, magnificent old cove over six feet, is I am told the original of old Newcome. He went over to India with Thackeray's mamma, with Thackeray already conceived but not yet born, fancy *his* having been a foetus! Mrs. Gurney, newly married sister of Prinsep's, very pretty, came up into Prinsep's room when we were smoking and spooned with her husband till I was hardly continent! c'était cocasse, hein? Somehow in the very delightful atmosphere of this house, I seem to perceive a slight element of looseness, hein! which I don't sympathise with—when I say delightful, it isn't enormously so to me, but could be if I were a 'gay' young bachelor.

I have also (by Leighton & the *delightful* & *refined* author of Rita, Confidences, Carr of Carrlyon) been decoyed into the Sartoris's. Clever people very; Mrs. S. no longer fit for Norma; fat red face; Leighton looks so pretty & fresh by the side of her, and the contrast naturally suggests itself when one has heard all about them. Verb. sap.—Le monde me dégoûte, quoi. Mrs. Prinsep & Mrs. S. awful enemies I fancy but very loving to each other.

Give us a cot beside a Hill etc.

Val who is a stunner in every way has introduced me to Burne Jones who is simply an angel and *what* a colourist. I had told the noble Val all about Emma's having a notion of engraving and he went & confabbed about the possibility of the thing with Mrs. Jones who is an amateur engraver; consequently Emma & I went there and coached up all sorts of information; the result of which is the enclosed performance. Emma bought herself the necessary tools and engraved a sketch I made; we are going to take the block to Mrs. J. this afternoon for approval & correction. We have been fraternising with the Solomons too, and are going to their little family conversaziones on Saturday evenings.

I've not been getting on so well as I wish quite lately; two or 3 Punch blocks have been returned—rather wantonly I cannot help thinking. Once a Week is very nice and has just sent a choice of work to me & Poynter. We shall take chambers; most of the furnishing will be done by Pa & Ma, who are very kind and all that. I am awfully anxious to get married; ce n'est pas une existence que je méne à présent. Not heard very lately from home; when I last did they were well & jolly; I suppose they have written to you by this time, as they said they would. My mother's letters are very amusing; they've been fraternising with all sorts of German Princes; my mother always in a funk lest the noble Holstein should come in and find them drinking tea out of the slop-basin and fighting for the cold remains of the early dinner, as is sometimes the custom with the noble but bohemian house of Busson. Also great friends with all the English. But I would give anything to have them over here, to trascorrere la vita unita (Verdi).

Old Bill is going on tranquilly and making his little old man of a way; I shall go & see what he's doing Sunday morning. He is at present labouring under a dreadful boil at the back of his neck—the fruit of too much virtue. Moscheles has a class of painting for young ladies; I've taken him to Lewis's but he has been abashed and did not produce himself; all the fellows like him immensely. Marks is the great man at Lewis's this year; last time he got drunk and his humour was terrific. He is a very stunning fellow, with a very big brain. Morten has somehow conciliated all our dislikes, and we see very much less of him.

I suppose you would like to have seen the sale at Christie's; Plinth's pictures—one of the jolliest and most interesting exhibitions that ever was; I went there with old Keene, who humbled himself before almost every picture in the Room. Saw the famous early Millais, the Carpenter's Shop—toute la sainte famille y plombe des arpions.

I am going soon to dine at the Tennants' with Gustave Flaubert, a great friend of theirs who is coming over, and whom I am rather curious to meet.

I look forward to seeing you early in May, old fellow, and I've no doubt we shall have lots to talk about with all the fellows. How I wish you could stay in London; for I can see every day of how great use it would be to you and I think if you once made yourself comfortable here you old sybarite and managed to keep in tolerable health you would enjoy it wastly. Nobody appreciates more than I do the warm and genial atmosphere of the family bosom, but I am afraid it is rather fatal to the artistic tendencies.

The fair Emma sends her kind remembrances and begs you will send her a carte de visite for our own particular album, which contains merely her friends & mine.

And now my dear fellow, I have told you all I can think of at present & will say good bye; let us know when you are coming, and I will try & get you a bedroom in the house. I have my old room on the second floor you know, so that you can paint if you want to in my gorgeous front room.

Yours ever

K

Saw Oakenshaw at the sale—fraternised.

The enclosed proof is not very well *printed*, as E. & I had to make out own dabber, and print it with a paperknife out of the depth of our own consciousness; but though the lines are rather jagged, the expression is preserved exactly.

[March 26, 1862]

My dearest Pem,

Much as I love the dear Tulse Hill people, I've been devoting them to the devil all the morning, for I never felt less inclined to pass the evening away from my dear inseparable as I do today; for I slept wretchedly and have been restless all night and all day, and there is nothing for that but to put my head on your dear shoulder.

Henley is not coming with me to the Greeks; the poor fellow writes that he has a boil as big as an egg on the back of his head, which unfits him for dining out; he's coming Tuesday if he's all right, and I suppose he will be by that time.

I didn't walk last night, but came home and read far into the night. I have put the sketch on the block but it doesn't come well. I am going to get Poynter to come with me.

I wish my darling that instead of being here yesterday you had come today; but I look forward all the more to seeing you to-morrow, and shall wake happy. I suppose you've taken Annie back to Brixton and not been able to engrave today; but I hope that there will be sufficient for us to print to-morrow evening, as I am very curious about the result. I also hope that you will miss me this evening as I shall you, my dear Pet. I feel awfully stupid and headachy; and have no news whatever to tell you; nobody has been. Give my love to Maman Bellemère my dear good angel, and wish for your ever loving and most affectionate

Kicky

". . . ." the Greeks!

Darling I have thought of you and loved you all night and all day.

In April of 1862 *Kicky was attacked by a strange disorder of the liver, which upset him both physically and mentally. Whether it was a form of jaundice, coupled with a slight nervous break-*

down, it is difficult to say, but it is evident that he was passing through a period of emotional strain. He tells the bare story of it in the following letters, and one is inclined to wonder if those evenings at Little Holland House, without Emma, the guardian angel, were proving a sore temptation to what he believed to be his better nature.

[April, 1862]

My very dearest Pem,

I have passed a pretty good night, and took the draught this morning. I of course feel very sickish, but shall be all right soon. God bless you my dear love for your kindness; I shall come early to-night.

Yours ever lovingly,

Kicky

[April, 1862]

My dearest Pem,

I must just run out and see you for a moment, or if you are out leave this to tell you that I am very well and quiet this morning, though weak from last night's and this morning's *wiolent* medicine. I shall return immediately to my work and come back to you about ½ past 4, or so. Prie pour moi, dear angel; and know and believe that you have got and are getting closer round my heart every day, and that I am permitted glimpses of such future happiness for both of us that I almost curse the slowness of the medicine which is getting me all right again. Love to Jules, and to M. Bellemère if you write, and tell the old Governor he's a muff.

Your deeply loving Kick

91 Newman St.
London
Thursday
[April, 1862]

My verry dear ole Moder,

I am now going to treat myself to an hour's chat with you, and tell you all the news.

I have just recovered from a strange illness which only lasted 4 or 5 days but on looking back seems to have absorbed quite an age—and which without giving me the slightest bodily pain or weakness, had inflicted on me suffering I had never dreamt of, and which now I can't realise. Don't let this alarming début frighten you, but you must know that without noticing any symptoms of disease whatever in my old carcase, I have been slightly disinclined to work lately, and irritable in my temper without due cause—and figure to yourself that on Friday evening as I was sitting with my dearest and most beloved of Pems, I felt all my affection for her, you, Isabel, and my friends, cease as by enchantment; yet my powers of reasoning strange to say were by no means impaired; indeed remarkably clear and active. Well, as you may fancy I went home and to bed but in such despair I cannot realise it! I awoke early to the same fearful state, feeling myself utterly lost for ever and ever, dead to all natural affection, and resolving hard to lead henceforth a life of martyrdom to duty—at length a faint glimmer suggested itself to me that perhaps some internal derangement, of which I was unaware, was the cause of this hideous state of mind—and catching at this straw of a hope, I went off to Haden's (may his name be ever blessed and his shadow never grow less!). He explained to me that my liver was altogether in a disturbed state which has been coming on for some time, but which had given no warning of its approach on account of the peculiar insensibility of that 'ere organ, but promised me faithfully the most complete relief in a few days, and prescribed strong remedies. As soon as I left him I didn't believe it any longer—had no faith, but got the medicine nevertheless, and carried my pills and unutterable misery to the Wightwicks, still feeling that there was not one place on earth for me to lay my wretched head.

How I have made poor dear Emma suffer you may fancy; for two dreary days she never left me, came with me to Haden's and waited outside—saw the prescription cashed at the apotheke's; watched and prayed and cried, for I was as hard to her and as insensible as a flint; gave me all my medicines—with a large black rim round her eyes like you when any new symptom in my eyes used to terrify you. At last an hour's relief came on Sunday evening when the neck of the disease broke, and I buried myself in my dear Pem's arms in a passion of hysterical sobbing, which I can scarcely bear to think of. I had two or three relapses after but rather less violent, and shorter; the medicines I have been taking are of the strongest nature, and I have a course to go through, and rules of health to follow for a time to insure me against any future recurrence of the complaint, the remembrance of which gives me a strange shudder. How I longed for frightful bodily pain and revelled in the notion of death (not that I should ever have touched myself, as that was not the temptation). I feel myself restored to everybody I care about with new intensity, and as for Pem, you may fancy how I love her. I feel myself so surrounded, wrapt up, hedged in, by her powerful affection, as if it were an immense thick strong-hooded double-lined-with-fur-and-silk blanket cloak of a material which will last for ever—to roll myself up in and go to sleep, or wear jauntily with the fur and ornaments outside when so disposed—but knowing alas that having purchased and worn this rare garment, should I ever lose it, I perish by the cold. There ma'am, what do you think of that for a poetical description. The only way I can express myself about this kind, constant, passionate, simple, pure-minded angel—Damn it Ma'am, I don't mean to flatter either, but I think she'll be doocid like you, si Dieu lui permet d'atteindre ton grand age. So much for the mysterious link between Pemkick. Now Pemkick is happy again and their native facetiousness being restored they are deep in anatomical studies of the liver, health, food etc. in any books they can find; health, digestion and the liver has quite become Pem's monomania in fact, and between engraving and reading hygienic treatise in old Cornhill Magazines she will have plenty of occupations.

I suppose she has written to Isabel and told all about the engraving and the Jones's. I enclose her maiden proof, which she has done without any assistance from anybody;

the lines as you see are rather rotten, but she has preserved the expression exactly. I've no doubt in time she will become a very clever engraver as an amateur for it is very hard work for the eyes—she will do my pet things for me—besides which it gives her a greater understanding of my peculiar branch of art which is uncommonly pleasant for both.

I must tell you that I have been in uncommon aristocratic society (like vous autres). Last week a large card came, on which the Earl and Countess Somers requested the honour of Mr. du Maurier's company at dinner on Wednesday the 9th, which was yesterday. As the card came during my attack, I didn't answer it, feeling at the time that if there was anybody I particularly loathed, it was that particular earl, and that particular countess. However I did go and made it all right with her Ladyship. It was a dinner à la russe, 12 people, greatest state of sweldom these rustic eyes ever had the pleasure of beholding with mild surprise & of inwardly laughing at. Milor is a jolly sort of a little fellow with a squeaky voice; Miladi very handsome woman; but she & all the women were décolletées in a beastly fashion—damn the aristocratic standard of fashion; nothing will ever make me think it right or decent that I should see a lady's armpit flesh folds when I am speaking to her. About 30 or 40 upstairs after dinner nearly all in the same state of partial nudity as per diagram. Lots of swells, as you may fancy—damn their style, etc. I who feel so small at Lewises felt myself quietly & mildly big at the Somerses; as if it would be something too absurd for me to be patronised by people whose dinner conversation was such as I heard last night—not but what they were very flatteurs & charming in the extreme and nobody tried to be swell except an imperious old maid Miss Duff Gordon, who patronised my Gordigiani's rather, and was put down with irresistible tenderness and simplicity. Lady Somers wants to know Pem. Jolly Mrs. Prinsep drove me nearly home though quite out of her way; so droll—she & Dicky Doyle in the back seat, Val Prinsep & I on the other

smoking two enormous cigars we had stolen from Milor, and Mrs. P. cuddling poor Doyle because he couldn't bear the smoke or the window being open. I'm getting amazingly fond of Mrs. P. who seems to be getting deuced fond of me. Holland House will be a nice Sunday Haunt for Pemkick, & for I. when we are all together again. I like the men better than the women—they are manly, muscular & simple. There was one fellow I liked immensely, Sir Coutts Lindsay, who strange to say is a wonderfully handsome likeness to little Lindsay the Harchitect, so that I am convinced they must be of the same stock. Isabel with her playing & nice manners would have been a Goddess last night; Isabel & Pem are two of the best mannered girls I ever met (I'm another). Miladi made the most charming overtures to intimate friendship, mais je doute de sa sincérité; for I'm an uncommonly useful fellow at a small tea-party, among people who are sick of Verdi, Bellini & Co, and like peculiar music, and my experiences of life being unusual, I suppose my talk is rather an institution among critters who are all like to each other as Sterne's shillings or francs, which is it? But if Miladi will ask Pem, I'll go as often as she likes (in moderation, bien entendu), for I shall find people who'll buy watercolours, or sketches when I make them, and like to have it spread among publishers who are great snobs that D. M. disporteth himself among swells. If you read Philip you will become keenly alive to this advantage.

That naturally leads me to business, which is so so; of course I have done little this last week or two, but have just finished a jolly drawing for OAW—will send you yesterday's & last week's. I may have to take a week's spell in the country but I think that my work will be of better quality and more profuse and spontaneous after this clearing of the brain and biliaries. Punch and I un petit peu en froid, but I do not think it will last. I am going to get up at 7 in the morning. I did this morning and yesterday and took a long walk through the rain which gave me a wonderfully healthy relish for my breakfast. My eyes are all right.

Now old Lady, write me the news about yourself and

yours; you have no idea how welcome some 50 or 60 pages in your fist will be. Tell me all about your health—Isabel's and everybody's—and I want you to get a little vignette photograph of your old face done at Severins, trois quarts, with the chin rather up, so:

Love to all—I'm going to write to Eugène—not exactly in this strain as you may fancy.

With best love

Your ever affectionate son

K

Thursday
Brighton
[April 21, 1862]

My dearest Pet,

You will be pleased to hear that relief has come to me at last and that today I am much better, although perhaps only for a few hours. Indeed, I have been quite myself for a little while, feeling only that I have been most fearfully shaken; and of course my native facetiousness has been frightened out of me for a little while. I received your dear affectionate letter and also one from Maman Bellemère to whom I am going to write.

I have not yet made up my mind how long to stay, indeed much will depend on what Traer writes tomorrow. As you may easily fancy Brighton is not a very amusing place to me; for when I am well my idea of amusement is inseparably connected with you. But if this sea air, out of door life and lots of exercise are really doing me good I think I had better stay a few days longer. Should I make up my mind to leave on Saturday night or Sunday morning let me know if I could go and dine with the Mosses and meet you there; but do not return to Grosvenor St. on that account as it is so undecided whether I shall stay or not.

I shall have lots to tell you about the Bakers[1] who are excessively kind, but will write no more at present.

Pray for me my dear kind good angel—*I* do most fervently both for you and myself—and with kind regards to Mr. and Mrs. Moss believe me my darling Pem most lovingly and affectionately

Yours Kicky

10 Norfolk Square
Brighton
April 23

My dearest Pem,

I write a hurried line now (10 o'clock a.m.) in case I should not be able to do so again today. I am going to the review with the Bakers. Today I am a good deal better—a sort of languid lucid interval—yesterday was miserable. I hope you are not making yourself very uneasy. Traer gave me such assurances of recovery—I have to eat enormously and take quinine for some time in great quantities. This morning 3 miles and a bath before breakfast. I suppose you are at the Mosses by this time. To-morrow I shall have time to write a much longer letter. Baker lends me a pony—they are waiting. Love to all, my dear angel; pray for your Kick and hope for better days.

In great haste for the B's are waiting for me
Your ever most loving
Kicky

April 26, 1862

My beloved Pet-Pem,

I have had a few hours relief and then dropping down again into wretchedness. God knows when and how it will end. With your dear old scrawl came a most encouraging note from Traer, which I enclose for you. At present I have just taken a draft of bitter beer which has enlivened me for

[1] With whom he lodged at Brighton.

a few moments. It is half past 5 and we are soon going to dine.

I have been out nearly all day; have begun a sketch of Rosalie Baker on a pony which will be good I believe. All the afternoon I have been on pony back, with a fit of the blues, cutting the accompanying fascinating figure among the swells on the parade.

I am getting very fond of Mrs. Baker, although she is sometimes almost uncouth in her excessive straightforwardness. Baker is in London—there is a Miss Otté here who passes for a great flirt, mais qui ne m'amuse pas énormément comme tu conçois. Yesterday I met Tuffnell and went to his hotel in the evening. You will be pleased to hear that yesterday and today I have confined myself to a cigarette after breakfast and one after lunch with 3 in the evening—I assure you the effort to me is quite terrific.

Darling, I shall remember Brighton as the place where the most unhappy hours of my life have been spent. I wonder if I shall get really well again and once more have confidence in myself and self respect and courage to struggle and work.

I can see from your affectionate letter how you miss me; but, darling, it is better that we should become able to do without each other for little spaces of time, and not depend so utterly on each other's society. Now I find myself utterly lost here and occasionally bored as I sincerely hope you will never be in your life. I pray most fervently for better days every night and morning, am up long before breakfast walking and trying to get up the appetite recommended by Traer.

I will now say goodbye with many kisses, my angel; believe me your ever loving and affectionate but sorely afflicted

Kicky

Tuesday
[April 27th, 1862]

My darling Pem,

I have just come in from a long ride over the hills. I am

constantly fluctuating between the blues and the other thing, but am beginning to acquire more command over myself rather. This morning after breakfast I had a strong temptation to go off by train to Norwood and dine with you, but think Traer would not have been pleased. We are all of us now going for a walk, it is lovely weather; how lovely Norwood must be! Oh to get well and back to Pem and my work again. I don't know yet how long I shall stop, but think that as I *am* here I had better give it a good trial. Strange to say the wretched fit comes on during the digestion and is accompanied by constant *rumblings* and a slight weight. I fancy that great care and a long time must elapse before I am thoroughly well, but I hope to be back to my work in 3

After Riding
For Maman bellemère—great care to be taken when you sit down—choose a soft chair, and mind the expression of your face does not betray you.

or 4 days. I think I shall walk to London. I wonder you had not received my letter, but probably got it after sending yours; I also wrote one yesterday morning to Grosvenor St.

It seems funny to be so long *unkissed!* doesn't it.

Adieu my darling, love to all,

Your loving and affectionate

Kick

If I had written this this morning after breakfast it would have been much longer and merrier, my Pet.

Monday

[April 28, 1862]

My darling,

I am altogether a good deal better today than I have been yet. There has been no letter from you, on account of Sunday, but I suppose and hope that you are all right. Baker has gone back to town today and I am the only male in the home. To tell you that I bore myself is but a mild expression, but I am so thankful to feel myself getting better I would gladly stop here a month. The weather is most lovely, and today as I roasted myself on the sands and flung pebbles at the sea which was as smooth as glass, I felt the want of my old companion very badly.

I've not heard from Traer since Saturday.

I rather fancy that I shall be in town on Wednesday but can't say for certain. You will find me jolly brown with a red nose from the sun and mahogany hands. I shall have lots to tell you—but these fits will go on occurring occasionally although in a slighter degree till I am quite settled into myself and have no more rumblings, or dyspepsia—but I can command myself better when they come and that is a great comfort. Perhaps there will be a note from you tonight to say you are all right and in London. Do not make yourself anxious my dear old gal. I trust in God that I shall be all right and make you jolly again.

I am now going out for a long walk.

Addio, darling—treasure—pet—all the world—couldn't do without you

Your Kicky

Best love to the old 'uns. Maman Bellemère said she'd write. Why doesn't she?

Tuesday Morn.
[April 29, 1862]

Dearest Pet,

Still progressing—have thoughts of going to London to-morrow, but am not decided. Getting to miss you very dreadfully Miss, but half a cure won't do. Facetiousness not returned yet, but am rather longing for work, which I can't do here. Spend my days tearing about the downs to get up the necessary appetite to follow Traer's prescription. Heard from him last night, he wishes me to write to Haden. If by any chance you should meet the latter, don't mention Traer.

Next Monday at the Academy with you, my old Pem—won't it be jolly. I shall eat nothing the whole day so as to have no digestion to embitter my existence—Hélas! hélas!

Cornhill comes out today—desperate temptation which I shall however resist, as I want to read Philip with you sitting by (and an empty stomach). I am also now going to write to Lucas. (There's a shop here kept by one Lucas, No. 48). I hope I shall see you looking well; I suppose you will have one of those darling muslins on when I come back.

With dearest love, my good angel

Your ever loving and affectionate

Kicky

91 Newman St.,
[May 19, 1862]

My dear Mamma,

I dare say you are getting anxious about not having heard from me. The fact is I had a relapse of that beastly liver complaint I spoke of in my last, and so severe that I was ordered to go and spend a fortnight in Brighton doing nothing but take immense long walks, bathing, eating 3 or 4 meat meals a day and taking quinine. I am now recovering gradually but surely as far as I can see, and can scarcely realise now the wretched state of mind I was in at Brighton—evidently a sort of strange aberration of mind. They say it is a thing which only occurs once in a fellow's life if he only takes proper care of himself. The causes were want of air and exercise, anxiety (which was needless) and above all the want to be married. I am still going on with my quinine, taking cod liver oil and plenty of exercise—of course I am also working hard to fill up arrears—for this unlucky state of things and the consequent expenses have thrown me back a good deal as you may fancy.

In Brighton I stayed with some people of the name of Baker, friends of the W's. I wouldn't have dear Emma with me as the distress of mind I caused her made me worse than ever. Since I have had this, I have met lots of people who at one period or another of their lives have suffered the same thing. Now the fits are less frequent and I can command them; and in another month or so I hope to be quite free; poverty of blood, exhaustion of the brain in a very excitable temperament etc. . . . I had no pain whatever but slight dyspepsia after meals. But the agony of mind was worse than anything I ever experienced from my eyes in Malines. It seemed to me as if my heart was changed into a stone for ever towards everybody in the world, and I thought at the time it would never get right again. Indeed I can't quite understand now what I thought; and were it not for the intense anguish I felt and can remember I should feel disposed to laugh at it and see it all in a humorous light.

I can't write you a very long letter—indeed there is very little news to tell. One thing will rather amuse you. On Saturday week I went with Emma and Ellen Levy to the International Exhibition, the latter having press tickets to pass us through—and in the picture gallery Emma said, "There then I've just seen Miss Lewis, and after looking at me she turned away her head in another direction." Now

Miss Lewis has uncommonly good sight, and very likely cut Emma on purpose—consequently when we afterwards met them, both Isabella and Louisa, I obstinately stared at some pictures above their heads, so they may if they like believe I really didn't see them. But you understand it was very awkward, and I wasn't going to stop and speak or even bow to people who might have intended cutting Emma.

Since my return I have done a drawing for OAW, 3 for Punch and some initials. I am going to try and get work for the Illustrated, for whom I did something six weeks ago, and also to paint some watercolours.

Nothing would do me more good now than a jolly long letter from you and Isabel with all the news and chit chat of Dusseldorf. Pem and I have been out to one or two very nice artist parties at Jones's the prœraphaelite's and at Solomon's meeting all sorts of celebrities vocal, artistic and otherwise. I have lately had a great accès de voix and been singing in a manner that smashes everybody professional or otherwise.

Not heard from Tom lately. Hasn't sent a picture—all the other fellows have got their pictures in. Moscheles' picture has been very favourably noticed in all the papers, and on the private view he had sold it to a fellow for 50£ who sold it to another for 100£ who again sold it for 125£.

Val Prinsep and I getting very thick—Emma quite in love with him. How's Aunt G and Bobbie? I suppose the Schadow strasse concerts have begun again. Tell me all about it and everything else. Indeed it seems ages since I have heard from you. Give my love to all. I will send you anything that comes out—probably to-morrow Punch will have some things of mine and perhaps OAW. Tom J. has sent me some sherry, which is very kind, but I do wish he would not be such a little snob and idiot for all the fellows to laugh at him and make fun of him to his very face.

And now my very dear Mamma write soon to your ever affectionate son

K

Saturday
[May, 1862]

My dear Tom,

Received yours yesterday with Bancroft's. Will do what he wishes & write, shall be delighted to see the old fellow & get all the fellows to exert their utmost fascination over him & prevent him from going to America. Hope you'll be in town too.

Lots to tell you. I didn't write in the first place because I thought from your last note you were going to write again —secondly because I've been beastly ill of a strange & weird malady which began about six weeks ago. My brain suddenly got affected by my liver it appears and I fell into the slough of despond, but, vois-tu, in a way I never saw or heard of in anybody else. I was first treated by Haden very violently; finally Traer took me out of his hands surreptitiously, sent me down to Brighton for a fortnight, to do nothing but walk about the whole day, eat 3 hearty meals of meat & take loads of quinine. Enfin I am getting better but am not myself yet—c'est drôle, hein? It appears I am built of strange materials, but they assure me that my brain itself is perfectly healthy and sound. The agonies and tortures I have endured are beyond all parallel in my experience—brought on gradually it appears by lack of air & exercise, overwork, anxiety, insufficient food & the admirable purity of my morals, my boy. I am now taking codliver oil, and 15 grains of quinine per diem; and have exchanged my fearful state of mind for the delightful luxuries of a boil on my ancle & a cold in the head. All this will account for my not having anything out, as you may fancy. Indeed this last month or two have been disastrous; nothing or barely nothing done, and great expenses—Enfin! Tout est pour le mieux dans le meilleur des mondes. When I am thoroughly myself again, say in another month or two, I think my work will have improved. This last fortnight I have done a good deal. Marriage, so says Haden, would be a radical cure. Emma has been dreadfully shaken by this wretched state of things, and looks very ill; I was all the time away from her in Brighton, for the misery she could not conceal at seeing me in such a state made me worse, and I did therefore tear myself away for both our sakes like a veritable brick.

On Good Friday I had to do a block for the News; it was all done but a few hands, when I felt such a rush of misery & madness come over me that I gave it up & spoilt the whole thing to rush off to Haden. I believe I fell down on my knees to him or something & cried!—Why the devil have we got livers & things?

First I must tell you the object of my writing so soon. Morgan is getting up an exhibition in Berners Street—Jimmy's white woman & lady at the piano are there, and everybody has sent things so that it is a first rate thing (to open on the first of June); so send up anything saleable you have before that time, consigned to Matthew Morgan Esq., 14 Berners St.—only let me know first by return if you are going to send and I will try & secure you a good place.

All the fellows have been very lucky this year. Moscheles the most lucky of all—picture sold at private view for fifty, resold immediately for 100, next day for 125—besides has lots of commissions & a painting class of young ladies which brings him in 5 guineas a week. Poynter sold his picture I am told, Henley got two in, etc.

On Sunday we are all going to have a reunion at the Greeks'—Keene going & I'm going to take Val Prinsep, my pet giant strong man and best of good fellows. I wish you were coming. Been fraternising lots with the Prinseps & Somerses. Got a large placard on which the Earl & Countess in Capitals request the honour of my company to dinner in small print. Diner à la russe—awfully swell; sat next to Dicky Doyle who's a stunner. But found it awfully slow I must say. Not so at Little Holland House, but just like the Greeks', smoke in a comfortable state, pelotage with the ladies after dinner—Mrs. Dalrymple awful pretty—Miladi idem—Milor

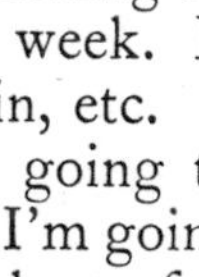

Also go (with the fayre Emma) to Solomon's at homes which are delightful; the best of professionals there—old Joachim, and all sorts of swell singers (including me). Also had a delightful Evening at Burne Jones's, who's got the jolliest wife & sisters-in-law imaginable (Poynter head over years). Met lots of jolly fellows there—William Rossetti & his two sisters etc (my Adelaïde, accompanied by the future Missus, met with rapturous & well deserved applause—tears, hysterical sobbings & final swoonings).

In fact old fellow, I very much wish you pitched your tent in these diggings.

The other day I was walking in the International with Emma & one of my friends the Miss Levys (who passed in by favour of the Daily Telegraph Press ticket) when suddenly Emma said: "I have just seen Miss Lewis, who looked at me & then looked another way!" Beastly awkward I thought, knowing Miss Lewis to have a remarkably long sight and good memory; so presently when we passed them I thought the best thing to do would be to be enormously interested in the beautiful roof of the building, so that I didn't see them at all—wouldn't do to run the risk of a cut from them, you know. Well since then Isabella has written to my sister in a sort of delightful cheeky manner to ask (with her best love to me) why I did it? and wishing me all sorts of happiness—but from what she said I am pretty well convinced that Louisa *did* cut Emma, which is excessively undignified & foolish, and makes all sort of awkwardness; and Isabella very sensibly writes so as to try & cloak this freak of Louisa's. Did you ever know anything so damned awkward? What am I to do if I meet them again? They are stopping at the General's who's very kind to them.

My aunt is over here; she is come over to say farewell to her parents who are going to India & then very much to my mother's displeasure going back to Dusseldorf. My mother & sister not at all well it appears. Pork beginning to tell on their constitutions. How I wish I could get them over here—Beef here, & mutton, underdone.

My brother is broke for debt, & writes to me that a

friend of his is going to buy him out of the army and they are going into business together, and that I'm not to write a word of all this to my mother. Did you ever hear of such a thing? I am expecting to hear from him every day, and I suppose I *ought* to write to my mother about it. I've now told you all about myself, and will tell you about the fellows en détail.

Poynter's picture the Bunch of blue ribbons is out & out the best thing he has painted, hung below the line. Modern subject. His angel, fortunately for it I think, is quite at the top. He has done another thing for OAW (not so good as the last though) but is doing lots of etchings from old masters for Lady Eastlake who is getting very fond of him it appears. He is getting gradually out of his troubles, but I am afraid is overworking himself terribly & looks very ill. Mrs. Bell has just had a little girl. Henley has two little pictures in muslin beneath the line, very pretty but rather weak. His best picture Miss Denrich & the one you sent, at Morgan's. Jimmy has just done a first rate drawing on wood for OAW. He has been trying to paint little Ossi Coronio but has given it up in disgust. He is in his furnitures somewhere with Joe, qui devient de plus en plus insupportable et grande dame I am told. His pictures have met with no mention as yet I believe but they look glorious. Leighton has some magnificent things, I must say. Millais' "Trust me" the finest thing there. Morten pottering about in his old way. Tom Jeckell's 'Norwich Gates' for a park are one of the finest things in the International, and he is making lots of money. Getting very unpopular for he tells such colossal lies & talks so beastly big about his friends Wales & St. Alban's. Charles Keene unchangeably jolly & mild sunshine as ever. Marks got a very clever picture of a mediaeval jester which is well hung (both jester & picture) & consequently sold (to a lady of rank I suppose).

Smoking half hour at Pamphilon's always uncommonly jolly—everybody seems on the whole to be getting on. I'm not, as I would wish—ce cochon de Valker! I am going to do some watercolours. I think Punch snubs me a little.

OAW inquire tenderly after my health, and shew great consideration in not overworking me in my present delicate state—Emma getting on very well with her engraving—is much delighted with the portions of your book which she can understand; I think it delightful, but will own that there are questions discussed in it that are almost above *my* lordly comprehension. The loves of the barrister & German girl most exquisite little story. I'm trying to get up the Japanese business again for OAW. Would I could marry! I could work more & better—should be rid of ennuis beaupaternes et bellematernes, and live with the dearest goodest kindest woman I ever met—who sends kindest regards. Till I hear from you again, & hoping to see you soon

ever your K

[May 23, 1862]

My dear Mamma,

I received your letter two days after I had posted mine, and was much distressed to learn how anxious you had been. Indeed I cannot understand how I had not thought of that, except that I was so wretched that I had lost all note of time. The first day for a month that I have been thoroughly myself again for the whole day was last Sunday. Indeed now I am far from well, although so much better and nearer complete recovery that I am very thankful. I fancy I must have passed through that jolly state of mind which our ancestors, ignorant of the anatomy of the liver, used to call possession by the devil. I am very sorry to hear you and Isabel are poorly and that my silence has in some degree contributed towards it. I would not let Emma write either —why, I really don't know. First I hope to send you either 5 or 10 next month, as I have been working very hard these last three weeks; but don't know as yet whether my last 2 drawings, 5 guineas worth, are accepted by Punch or not, and have a slight presentiment they will not be, somehow. Mark Lemon is so very capricious. Nothing whatever of mine has come out this week, or I should have sent it; but I think that next week will bring out something for certain which I will send.

My Aunt[1] came here yesterday afternoon but I had left—she went straight away to Emma, where she stayed half an hour and from thence to the train for Hastings. I wish I had seen her, but she gave all the news I was anxious to hear to Emma. She says Isabel has grown very thin, and that you are poorly; she found Emma it appears very much altered—no wonder after the worry she's had on my account. Fancy my being 10 days away from her, she knowing that I was ill, when she will almost go into a fit from anxiety if I have a slight *stomach-ache*! (Yes, Isabel, to such details the most romantic attachments will finally condescend.)

I will now tell you about Johnny.[2] I went there to lunch the day I had your letter; charmingly pretty house in Mitton Place, not *street*; 3 horses, lots of pet bull dogs. Missus very elegant pretty woman. Johnny a little bit less robust than I remember him years ago. They received me very nicely, and now and then I will go and lunch with them; but they will never be of any great use to me or me to them, for we haven't got many notions in common. However if he takes me to Tattersalls and puts me up to a few horsy jokes for Punch that will be something. He reminds me wonderfully of my uncle in manner and way of living—and seems a peculiarly happily constituted individual. Inquired very warmly after all of us. They appear to be most worldly people, and I shouldn't think they belong to a very intellectual set, nor I should say a very high-principled one. They also enquired very kindly after my Aunt. I suppose the departure of that little lady is a great relief to you for a while; but from what she said to Pem she seems to have completely made up her mind to return to Dusseldorf; and I really don't see at present what means I can very well employ to prevent her. I suppose you could not endure the idea of living over here with her either. I shall see her on her return from Hastings.

[1]Georgie Clarke, back in England for a visit.
[2]A Clarke cousin.

It appears she looks wonderfully fresh and young, and says she is growing so fat she is quite ashamed of herself. I am very sorry Isabel neglects her piano, which would be a great thing over here—besides being such a recourse for herself against ennui. Curiously enough when I was ill, in the milder moments I had that expression of listless languor and blaséness which characterises Isabel, and was able to realise as I fancied her state of mind when she has no excitement to look forward to; and that set me speculating a lot about her. I think that her liver must be a good deal out of order; and I should say that a long course of exercises, quinine, and alas! *good food* would set her all right; and also plenty of occupation for the mind. That hard work and exercise are the only healthy conditions of happiness, except for some peculiarly constituted individuals, I am thoroughly convinced. I overdid the hard work, and completely neglected the exercise—consequently my liver became inactive and suddenly drove floods of poisoned blood into my brain. I think Isabel would find it very slow over here at first.

On Tuesday last I dined at Little Holland House; what a lovely place it is. Mrs. Dalrymple was there—such a handsome woman—also Lady Somers, or as we call her 'Miladi'—both dressed—mais fallait voir! On Sunday there is going to be a réunion of all the old set at Tulse Hill, and for once on Sunday I am going to be unfaithful to Pem, and dine there. But I am not in a state of mind to enjoy these festivities. Very anxious about the future, when not depressed from liver causes. In terrible want to marry, besides. My doctor says that health and peace of mind will return by enchantment under those circumstances, and I should only have natural and healthy worries to look forward to—that of providing the daily bread. Oh that we four were united or near each other; we would make a happy home.

I often think that Emma and you, and one or two other people I know, are made of happier materials than anybody I know—with this drawback, that exterior circumstances have the power to make you happy or wretched as the case may be—to be able completely to forget oneself for somebody else must be the jolliest constitution going though it may not seem so for the people themselves. If I am looking a little better or in better spirits for a day Emma seems to enjoy such exquisite happiness from it that I get quite envious of her.

The Doctors, both Haden and Traer, laughed at me and said that my disorder was purely physical. Do you know what it seemed to me at the time, for I could not get myself to believe it was physical till I actually felt that physic was getting me round? It suddenly came across me that I was a thoroughly bad man who had by a marvel been sustained by good example until now, and that the original badness of my nature was just going to break out at last like a regular conflagration, and that the last year's virtue had been the crowning point of my goodness on the earth—a temptation suddenly to break loose and indulge in every riotous excess, drink, opium, and the most shameless intrigues, for I felt that come over me (*as it seemed* you know) that no woman in the world could resist—and that when I felt downright madness reach me, as it would inevitably have done according to my theory at the time, I would kill myself and escape the asylum.

My appreciation of all Emma's qualities strange to say got stronger than ever, and the fact of my conscience suddenly becoming painfully and morbidly acute was the real torture and agony. I felt I hated Emma, you, and all those of my friends I admire the most for being so naturally and easily possessed of qualities which were denied to me, and envied you all to an extent that was a downright anguish. The great kindness that was shewn to me by everybody, and the wonderful devotion of dear Emma made me worse. I kept on saying to myself: "Oh unlucky girl if you *only* knew me!" or else "How blind these fellows are not to read me through and through as I really am and cut me!" So you can fancy what I felt when I went tearing all over the Brighton Downs, miles after miles, or getting up in the night and throwing myself on my knees praying in down-right despair. It all seems like a dream. Since, I have met other men who have suffered in the same way, at some time or another—Charles Keene's brother was like this for a year. Then there was always the good principle struggling in me, but somehow so completely clouded that I was quite in the dark. Both Haden and Traer say that I am a very peculiar temperament but that there isn't the slightest trace of unhealthiness in my brain itself; dreadfully impressionable and passionate from being almost purely nervous (a constitution which I inherit from you) with the additional causes of excitement which result from my temperament being highly artistic and overwrought—all of which sounds rather romantic, like an artist in a novel, doesn't it; but such is the diagnosis of two very practical and unromantic men. Add to that the concentrated state of pent up excitement I have lived in for the last year, insufficient food and exercise, overtaxing of the brain to produce Punch jokes etc. when not in the humour, and all this coming on after the quiet and idleness of 4 years. If I had not been engaged to one of the dearest creatures that ever lived I am afraid I should have gone thoroughly to the bad and injured my constitution for ever and ruined the proper healthy tone of my mind and lost all chances of happiness. Once married I am safe—so say my doctors—but that can't be for some time. Now thank God I am nearly all right again. Have been dreadfully shaken and all that—and do not feel peculiarly bright or facetious as you may fancy; but in another month or so I daresay all my native facetiousness will return and I shall get on well.

I will now shut up as I am going to Traer's to lunch with him and ask if I may not leave off quinine—which costs lots of money—and so my very dear old moder, hoping to hear from you soon, and with kindest love to Isabel

Your ever affectionate son

Kicky

I shall probably get in my accounts within the first 10 days of June and will send accordingly.

Always send your love to Pem when you write.

[June 2, 1862]

My dearest Idiotic Pet,

I've no news at all to tell you except that I've slept very well and feel all right—and that I'm *beginning* to feel much bored at not seeing you to-night. This is the sort of weather for you and me to sit out somewhere in the country with my head buried in your muslins. I have been altering Miss Sims's arm for the benefit of Mr. Swain—all of it engraved except the arm. I am now going out with all my drawing materials. Shall take the Chelsea boat, find out a spot, work hard—and if I see some very pretty place, we'll try and have a day this week or next, if we can make it compatible with work. Won't you miss me this evening, that's all!

So goodbye my dear pet—I loved you dreadfully all day yesterday and still more today. Your ever affectionate darling

Kick

D . . . the Caughts!

I do hope I shall do some good work today to show you to-morrow—à demain six heures.

[June 13, 1862]

My dear Mamma,

I have just received your letter enclosing Gyggy's, with

which I am not surprised as he had written me all about it with the express condition that I was not to mention a word to you on the subject as yet, and I was deliberating whether I would or not just yet. I will write to him immediately. I think it is great madness on his part, and there is an inconsistency about his letters (whether they contain truth or falsehood) which I very much mistrust—for instance he says that a friend of his "qui lui est devoué jusqu'à la mort" advanced him money sufficient not only to pay his debts but to buy himself out of the army. If such is the case, he should pay his debts and remain where his bread and butter is, and my letter to him will be strongly to that effect although I fear it will be of very little use. His notion of coming over here to meet you is founded on what I must have written to him several months back when I took a very sanguine view of my own affairs, and thought your coming over here an event likely to happen sooner. He also states that his friend and himself with a certain small capital of money and a large capital of brain and experience in affairs are going to start as men of business of some kind or other; I shall certainly discourage any attempt to come here on his part, as it would be sheer madness. There is one thing to say, he would precious soon wish himself back again—and I will express myself pretty strongly about his going to Dusseldorf, not that I think it likely at all. If I could afford it I would go over to Paris immediately, but I daren't just now, and I don't know that it would be of any good. One thing is certain—I can't send him any money. Every bit I can spare I must send to you. I was only waiting for my Punch a/c to send you 5£; I had hoped to send you 10£, but one large drawing was refused, and the bill for my lay figure 4£ 15/- for six months is just come in. The Punch a/c will be paid in a day or two and you shall have the money directly; I have lots of trouble with the people about the simple thing of settling accounts, they are so dilatory and unbusinesslike with young and unimportant men. I should like to see them make Leech wait a day beyond the time.

My health is improving gradually and my spirits with

it. Traer recommends three meat meals a day, I eat two—a large mutton chop for breakfast ditto for dinner unless I dine out, and this is working wonders in my blood, which was dreadfully impoverished by want of air, insufficient diet (arising from my having no appetite) and anxiety. I am much distressed at what you write about Isabel, and the effects of bad food on yourself and her. Fortunately she gets plenty of open air, at least I hope so. As for her being consumptive—that of course is nonsense—all foreigners have a theory that English girls are consumptive. ("Ces belles jeunes *Meess* poitrinaires et rêveuses qui boivent du thé toute la journée, et soupirent en regardant la Tamise du haut de leurs fenêtres sur le pont de Londres.") That Isabel's liver is not in first rate order I have no doubt, want of food and want of proper occupation for the mind will soon bring that about. I hope she does not neglect her piano now that my Aunt is gone. If she could force herself to practise a certain amount a day at regular intervals, she would get into the habit of it; and it would be almost a stock in trade for her over here if she reaches very great perfection—making her welcome everywhere. But if she *were* over here, and did go everywhere she would be heartily sick of it in a few months I believe, unless she took interest in something, piano for instance, for its own sake.

I have had peeps at swell society, and would certainly not wish Isabel to become a favourite there; from what I have seen, it appears a vanity of vanities where nothing is solid except plenty of money, and to the poor all must be vexation of spirit unless they have something very serious to fall back upon—amusement and excitement are things that pall fearfully, which wouldn't matter if they did not unfit you for everything else.

I was at a very interesting evening last Tuesday at Mrs. Sartoris's in St. James's Place, about a hundred and fifty people; musical evening. Lots of swells of every sort. Male and female Markises, as Sam Weller calls them, writers, painters, poets, composers, Thackeray, Browning etc. etc. I did not sing but shall sing next Tuesday. Much of the singing was professional and very good of its kind; but an amateur Miss Brown by name, sang with a charm and perfection that I have never heard equalled in my life; so that I could have cried and laughed at the same time. That girl must make a hobby of her voice and live for it, I should think. It's all a mistake to think one need keep up a respectability or position among all these clever people. My uncle's wretched theory on those subjects is of a rottenness that seems laughable over here. All that is asked of you is that if you are English, speak it correctly. And as far as the pleasure that is to be extracted from these sort of gatherings, it shrivels up to nothing unless you go very seldom indeed. Like that fine sensation you get at the opera, only on the first night of the season. As for me, I am scarcely ever amused; the only way I can ever feel happy now is when a hard day's work has turned out successfully, that I have felt my progress in drawing and done 2 guineas worth of work in a day. Then I am much too exhausted to go out; but a cigarette in the Park with my dear Pem and a comfortable chat about the future, or you and Isabel or the fellows, and to finish up a peep at the Times or one of the reviews, et voilà!

As for marriage for which I long so, I can't say when it is to take place; I have no doubt old W., poor as he is, would do something when the time comes, that is furnish the rooms or part of them, and allow perhaps 50 pounds a year towards the ménage. But he is in no hurry to part with Emma, and can't sympathise with our hurry to get married. If we could only be married for the winter! I look with terror on the long evenings wasted, for I cannot work at the Wightwicks, and to sit here and work alone is out of the question; the loneliness of the day is enough. I have much to write and it would add considerably to my income, and as I want the day to draw it could only be done after dark; and then I would much sooner use Pem's eyes than mine. I have one idea for a book which I shall try and write this winter, and if I can carry out it would be very successful and of an originality unheard of; it will require reading up for at the

British Museum and taking notes on various subjects, and I think I shall manage for Pem and myself to pass our winter evenings at the reading room there unless we have a home of our own to do so—work, work, work! Je ne vois que ça et je n'espère que ça.[1]

It is a fortunate thing that Pem doesn't care for amusement of any kind and is always so tremendously delighted if she can help me in any way; indeed she has no other thought but me from morning till night.

There is no drudgery or privation she wouldn't be delighted to go through to be with me, and she is so unselfish and cheerful, all she wants is to be enormously loved (as most women) and told so occasionally, and then she is busy and facetious from morn till night, always doing some little service for somebody or other (who is generally myself) and funking nothing. What she has to put up with at home is enough to sicken the very devil at times.

Bancroft has come over here, and I expect T. A. will be up in a few days to meet him. T. A. seems to lead an unsatisfactory and unhappy life. He seems to lack some kind of practical energy; what I am learning and find it so hard to learn. What a lesson it is to have to depend upon yourself! All the little annoyances that are added to the one great anxiety. The depreciation of one's work that comes to one indirectly, the unfairness, the tyranny and bullying of publisher and editor, the little désagrément of not getting one's tin when due etc. etc., and above all the damned instability of everything till your name is well and thoroughly established; fortunately some little success comes now and then to wipe it all out (and prepare the slate for another series of disagreeables). By jove, life isn't a joke after 5 and 20. The very act of going to a dinner party among the most amusing people becomes a sort of hard work. Fancy after an unsuccessful day, when all one is fit for is to lie down on a sofa and be read to, having to go and sit next to Tom Taylor, whose good opinion about oneself and talents one

[1]This may have been the first germ of *Peter Ibbetson* and "dreaming true."

is peculiarly anxious to conciliate for very important reasons; before the soup is finished something comes out which damps some little hope one has been secretly entertaining on the subject of Punch, we will say. Deuced hard work to be lively and facetious then. I have been several times dining at Little Holland House lately, till indeed I am rather thoroughly sick of it, and yet I don't like to refuse too often. To-morrow morning I breakfast with Aidé who is anxious as ever to advance my fortunes. Also I am going to spend a day on the river with Val and Robert Browning, whose acquaintance I am particularly anxious to make. I believe I am going to get a ticket for Lord Lansdowne's great annual private concert. If I were a portrait painter or painted pictures, my fortune would be made, I am getting to know so many people; but unfortunately this kind of connection has no particular bearing on my line of art. I would sooner far be invited to the gin and whisky parties of the brothers Dalziel, engravers on wood, in Camden Town, where the Queen's English is solemnly murdered every other Saturday, I believe. The Levies (Emma is gone to pass a week there) seem anxious to get me on, and they have a kind of influence I fancy. Enfin Rome wasn't built in a day, and my position is immeasurably better than it was this time last year.

I wish it were possible for Isabel to make her musical talent of some avail; Clara Moscheles is earning lots of money by a singing class. I am going to try and get an appointment as solo singer in some swell church, and add 50 or 80 to my income thereby if possible. Felix is making lots of money; has a class for teaching young ladies painting, which brings him in nearly 300 a year and besides that has lots of orders for cheap portraits, which he paints very quick. On the other hand there is Jimmy, almost the greatest genius of the day, with scarcely anybody big enough here to rank by him, who isn't making a sou, and borrowed a shilling of me yesterday. Henley has just sold two pictures for 27 pounds; he has made 37£ since he has come over here. Millais makes 3,000 a year, 800 of which by drawing on wood alone.

Now my dear Mamma I shall shut up and write to Gyggy; I will send you the 5£ as soon as I get it, and also whatever comes out of mine. I have got an initial which must be done before dinner. Write to me soon as I like to get your letters so, and give my best love to Isabel. This autumn I will try and treat myself to a cheap visit to you as I want to see you both so much; I will not raise hopes of being able to bring you back with me, but I hope to be able to add to your means now and then, until by hard work and economy I shall see you safely landed here at some time not very far distant I hope. Among the many plans I am constantly building for the future, I have fancied the possibility of Isabel making some 40 or 50 a year by giving a few music lessons. She would be none the less welcome at the 'tables of the great' were she so minded—on the contrary! Oh that Emma had her talent and fingers! We should have been married long ago.

Your ever affectionate son

K.

[June 14, 1862]

My own dearest Pem,

What beastly weather; enough to give one the blues, as if it wasn't enough not to see each other this evening, and to have drunk arsenicated champagne last night. First I'll tell you the news. Silver has written to order an initial letter, Punch inviting the British Public to the Andel Festival. Had a letter from my mater, enclosing one from my brother who has told her of his intention to leave the Army, and she is very anxious and distressed about it. I have written 8 close pages to her, and a long letter in French to that young scamp of a brother-in-law of yours—really I don't think I ought to marry a girl with such a wretch of a brother-in-law, it is a positive let down to me, it is. Also wrote to accept Mrs. Bell's invitation, and to Silver, and to Swain. To-morrow morning I breakfast with Aidé, who is as anxious as ever to further my fortunes, that I may soon establish my happiness on the durable and solid rock of matrimony. If you take a proper and unselfish interest in me, you ought to sacrifice yourself for the same purpose as soon as possible. He thinks me it appears a far luckier fellow than Leighton with all his worldly success, and an example for young men to follow.

V. P. has just been in. Bancroft gone to International with Poynter. We shall all meet at Pamphilon's as usual I suppose. By jove, won't you bore yourself this evening without your darling, that's all! I've no idea what I shall do this evening—perhaps go with Bancroft to Poynters—perhaps come home here and work. How nice it would be to find my room enlarged, and you making the tea before our evening work.

My dear, I hope this little change will do you good; I suppose when you get home again and we are again alone together we shall appreciate it all the more. Last night's ride home was very jolly, don't you think so; it is no bad compliment to say that I wished the Robinses at Jericho, merely for the purpose of having a longer ride back to Grosvenor Street.

Have you taken your engraving to the Levies? I suppose though that you feel rather nervous about it with your finger not yet healed, my poor pet.

My mother sends her love to dear Emma, (so *I* needn't). She says Isabel is looking very poorly I am sorry to say, so much so that these German idiotic friends of hers encourage her with the notion that she's consumptive, which is of course downright bosh; she may be a little bit samperative but her bad looks come more from bad food, and want of proper occupation for the mind than anything else. I wish they were over here.

They are labouring under some nightmare apprehension lest my brother should take into his head that they would like to enjoy the charm of his society for a while, and go to spend a year or two at Dusseldorf.

I was awfully tired last night, and slept till half past 10 o'clock—and this morning I was quite spiteful to my dress coat, and as I put it into the drawer I said: "Stop there till Tuesday next and be d . . . d to you!" and ill-treated my dress boots so, that one of them tried to kick me, and fell into my bath in the attempt.

To-morrow evening at seven o'clock I shall come and see you (am I to ring the airy bell?) I beg you will command yourself and not indulge in any vulgar exhibition of delight before strangers; you must shake my hand and say: "Mr. du Maurier, your presence here, under the hospitable roof of my good friends, the Levies, although not unexpected, affords me pleasure, and I may reasonably venture to hope that it gratifies you likewise; the weather is more seasonable than yesterday."

I will now shut up with best and dearest love and many kisses, my pet—one for each eye, one for the mouth, and the rest to be disposed about your person in the manner most convenient to yourself, and most in accordance with modern prejudice—if you have one to spare, you may divide it between Ellen and Annie.

Goodbye my love, *I* shall miss you, you needn't fear.

Your ever loving Kick

P.S. Your letter has just come, and I performed the usual evolution with your name at the bottom (blowed if it isn't quite wet). I am delighted to see, Miss, that your ideas about the weather, the champagne and our mutual affection coincide exactly with those I have expressed upstairs—at the top of this letter I mean. There Pem darling haven't I written you a long one.

[June 15, 1862]

My deary deary deary,

I've just been drinking 2 glasses of wine and I'm very tipsy. I've made the pencil drawing of the people in the bo-(hic)-oat! already to ink. I've also designed some in-in-in-icshal lettush with which I am not quishatishfied but I think them goodnuff f'Punch.

Bancroft gone to the inchnashnal'shbishun.

Bancroft gone to the inchnashnal'shbishun.

So tipsy I can't help writing double. Take another glass of wine to set me all right. Here goes—

Shall go this afternoon to Swains to get some Punch blocks. Had no letters of any kind, but am going to send a note to T.A. to tell him his darling Bancroft has arrived. I suppose I shall have lots to tell you to-morrow my pet. I hope you'll miss me at the opera to-night. You ought not to be able to enjoy it unless you can squeeze my hand all the time Santley is singing (and all the time he isn't).

I shall try to see Walford about my ac/.

I've got such a charming little likeness of you in the boat scene (with such a nice little sore on the upper lip.)

Slept like a top, which makes me feel very well today. I've now told you all the news, my darling stupid and will conclude by saying I love you dearly deeply passionately all the world to me I couldn't live without you. Also that I feel very facetious and spooney and wish you and I were going to spend the evening alone together. So goodbye darling and think of me a lot tonight and I will of you.

Your ever loving and affectionate Kick

Shotipshy I've beenanddrawn 2 'nishaltettush inshtead of one—thirtyshillinsh—wery good.

[June 19, 1862]

Pet,

I forgot to tell you yesterday the very thing that would have interested you most, the Levies bored me so with their chaff—viz. Baker came at 5 just as I was going out, and we went to Morgan, who unfortunately had just shut up shop and gone away, so I missed my chance then. But he is very anxious to come again, and gave me what was tantamount to an order for a pen and ink drawing. He was very nice indeed.

Val Prinsep just been. Fancy, last Sunday Thackeray and Browning dined there—and T. wants to meet Jimmy, so V. P. is going to get them together at his rooms in Charlotte St.

I shall go there of course, and devilish glad of the opportunity. It appears that T. is awfully fond of music. (Cornhill initials, perhaps.)

I am now going to take six beautiful initial letters; if I

can get away in time tonight I suppose I shall not exactly *forget* to call in at Grosvenor Street on my way home. Anyhow to-morrow darling, with all our hearts. Give my love to P. and M. and believe me with many kisses and much love your ever affectionate

K.

Posted your letter last night at the British Museum.
Just paid for lay figure.

26 Charlotte St.
[June 23, 1862]

—Pleassir, fromBradburyandEvans pleassir!
—Hullo! you little fool, why the devil didn't you knock?
—Pleassirknockedheversomanytimessir!
—All right, cut your lucky—(Hooray, subject from O A W! won't old Pem be pleased!)

Pet,

I've been drawing here all the morning—one of my drawings for Punch already on the block, the other will be finished by 5—coming stunningly. V. P. put on corduroy bags and sat or rather stood for the railway official. Bancroft been sitting to Val for a beast of a duke who was cruel to his wife. Going on Friday to dinner party at Little H. H. to meet the Millais. Just had lunch; rather tipsy.

Had a long letter from my mother and one from my brother. Isabel is in Malines, actually staying with some friends there on her return from Paris; I think the whole journey was rather useless, but it has quieted their anxiety about your precious brother-in-law. I will tell you all about it to-morrow. He writes a most cheeky and amusing letter.

I've got nothing more to tell you except that as usual I love you d., d., pr, a.t.w.t.m., c.n.d.w. you . . . I've no doubt you will be able to put in the missing letters—and so my dear pet with many kisses, à demain, early.

Your ever loving K

Now going to do the other block. If I don't take them to-morrow I'll bring them to you.

[June 28, 1862]

My *dearest* Pem,

I've just received your note which was a very delightful little surprise, and suddenly put me in a good temper with Lawless who's been boring me for the last half-hour till I could have hit him, and he can't make out the sudden change.

First my darling, I must tell you that last night I found wedding cards from Levy and Miss Webster, and I went to bed envying their happiness. This morning I received a subject from OAW (upon which I immediately made the enclosed sketch). It's an italian story either by the author of the poisoned mind or the portuguese tragedy, George Lumley, who is a great ass; and it is so stupid that I won't send it to you, as with your usual conscientiousness you might take the trouble to read it through. Very difficult subject and I've been sketching for it all the afternoon. Got up early and did dumb bells like mad—consequence was that at 12 o'clock I was obliged to go and eat some beef; also invested in a bath, spunge and flesh brush (I hope these unromantic little details will interest you). And now my darling of darlings I have told you all the news, but I've not told you that you've been haunting me all day as usual, and that as the time draws near to dine with S (of whose dinner time, by the bye, I am quite ignorant) my heart is filling with hatred towards him for taking me away from you. But perhaps something may come out of interest to you and me on Punch matters.

I will now say goodbye, with many kissings and blessings, my dearest and best of all dear friends, whom I do always most affectionately and passionately love; wish for me this evening as I've been wishing and wishing for you all day, pray for me to-night, and try and dream of your ever loving and devoted

Love to Mommong bellemair. Just read your note over again, which I thought was werry jolly and kissed it—spooney, spooney Kick!

91 Newman St.
[July 16, 1862]

My dear Mamma,

I should have written to you before but that for the last 10 days I have been working without rest and have always been so exhausted after it that to write was impossible. As soon as my Punch account comes in I will send you another fiver, and next Wednesday I will get what things of mine are out and send them to you. London Society has once more taken me into favour and I have just done three drawings which will appear at the end of the month and in which you will still see great improvement I think, if they are well engraved.

Your account of Isabel's journey interested me immensely, and I have been expecting to hear the end of it. I suppose she is now with you, and I hope she is looking and feeling better for her adventurous trip. I hope she will soon write to Emma who is always much hurt when Isabel neglects her.

I am looking very well and have been so barring an occasional attack of depression of spirits, though very slight compared to what I have been through. Traer says there's nothing for it but time, and lots of bitter beer and animal food—je deviens carnivore.

I've no doubt marriage will set me completely right.

Bancroft left last Wednesday to visit T. A. on his way to America.

Moscheles is painting cheap portraits and making heaps of money; in August he will go to Antwerp with his gains and paint a picture. He thinks me no end of a great artist; I wish I could think so myself; but I shall become one some day I suppose—you will see me among the 'eminent artists' on the back of Punch which I will send you, an advertisement which has sent Pem up to the seventh heaven. But I am always knocking up against the pets of fame and that takes it out of one. The other day I dined at Little Holland House with Millais and Mrs. Millais and the sight of the fellow gave me the blues for a week. Doyle and Watts were there, but Millais was awfully big; such liveliness and vitality, such a spoilt child of nature and society and everything—and much of it owing no doubt to his astonishing beauty and naïf impudence—he is not more than 30. I was much disappointed in his wife (the late Mrs. Ruskin, you know). She is quite passée—wasn't she fascinated by my singing though.

Last Saturday week Pem and I went to some Private Theatricals at the Roches' in which Jimmy and Moscheles acted to perfection, in French. Next Saturday week I am going to act there I believe, shall be put upon my mettle. Pem fraternised with the Greeks.

I had a more sensible letter from Gyggy; I can't lay my hands upon it or would send it. But can say nothing as he has not left the Army *yet*.

I hope you are pretty well in health; I would much like to see you and hope to spare time and money for a run over soon. Please write me a long letter. Have you heard from my Aunt? I am now going to hurry off to the International to do something for the Illustrated Times. I did some cattle for them last week which were very badly engraved but very nicely drawn.

And now my dear Mamma with best love to Isabel and yourself,

Your ever affectionate son

Kicky

91 Newman St.
[July, 1862]

My dear Tom,

I haven't written to you for a long time, as I have been so hard at work ever since Bancroft left, that I literally have not found a half hour to spare. Nevertheless I have been cheeky enough to expect a few words from you to tell me how you are getting on. Your last letter seemed written in bad spirits; you ought to come and spend a few days in town, old fellow.

A fat blond of the name of Thomson has been fraternising with us all at Pamphilon's and favoured me with a call, stating that he is a friend of yours; he speaks very highly of your picture of the girl and helmet, saying that it shews the greatest improvement, and is particularly enthusiastic on the painting of the dress. I hope we shall soon have an opportunity of judging for ourselves.

I have been working for all sorts of things lately; have been retaken into favour by London Society; have nobly condescended to do an illustration for the Guide, journal à 5 centimes. Am illustrating a new edition of Diary of a late physician. Also swiss cattle for Illustrated Times; and drawings of a Dublin school for Ill. Lond. News, by our special artist. I think that I am improving; anyhow if I don't it is not from the lack of painstaking and conscientiousness. My health is conci-conça and I am often very much depressed in spirits, and nervous about the future; whereas my natural healthy state is to be tremendously sanguine and hopeful. I believe marriage will set me all right again. Never did a poor devil long for matrimony as I do, in spite of its anxieties and responsibilities; and both Emma and I are getting heartily sick of this desultory courtship, which we would gladly exchange for a garret, to be together and have nobody to worry us; car pour des ennuis, mon cher, nous en avons. Heureusement, of all the cheerful, plucky, affectionate and devoted women that ever lived, although I say it as ought'nt, etc.

I don't know whether you have lately heard from my peoplesh. My sister has undertaken quite a startling expedition to Compiègne, with the intention of inoculating the youthful Gyggy with fraternal advice. He is going to leave the army willy-nilly; as for what he will do I don't know, and my mother is awfully anxious. I wish he was your brother, old cock—but perhaps upon the whole you would rather not.

My Aunt who is over here returns to Dusseldorf next week. I hope to pay them a visit in August.

Henley is selling all his pictures like wildfire, and is consequently in a radiant state of mind and physiognomy. Poynter struggling hard—has just painted a beautiful watercolour. Jimmy painting river pictures for the Greeks—is going at last, so he says, to realise the Wabash bonds, and will start for Venice with Joe on the proceeds. I suppose Bancroft told you about Thackeray wishing to meet Jimmy at Val's. We went, but the old fellow never came.

Dined at Little Holland House a few weeks ago to meet Mr. and Mrs. Millais; was fascinated by the young god, as usual; the beauty, loudness, immense animal spirit etc. did envelop me, although his sayings were not awfully wise, as I found out next morning on recovering from my intoxication. I have really a bump of reverence, and love to worship heroes; but think on the whole that I do not care to mix

"A TIME TO DANCE"

Illustration to a poem so entitled, showing the influence of F. Sandys; from the wood engraving published October 1861 in *Good Words*

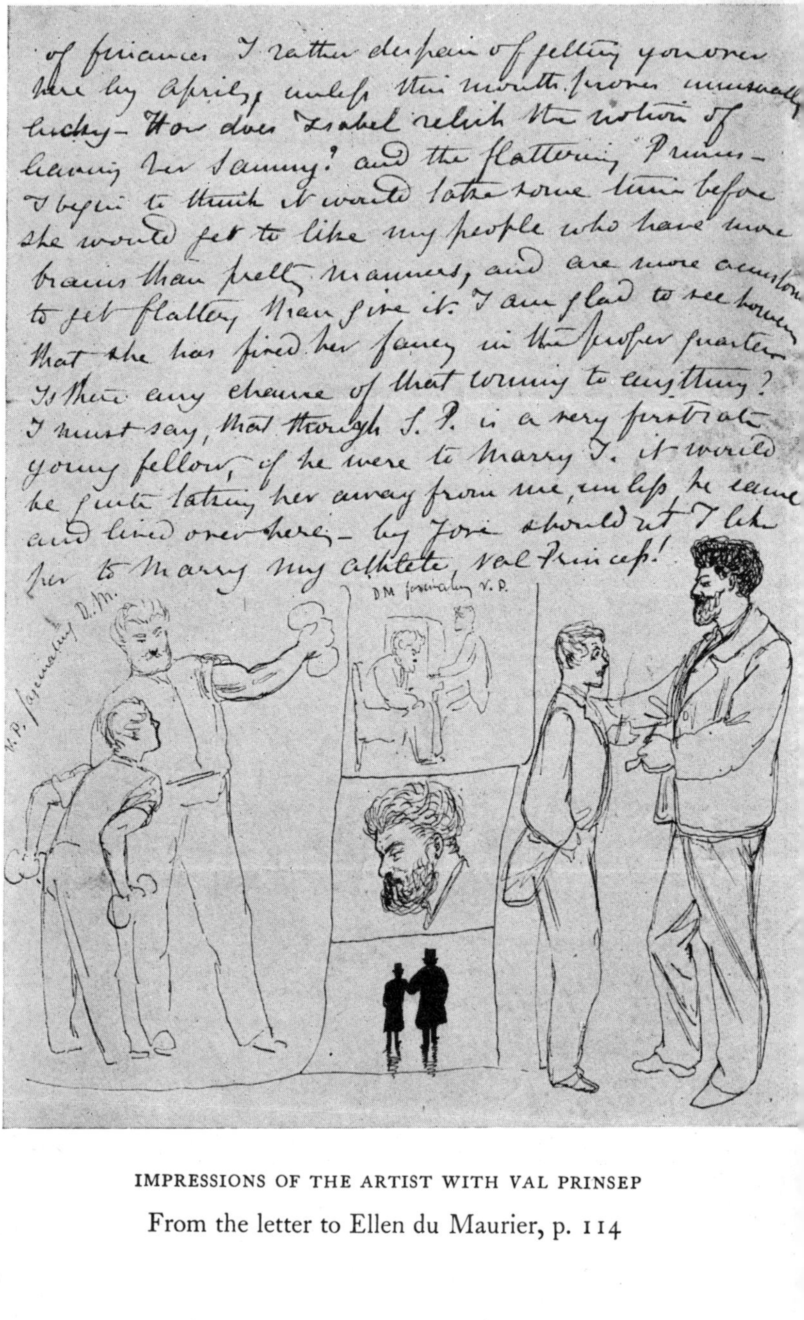

of finances I rather despair of getting you over here by April, unless this month proves unusually lucky— How does Isabel relish the notion of leaving her Sammy? and the flattering Prince— I begin to think it would take some time before she would get to like my people who have more brains than pretty manners, and are more accustomed to get flattery than give it. I am glad to see however that she has fixed her fancy in the proper quarter. Is there any chance of that coming to anything? I must say, that though S. P. is a very first rate young fellow, if he were to marry I. it would be quite taking her away from me, unless he came and lived over here— by Jove shouldn't I like her to marry my athlete, Val Prinsep!

IMPRESSIONS OF THE ARTIST WITH VAL PRINSEP

From the letter to Ellen du Maurier, p. 114

with them. ''Tis quite enough to see thee like a star' etc. (non satis). Bancroft, Poynter, Keene, etc. are unknown and obscure heroes whose heroism will wash and stand the test of familiarity—pour les autres, je n'sais pas trop.

Quant au monde aristo, tel qu'il m'est permis de l'entrevoir de temps en temps, il m'inspire un grandissime dégoût; se j'avais le talent je pourrais écrire des volumes sur une ou deux maisons; et M. Tackeré me parait avoir bougrement raison. Strangely enough I hear confidences de part et d'autre, à soulever le coeur. Val, for whom I have a great fondness, is great on the Sartoris faction. Little Captain Aïdé, who entertaineth, apparently, an immense affection for me, is most instructive on Little Holland House; everybody is the best of friends.

Sandys and I great pals; the Rossetti clique awfully droll, full of the strangest and most childish irrepressible affectations; to give you an idea of their tone and minds would take a quire—who's right and who's wrong? Hooray—whether it is prejudice or the result of early association, I never meet anybody to compare to the old clique taken all in all, and including Keene as the latest importation.

Dont auquel nonobstant quoi, as my brother says, may I soon lead a peaceful industrious and retired life, or I shall grow crazy; to cultivate the domestic virtues, filial, fraternal, marital and paternal, seems to me the noblest aim of existence; after which to devote especial care to one's liver, et puis, faire tout ce qu'il y'a de mieux en fait de petits bonshommes sur bois, en attendant autre chose.

And now my dear fellow, after all these excessively lively and amusing communications I will bid you au revoir; if you come up and see the International, we shall have many things to talk about.

Vale mon bon

Friday
[July, 1862]

My dear Mamma,

I suppose you were surprised at not getting the Punches; I went to the office in Fleet St. the other day, got them and as I was coming home they came out of my pocket and were lost, and I have had no other day to spare to go. I will get them now—the only place where you can get back Punches is at the office.

I have been working desperate hard; but cannot send you anything by this post, as I have not yet been paid.

I suppose Isabel has returned by this time. Why doesn't she write to Emma? I saw my Aunt the other day, she is now staying with the Vincents; she is going back to Germany in a week. Useless to attempt any dissuasion as she is bent on it, and expresses herself as being very attached to you! I told her that all my efforts were tending to get you over here as soon as possible. She said you would like it, but thought Isabel would not. Whether that is true or not I don't know—although Dusseldorf must be very agreeable to Isabel as she is made so much of there. I cannot see that she has any chance of marrying.

It is true that here she would not see very much society as we should have to be so very economical for the first year or two.

But I think both of you would enjoy much better health, having more wholesome food, and then taking the selfish view of the matter I should be so happy to have you both near me. I hope to see you soon and we will talk it all over.

My health and spirits have been much better the last few days. My last drawings have been very good—great improvement. They will not come out just yet. When they do I will send them. I have awful struggles against a sort of periodical and fitful disinclination to work which I always overcome in the most heroic manner. You really have no idea what it is to force your brain to invent when it feels utterly exhausted and empty. The more I advance and improve, the more I see what I lack, and the amount of uphill study before me for the next few years seems quite terrific—tu conçois, il ne s'agit pas *seulement* de gagner de l'argent. I want to reach the utmost perfection that my talent is susceptible of, and get to that point that every thing I attempt should turn out a complete and perfect work of art. Study, study night and day as soon as I am married, and quiet in mind, and all these agitations are ended. Heureusement, I shall be well seconded by Pem, who is indefatigable in help and encouragement. The very ideal of a wife for a struggling man who wants an awful amount of being taken care of, and to be completely understood in all he does.

You must have been very lonely when Isabel was away, and I am very sorry that you will have again to put up with society that you dislike so much. But there seems really no help for it just at present, and the best way is to swallow whatever contempt or dislike you may feel for ideas you cannot sympathise with; for by expressing them (a great temptation, I admit) you can only make matters worse.

I have had no news from Eugène—have you?

Pray write me a long letter—you will have lots to tell me about Isabel. I hope she is improved in health and looks from her journey.

I have not heard from T. A. lately. What is it you write about Isabel refusing him? I don't quite understand. Did he then propose to her in one of his letters? I hope Isabel in writing to him has not taken a serious view of mere hints, which he might afterwards say were merely meant in scherz!

And now my dear Mamma, must hurry off to Bouverie Street with next week's initial letter. Write soon, and give my love to Isabel. I will send you ten as soon as I possibly can.

Your ever affectionate son

K

In August Kicky went on a short visit to his family in Dusseldorf, and wrote before starting to Emma.

[August, 1862]

My own darling,

I am hard packing up, and among the things that I shall *not* forget will be your portrait, to perform upon in the way you directed—like an old spoon that I am.

I didn't sleep very well, but feel all right this morning. I hope you will miss me very much but that you will only bore yourself without me—and fancy how jolly Sunday week will be.

Goodbye, my own much loved pet. I will write again on Thursday. So with many nice warm kisses.

Your ever loving and affectionate
Kick

[August, 1862]

My dearest Pem,

I am sitting in the family bosom after a very fatiguing journey. I didn't get a berth on board and consequently walked on deck all night; fortunately I met and fraternised with a most delightful young parson, called Brook of the Kensington Church, and more stunning than any parson I ever read of; and we got so much fascinated with each other's conversation that the sun came up over the Scheldt before he retired to roost; and next morning he rose with rheumatism and the tic douloureux. I didn't leave Antwerp till one, on account of the first train being an express, and saw all my old Academy friends, which was rather fun; journey from Antwerp very tedious, only got in at 10 o'clock, and found them all looking well, I am happy to say. My Aunt so enormously fat which suits her wonderfully. And what do you think Miss? I saw somebody[1] at the station at Malines, and jumped from one carriage to the other without her seeing me; so you see I am as good as my word; it is true that it did not cost me a *very* great effort. Didn't get up today till 12 and am not rested yet. I suppose by this

[1]Possibly Carry, the girl in Malines, and the original of *Trilby*, whom Kicky had fancied himself in love with four years previously.

time you have arrived at Hampton and I hope you are comfortably installed. Been talking a lot about you Miss, and on the whole rather in your praise, although we have come to the conclusion that you are a heartless, silly and frivolous person, but that you will improve in time.

Isabel is trying to distract me by playing your minuet of Mozart, as she says to inspire me with proper feelings.

My mother is looking much better than I expected, and better than she did last year. Isabel is very thin, but does not look badly. They lead a very merry sort of life; the noble sausage-eating Prince Holstein is coming in the evening.

I have not yet been able to give the gloves and potted meat as I have not got my trunk from the hotel where I passed the night and so can only convey the thanks by anticipation. The sea coming over was as smooth as the river and I certainly should have enjoyed it very much if you and I had been together; as it was, it was very tedious except when the parson and I were settling theological points. He had a very nice young wife whom he had just married, and I am afraid I got into her bad books by keeping him up, when she went down; and I thought to myself how nice it would have been for somebody to be there who would bully *me* for exposing myself to the night air, and felt *wery* envious.

I have not begun to work yet; indeed today I am still stupefied, with great fatigue. I shall leave here on the Thursday morning, get to Antwerp on Thursday night, and start for London by the 'Moselle', by which I came on Friday morning, so that on 6 o'clock Saturday I shall be in Town, and will let you know whether I shall go to H. C. on Saturday evening or Sunday morning; most probably the former.

I shall have lots to tell about this fellow Brook, on whom I shall call (we exchanged cards).

I didn't make any sketches; c'est toujours ainsi. I hope my pet that you will take lots of walking and exercise; I declare if I find you looking well it will really almost double the pleasure of coming back to you. They find me looking very well indeed. My Aunt had given dreadful accounts about your looking so ill; Mamma said "no wonder, after my illness which must have worried you as much as it did her". I said still more, as you saw it all.

We are going to the concert at Geislers (don't you wish you were coming too?). I have not seen Best yet, but shall this afternoon there. Shall not hear from Tom till to-morrow I suppose.

The weather here is so awfully languid and hot. I think it would not suit me if I stayed a long time—6 months would do for me, and it's only on that account that I shall come back to England so soon.

Isabel is getting herself up such a swell for Geislers. She and Mamma send their best love and the kindest messages to you and Maman bellemère (in which I feel quite inclined to join); and now my dear old angel I will conclude this hasty scrawl in which I have tried to tell you all the news, and find I haven't told you very much. Write me a letter full of details, and look forward to seeing me again with as much pleasure as I do. I *do* so wish you were here with me, you would find it very jolly and I'm sure *I* should. I will write to you once again before I leave—recollect that your letter to me must leave *London* before 5 Monday at the latest, to be here by Wednesday. I am now going to rush off with this to the post; with much love and many, many kisses, my darling,

Your ever most affectionate

Kicky

Monday

[August 12, 1862]

My dearest Pem,

I was much delighted to get your letter a day sooner than I expected, and as for the photograph, we are all enchanted with it. It is *by far* the nicest that has ever been taken of you, and I am glad that you have stuck up your chin in the manner I like; the hands come out rather large and veiny, but you couldn't have chosen a better attitude.

Maman-bellemère's attack seems to have been a rather serious one; you must have been dreadfully alarmed, but I am sure that Hampton Court and the change will do her lots of good. Tell her with my love that I will be so awfully kind to her when I come on Sunday that she will get well in no time.

I will now try and tell you what I have been up to; not very much for I spend nearly the whole day at home talking to the maternal and telling all about myself and you. For the latter of these two persons she has quite an adoration, owing to the awful crams I tell her about your general jollity, which of course are all drawn from my imagination. She in return tells me all about Isabel and my Aunt; for the latter of these two persons she hasn't got any adoration at all—and old lady-like, makes out things a little worse than they really are—The devil not so lily-white as she paints him.

I have began my second illustration on the block, but am not very much delighted with it. Indeed there is scarcely time to draw, what with my having to call on people and their coming Borns Hall over me in return; I have already called on Perrot and Malvany. Saw the noble Sam, who seems smitten, and Isabel's another. The noble Prince Holstein spent Thursday evening here, and today Isabel and my Aunt and I are going to sup with him and Prince John at Gestein; the fair Nancy Malvany is also coming and will probably fall to my lot unless Isabel takes pity on me. But disquiet yourself not; the fair Nancy is dying of a love sickness for Cooper, and although I shall fall in love with her directly, as I do with everybody, she will keep me at a proper distance (as Nelly did the noble Somerset). In fact my dear, I am in a great rage at having to go at all, as I wish to spend every evening with my auld mither. I never saw such a romantic lot of people as here in Dusseldorf; everybody falling in love with everybody else because they've nothing else to do. Demned du maurialising as Millais would say.

I received by the same post a cheque from the Illustrated Times for £6.16s; they've taken off ten shillings which I call cheek. I have not yet heard from Tom, at which I am rather uneasy; I ought to have had his acknowledgment by Friday at the latest, and am going to write to him today. I have fortunately preserved the post-office receipt for my letter; but whether or not that would be of any use for recovering it should it have made fausse route, I don't know.

Best wonderfully improved and tremendously delighted to see me again and congratulated me; you know I didn't see him last year. He is always bothering them for your photograph, and expressed his opinion to me that you were a *charming* girl with an emphasis on the word which was most hearty. I of course told him that if he knew you as well as I did he would have quite a different notion; he also enquired most affectionately after M. Bellemère. He can read ordinary and even small print out loud just as anybody else, and walks by himself, and even recognises people in the street.

I passed at the back of funfanddreiser as Mrs. Wightwick calls it, and saw your old garden and the little arbour. As for wishing you to be here, I'm demned if I'm not wishing it all day. I should like to spend 3 months here together; but couldn't exist unless I worked very hard. You've no idea what a lazy place it is; we must try and spend some little time here next summer. I look forward to Hampton Court with delight, Miss, and hope it will be finer weather than here; I will come, D.V., on the Saturday afternoon or evening but cannot tell by which train yet as I may have business to attend to on the Saturday morning. If you come to the station I shall be under the disagreeable necessity of hugging you coram populo; shan't be able to help myself; feel the want of it every morning, afternoon and evening, altho' I have not felt at all spooney. (Et toi?)

My darling I do so adore your sweet little photograph you have sent that when I look at it, I can go without missing you for 5 whole minutes at a time; but I shall have to leave it here, as my mother won't look at any of the others after this, and Isabel raves about it. She was delighted with the gloves; and all four of us make dreadful pigs of ourselves every night with the potted beef. They live in such a funny Bohemian manner and when my Aunt and Isabel are there, the conversation is such, I am sorry to say, that Maman Bellemère would be in the seventh heaven of delight, and I should not like Poynter to be listening behind the door.

And now my *dearest*, goodbye till I see you again, when I will squeeze you quite flat (that's the way my Aunt accounts for your being thin; says I have "squeezed it all in"); I am dreadfully fond of you, fonder than ever, twenty times more than when I was here last year. Mamma sends her kindest love to M. B. and thanks for the P.B.; Mamma is very fond of P.B. Isabel is out (as usual) but would send hers too, and give mine to everybody, keeping the lion's share for yourself. Goodbye darling and bientôt.

Kicky

Friday
[October, 1862]

My dear Mamma,

I was delighted to get your letter which I had some time been looking out for rather anxiously. I have been thinking a great deal about your project of moving to Heidelberg, and think it a good plan since you will get into a still cheaper place and be removed from all causes of annoyance to you. But I must say it seems a long way to go, and I am afraid that Isabel will miss her Dusseldorf friends a good deal at first. But if you get into a nice boarding house you will have plenty of company. Besides which if Isabel were to be driven a little into taking an interest in something or other in which she could study and improve it would be about the happiest thing that could happen to her—except perhaps marrying the gentle Sammy. I don't want to preach—indeed I am afraid she thought I came the sermonising dodge a little too much over her when I was in Dusseldorf, for did she not say to me: "Dost think because thou art virtuous there shall be no more cakes and ale? Nay but ginger shall be hot i' the mouth too", or words to that effect.

I have been sticking hard at work though for the last week my work has not been quite up to the mark. I am as the Germans say strohwittwe, Emma having left for Ramsgate, et je m'empette, as my friend Haltenbourg would say. In fact I can't get on a bit without my Pem who is a downright angel, and I hope to go and spend 4 or 5 days with her at the lovely Mrs. Caught's before she returns (No. 5 Wellington Place, Ramsgate, should Isabel feel disposed to write to her).

I think I am improving in my work; for the trouble and pains I take are tremendous, and the anxiety, labour and time I bestow on all I do are not paid for by what I get; but that will be compensated by the progress I must make in consequence. Indeed the competition is becoming so pressing that it is only by unflagging industry I can keep pace. There is Leighton drawing on wood now for the Cornhill magazine, and other swells whom you have not heard of, who spare no expense in time, industry and models. There is little Walker who has greater talent than I (although Pem and T. A. won't allow it) and whom I can only hope to keep up with by straining every nerve so to speak.

I must also take models and indeed do hardly a stroke without (ça coûte le diable). When I go to Bouverie St. next week I will get the back numbers of OAW which you haven't seen and you will see the effect of this great care.

I went to Smith about the Cornhill. No chance for a long time to come—Millais, Leighton and Sandys have the monopoly of that at present. With Punch I certainly seem to stand very well as also with OAW and London Society. Indeed I spend so much time on my drawings that for a long time I have had as much work as I can do; and my chances of making a better income soon, lie first in raising my prices which I shall do as soon as I prudently can, and secondly in improving so much that I may do the same work in less time.

When married (I hope in January next) I shall be able

to work in the evenings and be altogether in a more healthy state of mind and body.

I shall soon too be able to work quietly and cheerfully—for alas! it is in my unfortunate nature to be more lazy and less energetic than any man I know, although I give the notion of being just the reverse, and the struggles I have to keep up with this wretched tendency embitters part of my existence, though much less than a short while ago. You can have scarcely an idea what it is to have to invent a thing and work it out within a given time, utterly against the grain; knowing all the while that if it is not up to the mark its publication will do you more harm than good. But when the thing is done the quiet and happiness resulting is greater reward than the tin it brings in. Although I don't know what it is to be thoroughly satisfied with a drawing yet.

Wednesday

I got your letter last night and it has made me very uneasy. You first write in great spirits about your proposed change, but now seem to take a despondent view and not be quite certain. I can give no advice in the matter being totally unacquainted with these German towns you mention, and besides you say your departure is irrevocably fixed. I need not say that when you want the money you speak of I will send it, for I think it hardly likely that I shall not be able to spare that. So don't entertain any desperate apprehensions on the score of money—at the same time be economical as there is no saying what may happen.

Your affectionate Kick

In October Emma went down to Ramsgate for a change of air. Kicky wrote to her nearly every day.

[October, 1862]

My dearest Pet,

Thanks for your nice letter which I had this morning and which I read in bed, as I used to last year, finishing up with the same absurd performance at the end of it, and blessing my darling with all my heart.

I will now tell you my news which are very good (except that I am still deaf, and that is a great bore, so I shall pay a visit to Squire this evening).

When your train vanished and the two red lights were no longer visible, I walked home, and found a block and a letter from Swain marked immediate, and containing a diagram of the Queen of Portugal's clock by Shirley Brooks; begging I would make the best of it in any way I could. So I have made an absurd drawing with two pages of explanation, amplifying S. B.'s idea. Whether or not it will do I don't know but I took it in today. Swain adds a nice little postscript—"the two socials have been accepted". I have also just received a letter from Silver to do an initial.

Yesterday I went to Bouverie St. for some tin, but didn't get it so will go again today. Called on Walford and Lucas who were awfully jolly, promising me another serial and also some smaller things, one of which I am to get today. Even hold out serious hopes of T. Taylor's serial, which however is barely sketched at present, nothing known of it beyond that the scene is laid in Italy. Am going off to see Hog today and get my money, also talk of Christmas which is to be entirely on my own book and with no letterpress whatever.

The evening at Bells was awful slow—a good dinner—old fogies—no smoke. En revanche I spent a jolly evening last night with Keene and Stuart, who is a stunning fellow in every way. Such a nice house—fancy darling if we were just married what an opportunity—6 months in a jolly well-furnished house, piano and all, for 20£.

I shall go and see Governor this evening before going to Squire.

Silver is coming to dine in Berners St. to-morrow and will very likely bring Shirley Brooks with whom he dines tonight in B. Street.

I hope you are taking plenty of air my pet; if the weather is the same as here you won't have much chance.

I need not say that I miss you very much, and shall do so more and more, but I am thinking so much of work that it absorbs me a great deal. No letters. Isn't it odd that Tom doesn't write.

I am quite well barring the deafness. I shall not be able to help coming to Ramsgate, but will not I think stop at Wellington Terrace; I do hope I shall have done lots of good work before-hand so as to enjoy myself with you with a good and tranquil conscience, and not grudge the time.

I am now going to Bouverie Street and Hog's, and will say goodbye my darling with many kisses; I hope I shall have lots more news on Friday when your letter comes and I answer it. Give my kind regards to the Caughts and Levies and my love to M. B. and believe me as ever your loving and affectionate

Kick

91 Newman St.
Sabaoth
[October, 1862]

My dearest Pem,

It was very jolly of you to write me such a long letter directly, and I ought to be very much delighted to hear that you are enjoying yourself more than you expected, Philosophina. I envy you very much, for, not having an over-well-regulated mind, *my* enjoyments at present are as delightful as those of a fish out of water—je m'ennuie comme un grand seigneur, and the cigarette-holding fore-finger of my left hand is of a rich mahogany down to the second phalanx.

My work this week has all been badly done and I loathe it, and it's a jolly relief to get out of this beastly room today and go down to Kew. I didn't think I should miss you so much, and must say that I hope I shan't be so unphilosophical next week as last.

On Thursday last I went with Keene to his lately married friend Stewart. They live in Chiswick Mall, and we had a very pleasant sort of chatty evening. I afterwards slept at Keene's in Hammersmith, and breakfasted with his mother and sisters next morning. It's a funny old tumbledown sort of house, just what one would fancy Keene living in; two nice gardens utterly uncultivated and overrun with weeds; one of his sisters rather nice looking—very plain and unsophisticated sort of people. What a splendid fellow Keene is, I like him more and more every day; I like big dark affectionate and sincere animals of either sex, as you know, my dear she-Keene. Next evening we went to Poynters'; Morten was also there, and we spent a very philosophical and musical evening. Yesterday I had the blues, and after dining and smoking with Keene I came home here and read Vanity Fair till 1 o'clock. Of all the magnificent works! It's as fine as the bible, perfect wit and wisdom in every line; that little angel of an Amelia, how she adores her snob of snobs! I dreamt afterwards that I had whiskers and you adored me in the Amelian style.

Yesterday I went and took tea with the Papa Beaupère who misses you very much, and expatiated on the merits of Lady Lee's widowhood which he was reading over again. He was afterwards going to Mellon's concert, and told me to send his love; today he dines at Clapham, and did not appear to look forward with enthusiasm to John Fitch's company.

I sent you O.A.W. yesterday and hope you got it all right; there is a new story in 5 numbers illustrated by Keene; after which a 12 number story by Walker; after which who knows? *I* may have a chance. Tenniel has just sent in his account for 215£ (43 illustrations to Silver); it appears that old Evans grumbled a little on paying it. Keene is now charging four guineas instead of three.

Poynter has just been in telling me I shall be late; that they expect me at one and it is now half past 12. Besides which he chaffs me about my merry and facetious appearance and says "Calypso ne pouvait se consoler du départ d'Ulysse."

The other day at Pamphilon's I had the honour of dining opposite Ciabato (is that the way you spell your beauty's name?) He is certainly a very splendacious animal, but looks stuck up and preoccupied with his beauty; Trentenova looks as if *he* didn't care a dem.

Pray write me a long letter, there's a darling; to-morrow I go to Bouverie St. to see if I can get my money. I shall try and cut off to Ramsgate as soon as possible but can't as yet exactly specify when. I think I have told you all the news. I shall be able to speak about you today, to that beloved little Mrs. Bell. Give my best love to Maman Bellemère, and kiss for me the precocious little five-year-old who has found out the magnetic virtues of the hand I miss so dreadfully.

I am in a bad temper with you for being away, darling, and a little bit for your not being as bored and blue as I am myself; but perhaps after all you don't love me the less sincerely for that, and I'm a selfish fellow etc.

Goodbye my dearest Lady Kick; think of me often, darling, as your very passionately attached and deucedly-bored-without-you

Kicky

Monday
[October, 1862]

My dearest Pem,

Your jolly letter came this morning. I have been working so hard all day that I shall not have time to write you a long letter, as it is just upon post time. Very stunning drawing I think it will be—cost me awful trouble and pains.

Haven't got very much news to tell you darling. On Sunday night I went to Henley's studio where I spent the evening. Saturday dined in Berners Street, Bell, Calderon, Poynter, 'Fun' fellows, everybody—Charades after dinner. Yesterday I moped at home and was miserable—read Tom Jones, and thought Sophia very like you. Dined at Bibia's and then went to Morgans where we had rather a jolly evening—nobody but Bill and such *lovely* children.

Morgan was deuced entertaining. This evening going to Val Prinsep's in Charlotte Street, to meet Doyle and Charles Halley. Tell Susie.

I will in all prob. come down on Thursday, but must try and get my OAW money first. I am sorry you are not getting stouter. We will have a few jolly days. I hope we shall never be separated again—I find it wretched. I am very well—still rather deaf—and now I will send Jemima to post this. So with love to all my own pet and darling, goodbye till Thursday (I hope)

Your ever loving and most affectionate

Kick

Isn't Walker's drawing exquisite?

On his return from Germany Kicky saw Mr. Wightwick, and told him that neither he nor Emma could continue with so long an engagement, and that they must be married by the winter. His prospects were improving, and further delay was absurd. Mr. Wightwick finally agreed, and the marriage was fixed for early in the New Year.

[October, 1862]

Mein lieber lieber Schatz,

Heut 'morgen hab 'ich deinen brief becommen.

This morning did I become thy brief—I am very glad the weather is decent and that you have some little congenial company in the Levies, and hope when I come down your cheeks will tempt me by the real colour of rose. First I have had a letter from Tom, but the beggar neither mentions you, nor your photograph, nor Isabel nor my mother. But the poor devil is so worried I don't wonder at his scarcely thinking of anything else.

On Wednesday evening I went to see the Governor whom I found in a fearful rage. He had smashed the teacups and given poor cook a black eye, and all because my Lord Dundreary had not come out. You must really write to him to be on guard against these dangerous excesses of temper. I told him all, after propitiating him by a liberal present of 10 and sixpence (I had just received some money), and said that January was the time. Oh yes, ses he, January twelve month will do very well. Upon which we had a little disputation, and although he didn't put the butter knife to my throat and say: "If you don't marry by January

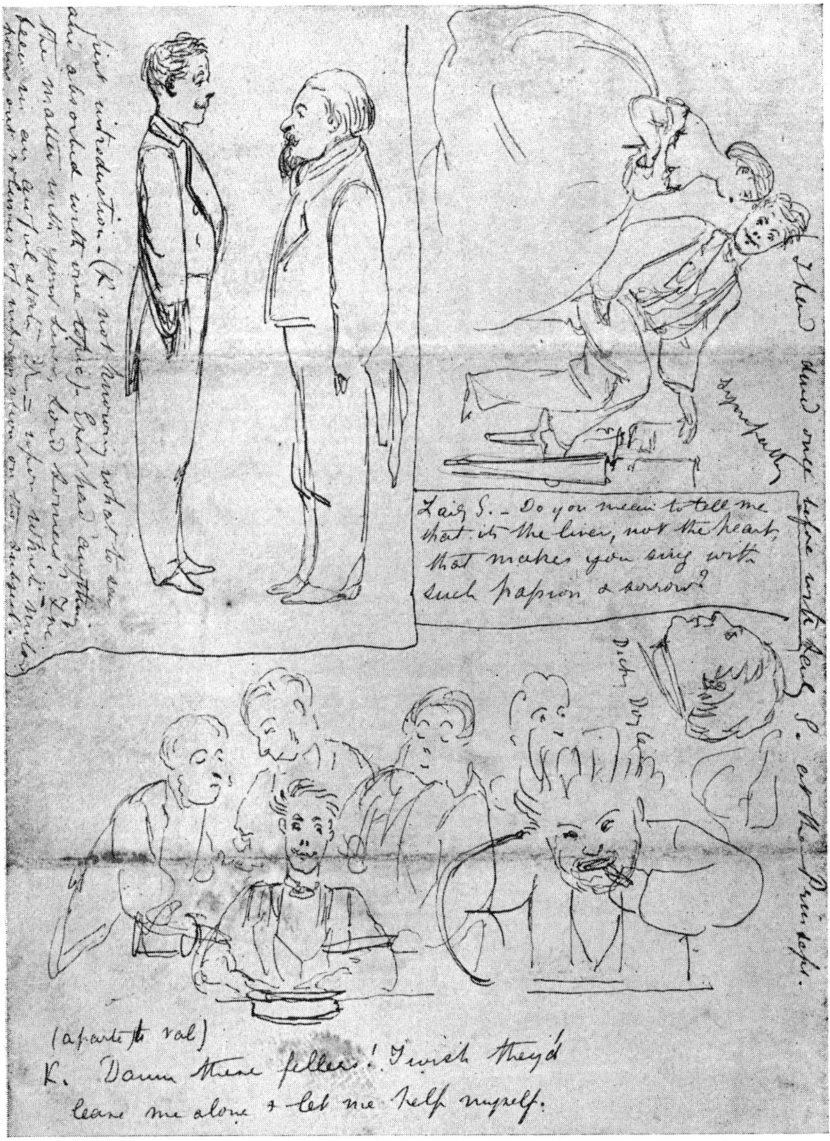

IMPRESSIONS OF LORD AND LADY SOMERS

From the back of the last page of the letter to Ellen du Maurier, *p.* 123

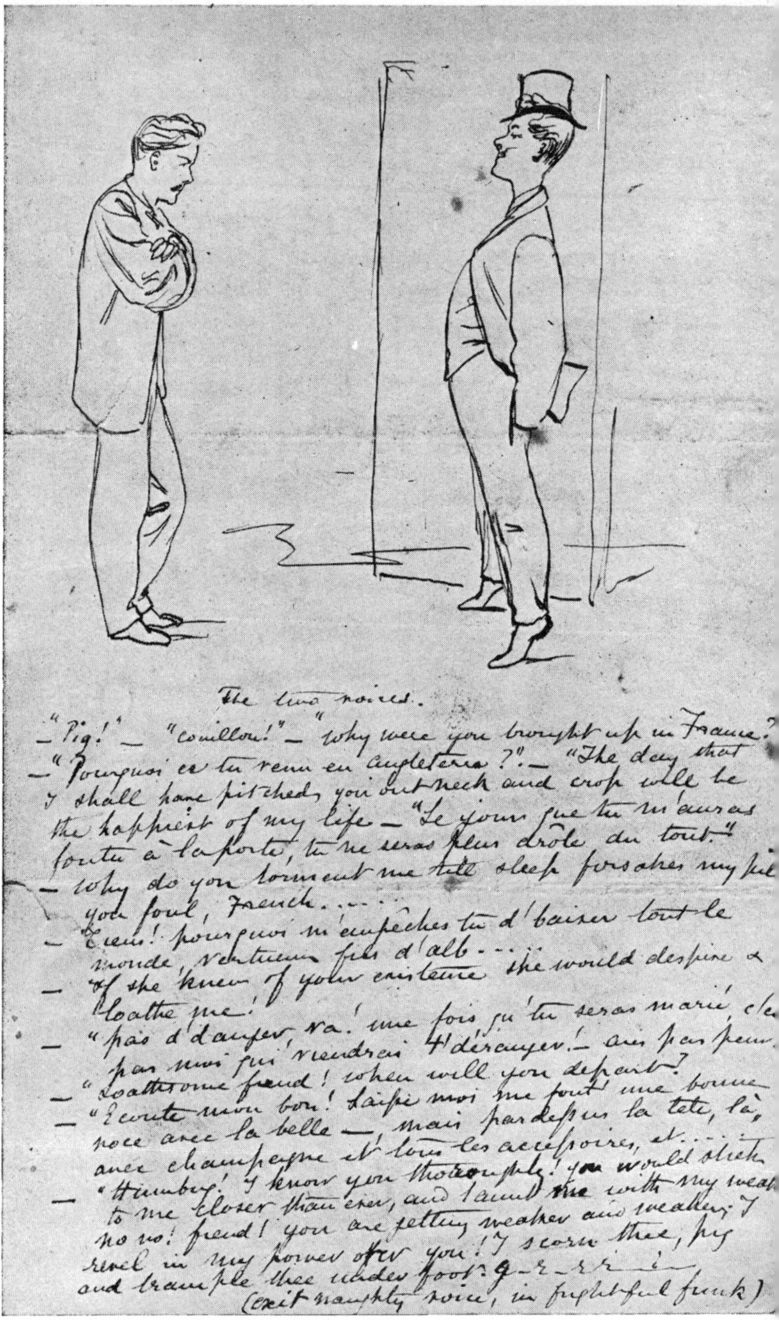

The two voices.
— "Pig!" — "couillon!" — "Why were you brought up in France?"
— "Pourquoi es tu venu en Angleterre?" — "The day that
I shall have pitched you out neck and crop will be
the happiest of my life — "Le jour que tu m'auras
foutu à la porte, tu ne seras plus drôle du tout."
— Why do you torment me till sleep forsakes my pil
you foul, French....
— "Crens! pourquoi m'empêches tu d'baiser tout le
monde, vertueux fils d'Alb...."
— If she knew of your existence she would despise &
loathe me!
— "Pas d'danger, va! une fois qu'tu seras marié, c'e
pas moi qui viendrai t'déranger! — ai pas peur.
— "Loathsome fiend! when will you depart?"
— "Ecoute mon bon! Laisse moi me fout' une bonne
noce avec la belle — mais pardessus la tête, là,
avec champagne et tous les accessoires, et...."
— "Humbug! I know you thoroughly! you would stick
to me closer than ever, and taunt me with my weak
no no! fiend! you are getting weaker and weaker. I
revel in my power over you! I scorn thee, pig
and trample thee under foot: q-r-r-r-i-i
(exit naughty voice, in frightful funk)

"THE TWO VOICES"

Dialogue between the English and French elements in du Maurier's character; forming an additional page to the letter to Tom Armstrong

p. 159

next it will be the worse for you!" he didn't seem to make any objections. I gave him a famous account of my doings and he was pleased to entertain a sanguine view of our future prospects. After which my pet I dined at Pamphilon's and coffeed in Berners Street. After which Bill, the reprobate, and I did accompany Morgan home and to supper. He lives looking upon the Copenhagensfield cattle market, a deuce of a way. Mrs. Morgan is a pretty clever little woman but of a vulgarity—you should hear her accent. Bill is quite the enfant de la maison—she calls him Henley, tout court or rather Heyneley, for she hath a musical drawl. I did not see the children, but was promised an introduction if I came on Sunday, which I shall do if it's a *foine dye.*

Yesterday I dined in Berners Street in company with Keene and Morgan, and afterwards went to Squires' to pay him two visits, one a professional one, t'other of friendship. But was successful in neither of these because he was not at home, and indeed is in the country for the whole of this week, so I shall try and get to Traer's for I am still deaf. I came home and read Tom Jones. Today have done a very nice initial which was duly fetched and continued working at a composition for O.A.W. which I began yesterday—a story in two or 3 parts (to be published, my dear, in one).

I have just received my L. S. money; and also my Punch d.b., amounting to about 18 pound. I hadn't a penny—six have gone to my tailors, and I have ordered a suit which must be gently broken to Ramsgate before I appear. I am detaining the rent from my Landlady in case the OAW money should not turn up opportunely. I have told you all my news now I think. As for this evening I have not yet decided what kind of wickedness I shall be up to.

The Governor said to me: "I suppose you find it very slow and dull to be in London without Pem?"

"Oh no"! says I—and that's the biggest lie I ever squeezed into so few words in my life my dear.

So now darling, I will say goodbye till Monday morning. Please to kiss the little locket you wear on your neck—and if by putting your head down with your hands, or by the help of Susannah, you could manage to kiss your dear neck itself for me, you will oblige your Kick. Give my love and remembrances in the manner detailed in my last and believe me my own dear absent darling

Your loving and affectionate

Kick

(who misses you enough to satisfy the most rampagious and exacting dispogician).

P.S. I was at a lecture of professor Owen's in which he said no relationship had yet been made out between man and the brute creations, for that between the lowest type of man, viz: the Australian savage, and the highest type of Ape, viz: the Gorilla, the constitution of the brain was so distinct as to make a difference of class between them, and that so it must remain until an intermediate link were established.

I politely interrupted him, and said that if he would take the trouble to make a post mortem on the Irish roughs I intend to kill next Sunday in the Park, he might convince himself that the 'missing link' had been found.

[October, 1862]

My dearest Pem,

I write you just a line to say that I shall come down to-morrow. I've not been able to ascertain yet about boats etc., but if it is pretty good weather and the boats run, I shall go by boat. If not I will come by an early train—shall have lots to tell you my darling.

I will not write any more as I shall see you to-morrow, and it is near post time.

So God bless you my darling and believe me

Your ever loving

K

I will accept Mrs. Caught's kind offer.

[October, 1862]

My dear Mamma,

I have just seen Isabel's note to Emma and had been

getting anxious about you both as I imagined you had left last Monday. I cannot understand whether you are going to remain any time in Coblenz. Since I have seen you I have heard more about Wiesbaden, and people don't seem to think it so particularly cheap; but I suppose you have had information on which you can rely. I am afraid it will be awfully dull, delightful as it may be to tourists during the summer months.

Do not be long about writing now you are on the move, as I get anxious.

I am very well and working very hard—have been better in health this last fortnight than I have been for months. Everybody notices how well I am looking. Pem is also looking much better. I am doing the initials for Punch's comic annual, no very great job but important so far as it is a slight promotion; and am in trial for a serial in OAW which will be splendacious I hope if I *do* do it.

Had 4 days rest in Ramsgate which I appreciated in spite of terrible weather. Saturday Tom Malvany and John Perry called about some Crystalline for the hair—they will take some over.

I have no particular news to tell you. Pem and I spent the evening at Bell's last week, and she is going to spend the day on Wednesday; Mrs. Bell as usual wanting to know when you and Isabel are coming over here. She tells me that her family, the Poynters, met Best at Heidelberg, and fraternised. I had a letter from T. A., fancy he is sulky rather. He had had a long letter from the Lewises to whom he had written. Has Isabel written to them? If she has not and is going to, I wish she'd say something about Emma fancying Miss Lewis had seen her and purposely looked another way, and that consequently I avoided seeing them, thinking they had made up their minds not to fraternise in England, or something to that effect.

And now my dear Mamma with best love to Isabel and hoping for a long letter

Your ever affectionate son

K

Wednesday
[November, 1862]

My dear Mamma,

I write you a few lines now for fear you should be getting anxious, as it won't do to wait till I have time to write properly, I see—and when I've been hard at work all day I'm really not fit for anything in the evening but to lie down in an abruti state and be read to. I have now as much work as I can do, and take enormous pains; you've no idea what it is to rub out a drawing that you've been hard at all day, and the state you are in after. The competition is getting tremendous; all the first painters are taking to drawing on wood; I never touch a block (unless it be an initial letter or something of that sort) but what I take a model—expensive but must be done. I am doing a serial in Once a Week, illustrating a book, and working for Punch. If I could only work as quick as 2 years ago I should be making a fortune. I have now been working 8 hours a day for 2 months, and shall have to do so till after Christmas; I shall then try and get married and take a fortnight's trip to rest my eyes and back. When in a new place I will try and work standing as it is better for the chest. But I don't mind the fatigue half so much as the anxiety and disappointment when the drawing doesn't come as I wish it—I get half mad at times. When Pem is living with me it won't be so bad, as she can always set me all right again when I get riled and morbid.

I am so glad you like Coblentz, as I much feared you would be regretting Dusseldorf. Isabel doesn't seem quite so enchanted—feels a little homesick for the other place, I suppose. Write me a long letter telling me everything as usual. I can't find Gyggy's letter, and must have a regular hunt for it among my papers which are in great disorder—and send it you.

Pem and I are going into furnished lodgings somewhere in Bloomsbury—bedroom, sittingroom and studio. Further than that I have no plans for the future, and trust to luck and hard work for everything to come right for all of us as far as money goes. But as for waiting any longer, I simply can't—should have another attack. I hope to send you what I said before April. If my position is as much better next year as it is this time compared to a year ago, there will be enough money for all of us to live in England should Isabel and you wish to do so. I needn't say how much happier *I* should be.

How are my Aunt and Bobbie getting on?

I will now hurry off to the post with this. Best love to both of you. I will send No. 11 of the serial. (Did you get the last all right which Emma posted?)

Your ever affectionate son

K

[November, 1862]
Tuesday

My dear Tom,

You have probably by this heard from Henley whose letter to you crossed yours to me. I saw him on Saturday; your pictures had not arrived; I will go again this afternoon, and if there is anything to say on the subject of packing will write.

I am sorry to hear about your being so knocked up, but you don't tell a fellow what's the matter. I hope the heart is all right, anyhow, and that it is no damned Rheumatism.

I am delighted to hear of Miss Lewis's engagement, and hope she will have a good husband as I am sure she will make a downright good wife—and hope that her sister will soon follow her example. I wish you could set it right about our meeting in the Exhibition; as Emma was under the impression that Miss Lewis had seen her and looked another way I thought it the wisest thing, in case of our coming across them again, to look altogether away and pretend not to see them, thus leaving them the option of coming up & recognising *us*. I thought it all the while *almost* impossible that Miss Lewis could have recognised Emma and willingly cut her without any reason, and indeed she afterwards wrote to my sister that *I* had *cut them*. I should like this to be set right, (not that there is much chance of our ever meeting them as I shall live entirely among artists), but for the sake of the great respect I have for them, and had for poor Mr. Lewis—and would like to know whether, should we accidentally pass them in the street, we are to exchange the friendly nod.

My marriage is coming off sooner than I anticipated when I wrote to you last. Mrs. Wightwick is going to write you to ask you to be my first man, and I should much wish you to be able to manage it if it is no inconvenience to you as it will considerably add to my felicity, old cock, and Emma has rather set her heart upon it. Of course there is to be no shindy—only you in church, and Poynter, Jeckell & Bill, who will come to lunch after. That is I mean to ask them—and Emma's friends to be the Miss Levies & two of her cousins, Douglas Fisher & Pa & Ma. Then we shall cut off to Dover & Boulogne for a week or so. The Day is at present fixed for the 3rd of January, and I do not think it will be altered. We have almost fixed upon our residence also—3 rooms second floor furnished & a jolly studio in Great Russell St. just opposite the British Museum, and a few doors from the Jones's whom we know.

I can't understand about my mother or sister not writing to you; they have not to me although I ought to have had a letter last week—and I am rather anxious. And last time I heard, my sister told me she was going to write to you next day, and send a new photo which she has had taken of herself. That must have been 3 weeks ago at least.

You do not tell me whether your Governor is better.

It is now post time so I will post this, and if there is anything about the pictures I will write again to-morrow.

Yours ever

K

I feel so damned excited I can't draw a stroke, and I've got to crowd a whole month's work in the next fortnight.

Friday
[December, 1862]

My dear Mamma,

I have been expecting to hear from you since my last; I

hope you and Isabel are all right. Poor T. A. is dreadfully ill, and can't make out why you or Isabel haven't written. You wrote Emma a month ago that Isabel was going to write to him next day and send her portrait. He has got a kind of fever and Influenza, and is very bad. Pray write immediately both to him and me.

Emma and I are to be married on the 3rd of January, we are going to live on a second floor, 46 Great Russell Street, 25 sh. a week, and I have taken a small studio in the same house, ground floor, for 25£ a year. It has a splendid light, all the ceiling being glass, and in time we shall be able to make it very comfortable I've no doubt, though not at all swell as you can fancy. The governor will give Emma a new piano; and will pay for her clothing; some 30 or 40£ a year that will be; and Mrs. W. will always be giving us things, what they call a 'basket fortune', so I have very little anxiety about our being able to get on. Of course I shall work like a nigger, and my work will be of much better quality.

I would give anything for you and Isabel to be here. We are going to be married by bans at Marylebone where Isabel was christened; I put up the bans yesterday. Poor T. A. was to have come up to town, and we shall be of course much disappointed. Bill, Poynter, T. Jeckell, and the Miss Levies, Charlotte Blythe, Julia Fitch and Miss Haslewood; voilà le programme de la noce. Then Pem and I will go to Boulogne for a week, although I shall try and manage a fortnight, for my craving for a little rest and air is uncommonly strong after these hardworking months.

Louisa Lewis is going to be married on the 22nd. of January to a Mr. Mirehome, General Lewis's brother-in-law. Isabella wrote to T. A. about the engagement and says he's a very nice man and that her sister has every chance of a bright and happy future.

When you write to T. A. you might thank him for the Saturday reviews, say that you have got them all bound for him (for I think you told me such was the case) and tell him not to send any more. As soon as we are married I will send it you. For in a letter a little while ago he said that he had not heard from you and had kept back the Saturday review.

I will also send you OAW and Punch as I think if I were to ask they would let me have Punch for nothing—they ought to—and I shall ask.

As soon as I see my way a little bit clear and get all my accounts paid I will send you some money.

I have looked everywhere for Eugène's letter and cannot find it, so if you know his address send it me as I want to write to him.

And now my dear Mamma, hoping to hear as good account from you as in your last to Emma, and with best love to Isabelle

Your ever affectionate son

K

P.S. How is my Aunt getting on by herself, and Bobbie?

Pem and I used to make castles in the air about going to Germany for our wedding trip and making you two come back with us and live in England. But that will come I hope, if you and especially Isabel would care to live over here.

Addio.

[December, 1862]

My dear Tom,

Your sister's letter yesterday, & yours this morning have been a great disappointment—mais enfin! The unfortunate thing is that you should be so ill. I can't see exactly what is the matter with you & what can have brought it on; I hope you will soon have some little change, and I think that in another month when you are quite strong again you should treat yourself & all of us to a trip up to London for a few days. I am sorry I shall not be able to offer you a bed, but if you are hard up you could put up at Bill's; his people are devilish jolly & kind. I have a great notion your pictures will sell, as they seem to be much liked, especially the girl in the Church. I will try & get hold of Jimmy & take him to see them & tell you what he says on the more serious part of the work—viz. the painting; as for the selling, cela regarde Morgan a good deal.

I determined yesterday to follow the advice you gave me to-day, and not sweat too precious hard for the next few days. However there are three things that must be done—the two last drawings for the serial & a sort of kettledrum thing for London Society. I am very glad you like my last drawings. It is more encouraging than the following extract from some Northampton paper à propos of the Xmas No. of London Soc.: 'We have no doubt Mr. du Maurier has his admirers—but we have never had the pleasure of meeting with any of them'. Sont-ils blagueurs! But the wound is healed by the next paragraph which goes into ecstasies about Florence Claxton I am told.

How do you like the Story of Elizabeth? The day before yesterday old Val came in & asked me to go that evening to dine & meet Miss Thackeray; but I was so seedy I hadn't the pluck to go. He says she's a tremendous jobber, and that if I get on the right side of her, I'm all right with the Cornhill—not a very noble way of climbing, mais je ne suis pas fier. Besides what the Devil is Leighton doing in that galley—certainly not good drawings on wood, and yet I believe he gets a most exorbitant price. I will devote a month if necessary to the block I have to do for them, and ruin myself in models.

How do you like Bill's drawings in Fun? they are most villainously cut; but when on the block they have a certain prettiness which ought to go down. Bill is doing the uxorious to an awful extent, and has got a very nice woman. Jimmy and Joe are as thick as ever—Jim going to retire from the world altogether and work hard. As a beginning he is getting up some private theatricals at the Greeks'. Poynter working very hard and getting on very well—went with him & Emma to hear the Messiah last night, with tickets given us by the Greeks. Jimmy had been also offered a ticket but an engagement prevented him from availing himself of the opportunity. I had a very nice letter from

During the Hallelujah chorus.

[*X., Aleco Ionides, du M., Emma W., Poynter*]

my aunt last night. She seems deuced lonely now my people are gone to Coblentz. But the maternal & she don't agree & nothing will make them. The bone of contention is the unlucky Bob, whom she doesn't adore with all that maternal fierceness my mother thinks proper. I think that if I had been constituted after the fashion of Bob when I was eight or nine years old, my mother would be little more lenient in this respect. But you see I was a most accomplished & fascinating infant some 20 years ago—there wasn't a place in the world of which I did not know the latitude & longitude. J'ai joliment dégringolé! My brother Gyggy, it is true—but I leave him to your imagination—he hasn't altered a bit.

The house in Grosvenor Street is not very gay just now—one has to go in goloshes & in one's umbrella. It's a devil of a thing to take away an only daughter, especially when she's the mother of her parents, so to speak. But I intend to be an awfully dutiful son-in-law. If the maman bellemère & I had one point of sympathy together this would be an easy and delightful task. But I'm holy water & she doesn't like it. When we see a little less of each other, however, I think we shall get on very well. And as for the governor, he's a devilish good fellow although powder was invented before his time, and he missed his opportunity.

Lewises evenings have begun. I'm going to-night, and was there last Saturday week—very jolly as usual, such splendid glee-singing—regaled the audience with Francs Lurons which was enthusiastically received. The gorgeous Leighton was there & the divine Millais & the noble Watts, who's one of the stunningest fellows out. The presence of Lord Gerald Fitz-Gerald made the wax candles unnecessary, and added considerably to the smoke. I've no doubt there were lots of other Lords besides, for Lord G. wasn't the worst dressed man in the room.

And now old fellow I have told you as much news as will come out of my revolving & excited brain, & will shut up. Give my best regards to your sister & thanks for her letting me know so kindly how you were getting on & accept the same yourself. Hoping to see you soon after since not before my wedding

Yours ever

K

91 Newman St.
[December, 1862]

My dear Isabel,

It is so rarely that you favour me with a letter that I answer you immediately after reading it, to show a due acknowledgment of the honour and to induce you to continue treating me to the same kind of indulgence.

I must first tell you that Pem has written to you today and will have probably told you all the news worth telling. So I will indulge in philosophical reflections. This is my last night in my bachelor apartment; I have spent most of the day in burning papers and packing up. The appearance of my dingy rooms in which I have lived so long, with everything in a horrible litter, and my lay figure in a white shroud (for the next drawing) is ghastly and calculated to inspire *SOLEMN THOUGHTS!* let alone the occasion of all this.

As you say it is a very strange thing and naturally enough I can think of hardly anything else. To think of the little girl in the brown boots by the Foundling Hospital etc. etc. and the wedding cards I saw to-night with 'Mrs. George du Maurier'. Does Mamma remember how we used to talk in Malines of such an impossibility ever happening? and here it is at last, but not without a struggle. If you had been my lay-figure, you would have seen the most terrific fits of discouragement and despondency and suspicion that I was only a duffer after all, and once indeed, almost a touch of insanity.

So morbidly does my imagination prey upon itself at any rebuff, or piece of bad luck or unkind criticism. When I am overworked and have been sitting alone all day over the drawing that won't come right and which must go to press before dinner—I can assure you if a stray friend has happened to look in I have sometimes startled him with the fervour of my welcome. But what if he tells me (as happened last week): I say my dear fellow, such a jolly paragraph about you in such or such a paper—it says:'We've no doubt Mr. du Maurier *has* his admirers, but we never had the pleasure of meeting with any of them'. The seven small demons enter my soul—I rush off to my Pem and bury my head in her faithful bosom and moan (the *burying* is of course a poetical figure of speech, for poor Pem has become so thin from anxiety, that sepulture in a literal sense is impracticable.) But often les misères du jour font le bonheur du lendemain, for I come home and find an order to do a drawing for the Cornhill let us say (and a stunning subject it is), or else go to Lewises in a desperate frame of mind and meet my editor who tells me I am to illustrate a long serial in OAW, à partir de Février. So on and off, in spite of many little discouragements, I see that on the whole my position improves month by month; and if I were not my mother's son I should have no particular anxiety about the future. To see Pem enter into details of household expenditure and cast up the probable weekly items of bacon, butter, cheese etc (this is always disgusting to me after a heavy dinner at a second rate tavern) would convince anybody as much in love as we are that a hundred a year will keep us fat and healthy and pay for many innocent pleasures besides—blague à part 250 will do it, and I can safely count on 300 now—barring accidents of course—indeed I *hope* to make much more than that soon. All of which goes to make one of the solemn thoughts. Then comes the question of the great trust and responsibility of another's happiness (this altogether a moral consideration); I have not very much fear on that score it is true. And then comes the thought of you and Mamma not being well off, one of the most constantly recurring of all thoughts—although Mamma told me on the very first day of my last visit to you, of your determination never to do such a thing as live with me in the event of your not marrying, and although you have shewn such a distaste to the idea of coming to live in England, I live in hopes of our all being, if not under the same roof, within a very few minutes of each other. Until that can be done of course every pound I can spare shall be sent to you; and if you get very hard up you will have the consolation to know that I shall be 'worser'; but I hope and trust that there will be plenty and enough for all of us soon—ça ne sera pas faute de travail et d'energie—for strange to say, I, the lazy Kick, have now got more a name for that than anything else, and I'm not likely to leave off now. Give me plenty of food and good light and a pair of dumb-bells, and don't leave me alone, and I will cheerfully work my 10 or 12 hours a day; and if I could have you two near me as well as the indisPemsable one, I think I should be *the* happiest instead of only *one* of the happiest men in London.

Don't fancy my dear that I underrate the pleasant life of Dusseldorf where I hope you will soon return; you are surrounded with very nice people of which you are the particular pet; but you did not seem to appreciate it so very much after all—et à quoi bon. But however it is no use my going on in this strain until there is a possibility of a change for the better, et alors nous verrons.

And now my dear Isabel I do wish you would write to me and Emma a little oftener; do not fancy that your letters will not be appreciated by us as much as by T. A. although the fact of your being a pretty girl will not have any weight in the matter.

You say Mamma has influenza, I hope she will take care of herself, and not let it get bad. Answered Best's letter, can't find Gyggy's. Hope yours will find him. Received my Aunt's letter all right. My candle is going out. Lots to do to-morrow—so goodbye old fellow. Best love to Mamma

Your ever affectionate brother

K

Saturday morning
[3 January, 1863]

My dear Mamma and Isabel,

This is my wedding morning; in another hour I shall be married, and I send you the last letter of the amiable bachelor known as Kick. I am awfully happy and dreadfully nervous, and have been thinking more of you in the last few days than ever. To-morrow I will write you a long letter from Folkestone, or else the day after from Boulogne.

So with best love, my darlings, no more at present from your

ever affectionate Kick

P.S. I have worked up to last night, and managed to finish all in time, and not scamp a stroke. I think another block would have broken the camel's back.

46 Great Russell St., Bloomsbury
Mond. 12 Jan. [1863]

My dear Mamma

We returned last night from Boulogne where we had a most delightful time of it, and now our brief holiday is over and I'm going to pitch into blocks again. I must give you an account of the whole performance for Isabella's delectation and your own. First let me tell Isabella we were much disappointed at not getting a letter from her on the eventful morning. She wrote to Jessie on a similar occasion, why not Pem? The event took place on the 3rd as you know. I arose and arrayed myself like unto the lilies of the field—grey bags and a sweet thing in neckties, blue. At half past 10, Douglas Fisher (my best man vice Tom A. on the sick list) came and we nerved ourselves with brandy and water; then my brougham came and we drove to the Church of St. Marylebone in great style (only one horse, but spif). Lots of friends had already gathered in the pews and my other fellows, T. Jeckell and Poynter, joyously bedecked, made their appearance. Then came the tribe of Levi. Then Mrs. Wightwick, looking very ill and much perturbed; we adjourned to the vestry and I tried to look as facetious as possible. When everybody had come, in walked Emma blushing quite white with the Governor. She was beautifully got up for the occasion, and then the ceremony took place—Mrs. W. crying dreadfully, Emma as white as a sheet; and I in an awful state of seriousness for it is an impressive performance. There were 4 carriages for the whole of our party, and when Emma and I had been made bone of one bone we drove round Regent's Park to get an appetite for breakfast.

Then came the exhibition of the wedding gifts, to be described after—poi the breakfast which was very merry in spite of Maman bellemère naturally being in rather an unhappy frame of mind. Douglas proposed our healths, I returned thanks. Capital breakfast. Then did Emma retire to change her dress and came down in the most stunning bridal-trip costume; I kissed everybody 'quite promiscuous' —painful parting for the Wightwicks père et mère—then drove to London Bridge and took the train to Folkestone where we were weather bound for 3 days. On the third day we rose again and ventured on to the Boulogne boat—in spite of terribly rough sea, weren't sick—and got to the old place safe—took 3 rooms on the Quay at the Hotel de Paris, a French Hotel, and a very charming little apartment it was. Such stunning little dinners at the table d'hôte where Pem and I were the only people who sat down. As for dear old Boulogne I don't believe a street escaped us and I remember every inch of it and felt quite like an old Thackeray. The first day we went of course to the cimetière to put couronnes d'immortelles on the two graves. My Aunt's tomb is in very good condition—indeed looks rather new. The difficulty we had in finding the other though! Got out the books and hunted everywhere—No. 245, no tomb only posts—at last Pem's eyes, which I wish I had, saw the number on the post of a tomb quite near the path and the Immortelle was properly put on by me and fixed there by the sexton and his wife. The moss I send is from my grandmother's,[1] the grass from my Aunt's. The sand is from Pont de Brigue, about three miles from Boulogne —if you recollect uncle G. took Alfred and Charley and me there for two or 3 days, during the funeral, and while Alfred fished Charlie and I made sand pies near a little watermill and my uncle laid himself down and cried as I very well perceived but I could not understand why. I made a mud pie there on Saturday (just 2 and 20 years after) of which I send you a small fragment. Though I had not much affection for any of them, all but Charlie, it made me sad to think they are all gone. I seemed to be in a dream of ever so many centuries ago, with a very delightful memento of the present by the side of me. As for my dear old Pem, of course it seems to me that I have a better wife than anybody I ever met—all fellows think so I suppose, but I really don't think it comes from the partiality of a nouveau marié. Though in reality the great struggle is to begin (let us say to-morrow or the day after) it feels as if all my struggles were over and I had got into port at last, and though I have tasted so little of married life I almost wonder how I could have existed unmarried. If I only had you and Isabel near and saw you both happy I should just simply be the happiest man in Middlesex, for my dear Pem looks happy enough! I know how much you like her—but you don't know how you would love her if you saw as much of her as I do—such a genial clever companion as she is and always so kind and affectionate.

We were quite loaded with presents. The Governor gave

[1]Mary Anne Clarke.

us a stunning new piano. We have a splendid sofa from Emma's uncle Noel. The Saynes's gave us tea and coffee pot etc. and a beautiful gold bracelet for Pem. Dinner and dessert service from the Levies, who have shewn the most wonderful kindness, also giving us the pass to Boulogne and back which saved us 5£; the Bells a charming tea service. Douglas gave us plate enough to feed a bigger dinner party than we shall ever give, I know, etc. etc.

Our lodgings are very nice and the studio will be a beauty in time. Now there is nothing in it but a lay figure and a carpet which Mr. Wightwick has given me. Mrs. W. is very unhappy at losing her daughter as you may well fancy. But we shall see a great deal of her and I intend to be a model son-in-law. She is tremendously kind always bringing things, and has had the rooms so nicely arranged during our absence. You will forgive the egotism of this letter considering the occasion I know.

I will go and get the back Once a Weeks and send them. In the tremendous flurry they were forgotten and there are two drawings you haven't seen I think; one number appeared without as the drawing was too ghastly they said. I worked up to the very eve of my marriage and got very seedy but am all right now. A few days before I had a letter from Mary Vincent asking me to go and see her—I wrote and made an excuse. I wrote to Miss Lewis and they both wrote to me. Had a very nice letter from Eugène who was writing to you by the same post. I shall correspond with him more regularly and hope to have a good influence. I hope you are both well and will soon be back in Dusseldorf. Though of course there is no chance before April, I look forward to our going to see you this summer. And now my dear Mamma I will shut up for the present. I have so many things to do I hardly know which way to turn. Pray you and Isabel write to us soon, we thought you would have written before. With best love to you both from Pem and me

Your ever affectionate son

Kicky

Henley's gone and made a foolish marriage, and we

cannot know his wife. His father and mother came to see me. They are utterly broken-hearted.

46 Great Russell St., Bloomsbury
Monday
[January, 1863]

My dear Tom,

Here we are back from our trip which was brief but delightful. I ought to have answered your jolly letter from Boulogne, but that kind of happy laziness came over me that I could write to nobody. The dreadful ceremony came off very well & everybody managed to survive it. You were very much missed, old fellow. D. Fisher was my best man. Present, the people I told you—17 in all, but lots of people in church to witness a thing of such European Importance. The breakfast was very jolly & though the Maman-bellemère cried dreadfully in church she kept up pretty well—she is much cut up, but I am going to be a very good fifi-beaufils, and edify everybody, in that as in all things. I will be unto thee O Tom as a shining light etc.

Henley was not present at the wedding, and if Poynter has not told you already you will be very much shocked to hear that he has married his woman—the same he lived with in London years ago. His poor old father & mother are quite brokenhearted; they came here the day before my wedding to pump me a little about her, but I of course pleaded ignorance as to whether or not she *was* his former London connection. They say they will never receive her. Poor old Langsdorff had aged 10 years though they had only known it a week. He told me he had left his country, worked & I don't know what and all to live near "that ungrateful boy" & then the poor old fellow broke down and sobbed like a child & his wife also. It would never have done for you to have been there in your present state, old fellow—I cried away like winking, regardless of manly dignity. From what Morgan says (& Morgan approves of it) Henley married this woman to "*do her proper justice before the world*", "*feeling that he owed her no less*" as if he didn't owe 50 times as much to his father & mother. I think his conduct has been as heartless as it is stupid, that such a nice fellow should be pumpernickled away from us all in this fashion!

Just as I was turning to the altar on Saturday & the Parson was clearing his voice I looked behind me; & just behind the group at our back, sitting just opposite the altar on a free seat, I saw the two poor old people looking the picture of despair & crying. It gave me a shock I shan't forget. Enfin old chap we'll talk of that & many other things when you come—I hope it will be soon. About painting in my studio old fellow I am rather afraid it's rather damp for you as it is quite new. *I*'m not afraid; but you are a bad subject for that sort of thing.

I have got to set to work immediately; need I say that I am just at present very unhappy & lowspirited, and that Emma & myself find living together a great mistake and intend returning to our respective homes?

Hoping to see you before that event, say in a week or so, believe me

Ever yours

K

Give our kind regards to your sister, to whom I will soon send my photo.

46 Great Russell St., Bloomsbury
Friday
[February, 1863]

My dear Tom,

I have not been able to write to you lately on account of work. Have been working this last week up till 11 or 12 o'clock every night. I hope you are getting all right again, and that we shall see you soon. I send you a catalogue by this post; I see one of your pictures is omitted; Poynter says by some oversight of Bill. Everybody speaks very highly of your pictures; Smallfield & Ridley whom I saw were quite enthusiastic about them. When I saw Morgan, he said that he wished the face of the girl in church had been prettier. He says the Exhibition is going on capitally; how far that is true I can't say.

I am getting on very well and am up to my eyes in work; have made myself much bad blood about the Cornhill block, and up to last Friday had determined on giving it up, when I at last made a sketch which seemed to do, and since then finished it. I took it in yesterday and believe it is accepted. Had I had more time it would have been much better, but they wanted it by Tuesday, for the March Number and I had to scamp the foreground, which I might otherwise have made stunning. Besides that I am illustrating Warren's beastly book, doing lots for Punch (which they send me) and have just received the great chapter of Eleanor's victory for O A W, which is a regular 3 vol. & will last a long time; also doing lots for London Society—j'ai donc grace à dieu les mains pleines. Everything seems at present too jolly & too good to last—and I keep often fancying some beastly piece of bad luck *must* turn up soon, or I shouldn't be Kicky.

We've been rather gay up to the last week or so, but are now thoroughly settled down to the earning of the d.b. First Jones gave a party, then Poynter gave one, & very jolly it was; little Mrs. Bell was quite charming, and we had quite an uproarious evening, about 20 people; getting very thick with the Bells who are Darlings. Dined at Little H. H. where we met Miss Thackeray; her august Papa was to have been there but wasn't. Mrs. Coronio, who is having her little girl painted by Watts, came here the other day & told us that he (Watts) had made up his mind on one point & that was that Thackeray & I were to be very thick and would do all in his power to promote my interest in that quarter—nothing like jobbery, is there? I feel quite ashamed; for I am pretty well convinced that Watts doesn't care much for my drawings.

Must put a stop to all this going out though, for it's quite incompatible with serious work, and I intend to take greater pains than ever.

I saw Miss Lewis's marriage in the paper, or rather was told of it. Has she sent you cards? If she has, & to my family, she has behaved very foolishly in not sending any here, especially after inducing me to write to her, & answering the way they did—we sent cards to them. I have made honorable amends for my rudeness by my letter—she's got a husband—je n'ai pas un reproche à me faire.

Haven't seen anything of Bill. Morgan told me that in a state of great rile he took his wife to his parents, forced his way into the house, & that old Langsdorff so far forgot himself as to strike her and that poor Bill was with great difficulty restrained from assomméing his step-father. I fancy that old Langsdorf's blow didn't amount to more than a push, but it's a great pity. I fancy Bill isn't getting on well; they don't like his drawings in Fun, Morgan says. He's working very hard—what a bad job it is altogether.

Poynter is up to his eyes in work & getting on very well. Jimmy is also working—got 300 lbs. worth of orders from the Greeks. His tone is rather changed lately—he has become more modest about his own performances. He was here the other night, and was peculiarly modest about his etchings.

And now old fellow hoping you are all right again, I will say good bye for the present, as I am going on a shopping expedition to Tm. Ct. Road with Mrs. Kicky (who sends all kinds of civil messages)

Ever yours
K

[February, 1863]

My dear Mamma,

I received your letter yesterday; I should have written this morning under any circumstances, as I knew you were getting anxious but I couldn't find a minute, and prevented Pem from writing as I always expected to write next day.

Your letter pleased me very much as there is a tone of much better spirits about it than when you were in Dusseldorf. I would not stick it indoors too much though. I hope to send you 20 pounds in April, indeed can almost promise it for certain as things are going on pretty well. You will then I suppose return to Dusseldorf for the summer. I will now tell you what news I can think of.

First let me ask you if you have received cards from Louisa Lewis. I don't know whether she has sent cards to you and T. A. but if she has, she has insulted *us* in the coarsest way and been a great fool into the bargain—for I wrote a long letter to her, being induced to do so from her sister's message to Isabel, and received two letters in answer in which they called me 'my dear cousin' and all sorts of things. Naturally enough we sent them cards—and a few days after her marriage appeared in the paper without the announcement of '*no cards*', as is usual when no wedding cards are sent; I conclude therefore that cards have been sent and we have been left out. If such is the case, it is a premeditated piece of impertinence of the grossest kind and the previous little attempt at reconciliation was got up to give it more point. If they have not sent you and T. A. cards it's all right of course: but I am nearly convinced they have to T. A. as I had mentioned the fact to him in my last letter and I got a letter from him yesterday or the day before, and he doesn't allude to it in any way. I merely tell you all this that Isabel and you should be on your guard about corresponding with them.

I have been working very hard lately and getting on well enough, but have been much worried with the Cornhill drawing; I was much hurried with it towards the close of last month and had to do it in six days. The consequence was that the Editor, Smith, wished to make some slight alteration although he said he admired it immensely, and I took it back—and nothing would suit me but to do the whole thing over again. I am hard at it now, and think it will be a stunner. It will appear in the April number, and I hope will do me much good. What I have learnt by it is immense, but it's been hard labour I can tell you. 20 guineas won't pay me, and yet I doubt if they will give me even that, but I hope it will repay me in another way. I have done my first drawing for the long serial in OAW. It will last nearly a year, and I do one drawing a fortnight.

The first number appears the week after next and I will send it. I will also send the March number of London Society in which I believe there is to be a large drawing of mine—also the sensation tale in Punch illustrated by Gilbert, Phiz, Millais, Keene and myself. My illustration comes out next week. There is talk about my receiving a regular engagement from Punch, but I have received no 'official' communication on the subject. As for writing or painting the Lord knows when I shall be able to do either; I have hardly time to turn myself about, and writing takes me immense time on account of my want of fluency; painting, on account of my lack of experience. But I must either do one or the other some day as I want to be something more than a draughtsman on wood.

One of the first steps to be taken is to get into a home, a thing we shall do as soon as we can get a few sticks of furniture together, for the rent we pay here is ruinous and Pem is in a constant fidget about it; fancy, it comes altogether to 95 pounds a year, for two rooms on a second floor (and the studio which I must say is perfect). The situation is peculiarly convenient to me—Enfin nous verrons.

My health is improving every day; I don't think I ever had such good health, and I am getting very fat; Pem is not gaining flesh yet and is still delicate, but is looking much better than before her marriage. I can work my twelve hours a day for a week without feeling it, and get awfully excited over the work into the bargain; all of which puts Pem into a terrible state of anxiety; but I only seem the better for it. Il faut dire que je ne suis pas mal nourri; and have nothing to think of but to draw my most and my best. Everything else managed as if by enchantment. Indeed so far I ought to go down on my knees every day and thank heaven for being one of the luckiest fellows that ever were—(Pem who is now in church is probably doing that part of the business for me). Je ne désire qu'une chose, to have you and Isabel here as soon as it can be managed; that is of course if you are both agreeable. I dare say that for the first month or two Isabel would have the mal du pays, and regret that pleasant lazy demoralising Capua, Dusseldorf, to which she seems so much attached; and then she would wonder she could ever have lived there. If she likes going out she would get plenty here, and she wouldn't lack for pleasant company. We have had to go out much more than we like, as we are rather addicted to liking evenings at home. Even then fellows are always looking in; Poynter, Val Prinsep, Keene etc. etc. To-night we dine at the Bells'; to-morrow we were to have dined at the Tennants', but an inexorable model (the beautiful and accomplished Miss Silver) is coming to sit for the principal figure of the Cornhill block and I shall have to draw all the evening. Last Sunday we also dined at the Bells' and afterwards went to the Levies' where we met Lord Dundreary (Sothern) with whom I had a long chat—nothing would suit him but that we must go and see him again this week so he sent us tickets and we went last night. Mrs. Bell who is a dear little woman has taken a great fancy to Mrs. D. M. and wants to get up duets and trios with her; she and Miss Poynter were here yesterday morning practising; Pem is not quite such an enthusiast, and we would much sooner dine at home this evening I must say—but I am glad they get on together, and couldn't wish Emma to have a better companion.

Maman Bellemère dined here with Douglas the other day; the Governor couldn't come. We got quite a nice little spread, and the table looked gorgeous—stunning plate, dinner, dessert, and tea service etc. all the gifts of friends—see what it is to be a nice young couple. She (Maman Bellemère) is all right again and seems jolly enough, although of course she misses her daughter very much.

Henley's mother came here the other day (we had called on her); she came to pour out her griefs; this woman that her son has married certainly justifies the poor old people in their wretchedness. Besides which I believe he is getting on very badly and not making a sou. What a dreadful thing, isn't it? I have not heard from Eugène to whom I owe a letter. I will write to him.

I hope we shall be able to pay you a visit this year, if things go on as they ought it will be easy enough.

And now my dear Mamma I will say goodbye for the present. Give our best love to Isabel, and believe me as ever your ever affectionate son

K

P.S. We can't get the Times but will send you the Daily Telegraph which is the next best paper after it.

Tuesday evening
[March, 1863]

My dear Mother,

Emma has just received Isabel's letter and photograph and will answer by the same post. I like the photograph very much, but next time Isabel is taken I recommend $\frac{3}{4}$ face or profile.

I can only send you 10£ I am sorry to say, as I have met with bitter disappointments in my accounts. London Society took 4£ off my bill, and I am advised to charge only 10£ instead of 15 for the Cornhill. 9 guineas makes a hole. But I will send another fiver in a month or two.

I am glad you like the drawings. By this post you will receive my famous Cornhill, which is just out and seems to have been a success. You see I'm in devilish good company —Leighton and Millais. Also the Once a Week.

Work is going on well, health also, although Pem has only just recovered from a very bad cold which upset her very much.

The Maman Bellemère has dined with us and is very well, although of course she misses her daughter very much.

We have been rather gay lately. On Saturday we went to the Majors' in the morning early, to see the Oxford and Cambridge boat race, and a very jolly sight it was. These Majors are most delightful people as are also the Greeks, their intimate friends. Pem and I have a general invitation to go on Saturday to Tulse Hill and stop till Monday, which will be very pleasant now the summer is coming on. If you move over here they would be stunning friends for

Isabel. Chariclea, the unmarried daughter, is fashioned after your own heart, the most studious girl, and such a linguist, has desperate ambition to be a great pianist also, and learns from Paul. She plays very nicely—but not like Isabel. Madame Coronio is also a very nice woman. Her sisters, the Miss Majors, are charming—very pretty, about 28 and 30, and most accomplished girls. Rosa Major writes very prettily—poems in Once a Week. Then we have Mrs. Bell, Poynter's sister, with whom we dine very often. She is nearly always in here; she is the cleverest woman of our acquaintance; she is going to give a café-clatch on Tuesday week, in which everybody is to read a tale of their own composition. I am going to write Pem's tale (if I've time) as it might do afterwards for OAW.

Our near neighbours are the Joneses; a name you have probably heard before, as the Papa Beaupère would say. Jones is a great genius, a prœraphaelite, and we have lately become rather frequenters of that clique, although I have few sympathies with them.

I have not heard very lately from T. A. and intend to write to him very soon. I fancy he can't be at all happy poor fellow, and is not getting on well, although he is getting on in years. Moscheles has just returned from Leipzig; *he's* got the knack of making money anyhow—too much ever to be much of an artist.

How do you like the great Leighton's illustration to Romola? It is the best he has done hitherto and I admire it excessively. The great Leighton actually honoured me with a visit the other day, and Pem was fascinated by the crichton. We are going to see his pictures before the Academy.

Saturday last after the boat race we went with the Ionides to the Dog show, where I caught a glimpse of Isabella Lewis with her uncle—she looked very pretty and did not see us.

Thursday

Got a letter from T. A. this morning to Pem. You will get the Cornhill the day after you receive this. I have just done a very stunning drawing for Punch and will send it you directly it comes out. Let us have a long letter from you soon, old lady (and acknowledge this directly as I shall be anxious).

I wish I could manage to make my letters longer and more entertaining, but I have so little time and in the evening am thoroughly done up; we often have to go out, but much prefer spending the evening at home. Indeed it's the jolliest part of the day, the summer evenings won't be half such fun; useless to repeat how much we both wish you two were here that we might make partie carrée.

I will now say goodbye for the present, with best love. I do so hope we shall be able to pay you a visit in the Autumn.

It will be a summer of jolly hard work, and I look forward to it with delight, although I am so tired when the day is done. Such a difference between working alone and having one's Missus with one all day. As soon as Gyg is settled in Provins I will write.

Kiss Isabel for me and believe me my dear Mamma your ever

most affectionate son

Kicky

46 Great Russell St.
Friday evening
[May, 1863]

My dear Tom,

I received your letter this morning, and am very much distressed at the account you give of yourself & your health; I have been going to write to you ever since the opening of the Academy to tell you all about it, but have been prevented from day to day. What a muff you are old fellow about the tin. Why, if I were hard up, I would write to you directly; ainsi ne te fais pas de bile à ce sujet; indeed in the course of the next 3 or 4 weeks, it would not inconvenience me very terribly to lend you another fiver, si la dèche devient très embêtante; as work seems to be coming in pretty fast just now.

I do hope the bad luck with your pictures won't last, it must drive you out of your mind to be constantly hoping & constantly disappointed. I almost think it would have been better to have tried the Academy; although you would have stood a very good chance of being some twenty feet over the line. You have of course seen the rows in the Saturday & the Times about the hanging; Brett whose picture was kicked out sold it immediately, which very likely wouldn't have happened had he met with justice. Walker's picture of the Lost Path (a girl lost in a snowdrift) is right at the top in the North room, with one of Sandys', and both are first chop—Walker's is his first oil-painting. Val Prinsep's right on the line, and I must say it deserves its position—his mother sat for the principal figure. How do you like Master Tom Taylor's allusion to his model? Mind you, dear old Mrs. P. has as much claim to be called a beautiful woman as I have. One of Leighton's best was kicked out, Salome dancing. His others have met with no end of praise—all sold I believe; je n'en raffole pas. Jimmy's Westminster Bridge down on the ground; Poynter's over the line in the big room, looks rather black & lacks interest —pretty girl with a book in her lap and her hand on a piano. Bill a small picture at the top & two turned out. Simeon Solomon's which is very good is under the line—you should only see some of the things on the line, it would make you sick. Jimmy who has had two refused, swears he's going to take a penknife & cut his picture out of the frame. All Millais' are upper crust. Poor old Turner has had all three refused. I don't know whether I told you in my last that I was trying to paint. I have had very little time as yet, but it doesn't seem to go on badly so far.

Old Poynter has got in a toile 10 feet by 6 for his Egyptian picture to which he intends to devote two years, never expecting to sell it. He intends to keep himself by 'wood' & 'glass'—he has done two very nice drawings for the illustrated Bible which the Dalziels are bringing out & which promises to be a very crack affair. I have just done another drawing for the Cornhill & Smith likes it very much, I hear. I am now doing two frontispieces (for new editions of Lady Audley's Secret & Aurora Floyd). Miss Braddon whom I last saw at the Academy was pleased to express herself very much delighted with the drawings to Eleanor's Victory.

We have been rather gay lately—quite dissipated. Last Sunday dined at little Holland House, played croquet on the lawn—last week went to a party at Gambart's, rather fun—Sunday & Saturday before at Tulse Hill. Very thick with the Bells, who I am sorry to say are going to move in another month to live at Kew. We are moving and are looking out for unfurnished rooms for midsummer—a very difficult thing to find, aperiently.

I hope your uvula will escape, for although I don't exactly know what it is, cutting it off sounds rather unpleasant. What a good thing you have not had another rheumatic attack! Smallpox is all the go here—we have just been vaccinated.

We hope to go to Coblentz, funds permitting, at the end of July; they are getting on all right. The Missus is rather seedy from her vaccination.

Tom Jeckell was in Town yesterday; Bill had spent the day with him; seemed in good spirit, but never alluded to his wife. I am afraid he's getting on rather badly; I've not seen him for an age; I wish he'd take it into his head to come & see me as he has Jeckell. Saturday night we treated ourselves to the Gallery at Covent Garden—Barbiere—of all the angels on the earth, little Patti is the angelest. She's *beyond* perfection.

I suppose you'll manage a few days here before the Academy's over, although you do not seem very sanguine—I hope so. Nearly a year since we've seen you—write soon old fellow.

This is a very stupid letter but I've been bedevilling my brains with Lady Audley's secret; & been drawing a sensation block (the ruined well in the lime-walk!!). The Missus sends all sorts of kind messages, which I do the same—

and hoping to have a more encouraging account of you very soon

Ever yours Kicky

P.S. Tell me in your next if your *principal trouble* is settled in any way satisfactory to yourself.

91 Great Russell St.
[June, 1863]

My dear Tom,

Your welcome letter came this morning (fiver included—I only hope the sending it did not put you out in any way). I needn't tell you how I sympathise with all your beastly worry about your big picture. Indeed your letter does not give cheering news about yourself; you evidently want a change very much. I can't say your plan of going to Normandy or Brittany strikes me in a very favourable light as I hear that there is great difficulty now in selling pictures there—so says a friend of Poynter of the name of Russell who seems a very good authority on the matter & who tried it himself. Of course much depends on the kind of painting I've no doubt.

I am very sorry we shall not see you—think: we shall be back three weeks after Thursday; will it be too late then?—as it would be so jolly having a little foregathering. If you must come before, my wife bids me say she hopes you will make this place your home for the time of your stay, as although we says it as oughtn't, you will be more comfortable here than in lodgings. Directions will be left to that effect with 'nos gens', and instruction to make you comfortable. (I need scarcely add that if you want really to look elegant & fascinating more than usual, my wardrobe, Sir, coats cut to my figure, will be at your disposal!!! but I believe you nourish some illusion that your own style is the thing.)

I can't tell you very much about the fellers. Jimmy is I believe in Holland, where he was to do an etching of the the big Rembrandt of Rembrandts. Old Bill will be delighted to see you—I met him the other night at Poynter's and he was as jolly as a sandboy the dear old chap. Poynter's picture has met with much praise and he is getting on famously. Have you not heard of his evening receptions through the medium of the fashionable papers? I don't think you will be much disappointed with Val's picture; it is truly a fine powerful thing. You mention William Rossetti's critique in Fraser of this month. Have you read it? I think he's the *only* critic who's not a hack and whose opinion are genuine & felt—and strange to say he appears to me to have wonderfully little party feeling considering his bringing up & associations. His article on Millais' Moonlight is enough to stamp him as a genuine critic to my mind—vide Fraser. As for Tom Taylor, snob & humbug—

(*don't, of course, mention or show this refined little diagram to anybody*)

you saw his allusion to Mrs. Prinsep, who sat for Val. Odd about old Tammy. I heard that he had married somebody with lots of money—so said Willy O'Connor (who's now in Paris). As for old Bancroft I am glad to hear that he has matrimonial intentions, for no fellow more wants marrying and I hope he'll get a good and charming wife worthy of him. My position as you say is improving. I would like to make certain reforms in my way of working—do fewer things and charge highly for them—ça viendra sans doute. I umbly ope new lights will dawn upon me and that I shall turn out an artist as I conceive the thing so called ought to be. I've had wonderful luck so far, there's no doubt.

How I wish you were coming with us to Bonn. We've been looking forward to this trip for many months; we intend to crush & utterly annihilate my mother and sister with our respectability. I hope that the beloved Bohemians will be able to come & live here soon; a castle in the air which my wife & I build at least twice a week, with all the most elaborate details of architecture. We are going to lose the Bells who are going to Kew—a great pity as we chum very much with them; we shall however often see them there. Our other neighbours & allies are the Joneses, whom I hope you'll see something of if you come: they live at No. 62 in this street. Val's been to Paris & has brought back a brother. We spent a very jolly day at little H. H. a little while ago. Our other great pals are the Greeks & Majors; and we lead a pretty gay life on the whole. I am very sorry to hear such a poor account of your sister—she should take another trip like last year.

No more for now, old fellow. Will give your love to all in Bonn

Ever yours

K

91 Great Russell St
Thursday
[August, 1863]

My dear Tom,

Yours to hand. I am very glad to hear about your pictures having sold, although very disappointed at your having chosen North-Wales instead of London. I dare say however you will have benefited much more by your fishing excursion, and trust that your health is already all right in consequence of it.

I am ashamed to say that I did not execute your commission *although* I went to Dusseldorf; for not expecting to go there at all, I never took your letter with me—in fact forgot it, and when I was opposite old polycolore's shop, I could no more recollect the names of the colours you wanted than I could have made them myself (or used them). We had a jolly time of it at Bonn although the tremendous heat, combined with the dainties of my mother's table made us, especially me, beastly languid and seedy; found them looking very well, and my mother quite an old beauty—like Jimmy's, a splendid piece of colour.

We had intended to astonish them by our appearance, I having had a uniform suit manufactured expressly for the occasion. Gad, my dear fellow, they were simply ashamed of us—and my suit with me inside was a spot among the brilliantly got up people of the country. Excursions to Drachenfels, Ahrweiler, Dusseldorf (where we saw a cricket match, which took place on a fearfully hot day near that bridge at Dusselthal where Henley stood & I drew him & you coloured him. The 11 of Dusseldorf v. the 11 of Bonn)—Sam Turner & Tait, and the reverend ass Cooper, who is breaking the hearts of all the girls in D.— De gustibus etc. Fraternised with the Malvanys who are devilish jolly people and have a splendid house & garden. Demoralising place, Dusseldorf; regular Capua. I perambulated here & there, and the remembrance of all of us fellows made me sad; I was devilish near hugging Tait.

I consoled myself by peeping over the wall & into the garden of the Frau Wittwe Kluth, funf & dreizig Kaiser Strasse.

Your old place is of a tremendous swelldom, and is the abode of a famous oculist, who has nearly cured Best. That capital old chap came to see us at Bonn and was awfully jolly, and inquired with warm affection after you; he will come over here in December, at least so he flatters himself.

When in Bonn, was taken to see the students' duels; 5 in a day; shall try and cook something out of them; fraternised with natives; Princes, counts & barons by the dozen. I have hardly recovered my tone of mind sufficiently yet, to write to a commoner like yourself. Passage home was simply Brutal, devilish good thing you weren't of the party, old fellow. We came by that beastly Rhine, & were six & 20 hours in the filthiest boat in Europe with the exception of the filthy boat laden with cattle in which we spent 2 & 20 hours the day after: you recollect the long room in the Hotel des bains? Supped there, and listened attentively for the ghost of violent & discontented Britisher, swearing in several languages in the passage. Hang it, how I love England more & more every day, and how I long for my mother

Q

& sister to come & live here—next year, please the pigs.

Working like bricks—just done 10 little sketches for the Cornhill with which Smith is delighted I am told. Spent a Saturday & Sunday at the Bells' at Kew; so jolly; what dear people they are, and such a stunning house. Last Monday disported ourselves at Putney with the Majors, whom we are getting to like more & more. Greeks have separated into different parts of England for the Autumn. Bill has gone to live with his Missus at Maidstone. Jimmy gone to Holland with Legros, to etch the night-watch. Poynter soon off too—'aïlle âme hirrre' as Fechter says in the Duke's Motto. We are however going to Brighton for a fortnight D. V. in September, for it is hot & enervating about here, and Eleanor's Victory has almost vanquished G. du M. Arthur Lewis has just established a splendid bachelor's paradise in Campden Hill—ah che casa! che giardino! All kinds of manly sports on the Sunday afternoon including claret cup & a jolly supper at eight, 20 fellows sat down to it last Sunday, and by Jove the number increased to 40 in no time.

Et voici mon modèle qui m'attend; adieu donc pour le moment, modèle des antiques vertus; ma femme t'envoie ses affectionnés regards.

Giving up hoping to see you soon

Yours ever

K

91 Great Russell Street,
Bloomsbury
[September, 1863]

My dear Mamma,

I send you a fiver; I should have sent you more but have to fork out 10 guineas to pay my entrance to a club, the United Arts, to which I had very foolishly put my name six months or a year ago, never thinking it would come to anything. I can't very well get out of it now—and it's a great nuisance as I shall very seldom if ever go there, anyhow for a year. By the same post you will also receive the

Cornhill with all my pretty drawings shamefully murdered by the printer—I only wish you could see the proofs I have. Smith is however delighted with them and very kindly sent me a cheque for 20 guineas although I had only charged 15—En voilà un gentilhomme. I am working very hard and we are both very well only Pem has been suffering very much from toothache. We have heard twice from Isabelle from Malines. In one of her letters she mentions the often heard question of wintering in Dusseldorf, and I really think you could do no better than pass the winter there. It will be very different to last year when you were in the same house with the great objection; you need see *her*[1] very seldom; and although she is not the best companion in the world for Isabelle the latter is too old to be influenced by her either one way or the other. Dusseldorf is the only place where Isabelle has friends, and a chance of marriage, according both to your shewing and hers; and I think it is rather hard to exile her from all this because she must meet a person whom you dislike, although I grant you that you are perfectly right in disliking her. The coming between the bark and the tree is I think an illusion of yours much more likely to be effected by persistently opposing Isabelle in what seems evidently to be her great wish and desire. I mention all this over again that you may think of it once more; if there were any object to be gained by constantly making experimental moves to new places, or a chance of really doing better than before, I shouldn't recommend you to return. Just see. Isabelle writes to me that she is slandered and that all sorts of frightful things are said of her. Is it not better that she should remain in a place where she is well known? I think steps ought to be taken to stop this slandering and to find out who is the originator of it. Isabelle says she is nearly sure of the author; if so why not settle the thing at once and have it out with her or him? She also writes that the Lecoqs and Mildays have cut her—Why is this?

It seems pretty evident that she will never be happy away

[1]Kicky refers to aunt Georgie.

from Dusseldorf—Je te conseille donc d'y songer, ma chère Maman.

We have been very quiet and stay-at-home for the last fortnight. Mrs. Wightwick is in Boulogne, which she writes is now a very gay place. Greeks gone to Devonshire. In a fortnight or so I hope to fish an invitation to Brighton from the Bakers. Just had a letter from Tom Armstrong, who says he hopes to sell a couple of pictures and if he does he will try and come to London to work; has also some thoughts of going to Algiers, as a friend would pay his expenses. Says he's going to write to you in a day or two. Wants me very much to paint in watercolours—haven't the time. Am working now for a penny periodical, the Sunday at Home, which I like as it makes one popular, besides of course other things. Eleanor's Victory finishes this month. I will send you all the drawings you have not seen in a lump. Have not been doing much for Punch. Pem takes lots of exercise and is looking very well. She is now (when is she not of late) making the layette and things for the son and heir, whom I am beginning to look forward to with a certain amount of curious expectation; I think he will rejoice in a very affectionate pair of progenitors. I want him to inherit the heart and bones of his Mamma, the flesh and brains of his papa, and I will love him (or her) as the apple in mine eye, which I love and prize more than most men, 'cause why? I have but one. We have already cast the eye

Here is my dream of bliss (rude illustration)

of future acquisition on a little Japanese chair, which looks like the legitimate offspring of a large ditto which I have just purchased for the better comfort of my back as I sit at my easel.

What on earth is as lovely as little children; one came the other day, of the age of 9 months; her Mamma, who is a friend of Pem's, came to help her and initiate in the mysteries of Lilliputian mantua-making etc. Such a little love—I wondered in my mind whether I would exchange the future possible infant for this ready made perfection, but decided I would run the chance.

And now my dear Mamma, I can't think of anything else at the present moment. I am sorry you've had to complain about the food, but hope you are otherwise pretty jolly and well. You will be pleased to hear that I've given up the glass of spirits at night and am very much the better. I've been remarkably well lately, and in very jolly spirits (a little dream is coming over me that I'm going to cut out Walker).

With best love from Pem and myself and hoping to hear from you soon

Your ever affectionate son

G. du Maurier

[October, 1863]

My dear Tom,

I have considerably added to the trottoirs of H—ll by my good intentions of answering your last; however better late than never. I need scarcely say I'm delighted to hear you mean to come here. Another fellow is no less pleased, and intends to take rooms with you if possible—no less than old Tammy[1] who has turned up here on his way to Scotland with his brother. That most unfortunate sufferer has however been badly laid up with an attack of erysipelas in the face which has kept him in bed for more than a fortnight at the Hotel & Tammy has been kicking his heels about

[1]T. R. Lamont, another friend of Quartier Latin days, later to figure as the "Laird" in *Trilby*.

London all the while. He means to quit Greenock and fix himself here, à partir of next February. He is not married after all, you see, it was a vile calumny which has been traced back to Willie O'Connor, who won't or can't give up his authority. The last time I was at the Greeks I heard a similar report about you, but stuck up for you like a man—nobody's safe.

Old Tammy hasn't brought any of his work and speaks in rather a despondent way; his trip to Spain was a failure—nonobstant quoi his jollity is as infectious as ever, and to see him hitch himself by his waistband into my studio was as good as lotion to my sore eyes.

The Missus & I returned on Saturday from a week's trip to Brighton, where we had been invited and had rather a jolly time of it.

Sunday 11th Oct

A whole week has elapsed since I began this, and I have been prevented from going on, partly by a Cornhill drawing for next month which was sent in at the eleventh hour.

Tammy has left for Greenock, intending to return very shortly & fix himself. I am going to propose him for the United Arts Club, of which I am myself an ornament. I don't know if you have heard at all of this institution, which seems to realise the conception of a club you yourself had, I recollect, a couple of years ago. The idea of it originated last winter at Lewises', and it opened a month or two ago. There are about 200 members—the entrance fee 5 guineas, and 5 guineas a year—good rooms, cheap dinner etc—in Hanover Square—mostly artists, but not exclusively so. I will send you a prospectus, and if you like propose your lordship. I, as you may fancy, don't often go, and indeed rather begrudge the 10 guineas I paid last month, but to bachelors it will prove a very comfortable resort I am sure.

Poynter, who is getting on famously, has just gone to Pau with his younger sisters. He has been drawing on wood for Dalziels' Bible, and very successfully. He sells them both drawing & block, and they pay royally. He has just finished one; they gave him 25£ for the drawing & 15 for the block; and it was certainly worth the money, being by far the best thing he has yet done.

Those Dalziels have snubbed me awfully, I really cannot think why, perhaps because I shewed myself too anxious to work for them. I had a drawing in Good Words 2 years ago, et voilà tout. I am doing one now, but for Swain who is going to supersede the Dalziels in the Management; this is as yet a profound secret, so please don't happen to mention it—I mean to Shield, or anybody in the trade—but it appears that Strachan the editor is awfully dissatisfied with the artists employed by Dalziel, and has settled that Swain is to remplacer him à partir of next January, and I dare say now I shall get work there pretty constantly. The other day the Dalziels did actually send me a subject (because it had been refused by everybody on their staff); I refused it also. I am now among other things making drawings for a serial in the Sunday at Home and taking the greatest pains with them; I have also to illustrate Mrs. Gaskell's tale, 'Sylvia's Lovers', for Smith & Elder, which I shall enjoy mightily. If everything only paid like the Cornhill, je deviendrais riche; but whether I get 3 or 10 guineas I take the same pains & time. You know those vilely printed little drawings to the Chalet des Chêvres 2 months ago—I charged 15 guineas; Smith sent me 21£; and was much pleased with them. I was also told by Swain that the noble Millais had spoken very highly of them, which was almost as good as the extra 5 guineas—mais nous n'avons pas toujours cette chance. However people seem to think that I am improving; quant à moi, je n'y vois que du feu; as generally the drawings that I like the most are the least approved of. Did you see in 'Fun' a week or two ago that amiable piece of chaff about me, and the other fellows who draw on wood!

I was much tickled at the notice of your picture in the paper you sent, and should certainly take it as a compliment, although perhaps the smart idiot who wrote it hardly intended it should be so. I should much like to see the picture and all that you have lately done; the last things I saw of yours were those 2 at Morgan's and they were a great improvement on all I had seen of yours before.

Before going to Brighton I dined with Jimmy & Legros; Poynter & Willie O'Connor were there. I saw some of Legros' painting which was very splendid; his etchings I didn't think so much of although Poynter nearly bust a gut over them in his enthusiasm. Jimmy doesn't seem to be doing much. He has bought some very fine china; has about sixty pounds worth, and his anxiety about it during dinner was great fun. He, Legros, Fantin & Rossetti are going to open an exhibition together. Jimmy & the Rossetti lot, i.e., Swinburne, George Meredith, & Sandys, are as thick as thieves;

Ces animaux vivent entre eux comme cousins;
Cette union si douce et presque fraternelle
Enveloppe tous les voisins.

Their noble contempt for everybody but themselves envelops me I know. Je ne dis pas qu'ils ont tort, but I think they are best left to themselves like all Societies for mutual admiration of which one is not a member. If said mutual admiration becomes a parti pris, I can't help thinking it is utterly valueless, and worthy of the motto 'asinus asinum fricat'.

I am indeed almost convinced that a mature man's best chance of getting to do his best work is by sticking very much to himself and of course working very hard, and I do believe talking very little about it—for the best quality of influence seems to flow through some public channel such as exhibitions or picture galleries, or even (if you are a poor devil of a draftsman on wood) the Illustrated Press—better than what comes from the lips of the two or three fellows one lives with. I wouldn't mind however working very hard for the praise of some very clever fellow who had a strong personal dislike to me, taking pains all the while to keep up the dislike—which would be difficult under the circumstances. Happy Millais! fortunatus nimium sua si bona nôrit—who ran away with Ruskin's wife and became the ideal theme of Ruskin's pen. Some people say however that Ruskin has a sneaking gratitude—ayant l'honneur de connaître la dame en question, je m'abstiens de commentaires, but by jove, *I'd* run away with her to be praised by Millais.

I had a long letter from the Maternal who is in Coblenz as you probably know. My sister is on a visit to the Malvanys in Düsseldorf. My aunt is going to live in England, and Bobbie has it appears become quite a sweet boy! By Jove Tom, you may perhaps become a moral man, after all.

Can you tell a fellow any books of any kind to get? The Missus and I devour novels of an evening & confound our tears. We have exhausted our circulating library and at least six months must elapse before we have sufficiently forgotten them to begin them all over again. I have been rereading all George Eliot and think her greater than ever. How did you like Miss Thackeray's tale, 'Out of the World'? pas si fort qu'Elisabeth, hein? Did you see that pretty article about Eleanor's Victory in the Times, in which the distinction is so admirably drawn between Eleanor & Hamlet; and the difference between Miss Braddon & Shakespeare explained to the undistinguishing public? Delane the Editor of the Times is a cousin of Miss Braddon's, and Lucas the writer of the review is the Editor of Once a Week. I tell you this that your opinion of the relative merits of the two authors in question may not be too much influenced by the article.

Did I tell you Lewis has taken a stunning house and grounds up at Campden Hill, and that his Sunday afternoons were such an institution? I go there to-day—games on the lawn, and a gorgeous feed.

There will be little difficulty about the lay figure I should think. Mine cost 15 guineas, I scarcely ever use it, and it is now disabled; can't sit on its chair. If you can be persuaded to choose Bloomsbury to live in you are welcome to it, on the condition that when I do want it I may come and draw it at your place. Should you prefer buying one I feel sure you could get a better one than mine for a fiver—second-hand of course.

Now old chap I'll shut up; the Missus has returned from her devotions and sends her kind regards, and we are going off to an early dinner in Grosvenor St. Give our united kind remembrances to your sister &

believe me

Ever yours

K

Let us hear from you soon.

[November, 1863]

My dear Tom,

I was very glad to get your note and hear your hand is all right again. I was under the impression you owed me a letter, but should have written nevertheless in a day or two.

You don't say anything about coming to live in town next year; I hope you still entertain the project. Tammy as you know is coming.

My sister is coming to pay us a visit in February, after a certain little event which is expected to take place early in January, and to which I look forward with pardonable pride and expectation. The ancient and noble House which bears the sable lion on the argent field will, if everything goes well, begin a new generation (say the 97th) early next year. Wilt be t'godfeyther? *There's* an inducement to come to London! . . . A chance you may not get every year. J'ai un pressentiment que cet enfant sera d'une beauté surhumaine.

I've no particular news to tell, been working very hard, except a very jolly week we spent at the Bells' who have a charming house at Kew. I've been illustrating Sylvia's Lovers by Mrs. Gaskell, among other things—also a serial for the Sunday at Home which will appear in the beginning of the year. I'm now working again for Punch; owing to Leech & the Almanac, drawings are sent to me to put on wood.

Poynter has come back from Pau, with some charming watercolours. He's doing blocks for Dalziel's Bible. Jimmy & Legros are going to part company, on account (I believe) of the exceeding hatred with which the latter has managed to inspire the fiery Joe: one never sees anything of Jimmy now; I have however been to dine with him a few months ago. Poor Aleco has been dangerously ill. The Herculean Val just returned from Venice et autres lieux.

I think I told you about our club, the United Arts. Tammy's going to belong; I hope you will be one of its ornaments some day; it's a very jolly sort of place; I occasionally lose a game of billiards there; c'est ma passion. Poynter is a constant frequenter; capital dinner for half a crown.

T'as dû joliment t'embêter avec les doigts en sautoir. What was the matter with you, panaris, witlow? I've been suffering from toothache, and have had two stopped.

I'm racking my brain in vain to find something to tell you. Apparemment je ne suis pas en train. You however really owe me a longish letter, for I wrote you a very long one a little while ago.

Donc, my dear fellow I will shut up for the present. United kind regards to yourself & sister.

Ever yours
Kicky

Friday, New Year's day
[1864]

My dear Mamma,

You are a grandmamma; my darling old Pem has just had a daughter after a long and painful labour. Yesterday morning at 6 she had pains which came on and went off all day; at 6 in the evening I went to the doctor who said they were 'false pains' and gave her a sedative which did not operate. At 12 I went again and he prescribed some laudanum, but she couldn't sleep and the pains got more violent; so I went to him at 4 this morning and he came and sent me for the nurse. It has come on 7 days before we expected; she was now and then made partially insensible with chloroform. The child's first cry saluted my paternal ears at half-past eleven. It is I am told, a large child which accounts for poor Pem's dreadful suffering; to me it appears very red. I recollect Isabel's elegant figure about 25 years ago having much the same appearance as she reclined in a state of nature on the nurse's lap in Devonshire Terrace:[1] its features seem to me very good, and the shape of its head very stunning, and its bust is most fascinating; but there is a mulberry appearance about the nose which gives me some uneasiness. Mine was however a *crushed* mulberry was it not? Clytie Maud's is anyhow not crushed, and gives grecian promises.

My dear Pem is very well now; I expect the doctor again every minute.

Maman bellemère sent last night to know how things were getting on but we were still under the impression that these were false pains. Tom Armstrong is to be godfather; he is coming up to meet Isabel next month.

I will not write any more now; I have been as you may well fancy in a fearfully excited state. Poor Pem's cries went through me. Si tu as souffert comme ça avec moi, ma chère mère, je t'en suis bien reconnaissant.

Give my best love to Isabel and believe me

My dear old Mamma

Your ever affectionate son

Kick

I will write again in a day or two

[January, 1864]

My dear Tummus,

Thanks for your very jolly letter, and for thinking of sending a telegram, you old trump. My missus was delighted. I may as well confess that the message had been revu et corrigé by the telegraphic clerks, qui n'auront probablement pas fait leur bachot-ès-lettres; *in nomine iantoe socie satis* was a puzzle, construed at last by your friend Susannah Caught.

Your goddaughter, I am proud to say, is well worthy of a latin telegram. She is of stupendous size and power of

[1] Isabel du Maurier was born in 1839 at No. 1 Devonshire Terrace, Marylebone, into which house Charles Dickens moved later the same year.

lung and appetite. In colour & feature she favours the type of her Bussonian ancestors, such of them at least as may have possessed extraordinary beauty; for everybody who has seen it agrees that it is a beautiful babe. As for the jambe de cour I am not quite certain; anyhow I am not going to descant about my daughter's legs with a young bachelor of notorious propensities. I can't say anything as yet about the qualities of the intellect & heart, it has not yet 'taken notice'; but from the shape of its head I believe it will unite strong common sense to a deep poetical feeling, and that it will make an excellent wife to the youthful Malcolm Bell to whom I intend to affiance it as soon as I have spoken to Mrs. Bell on the subject.

Blague à part mon cher, c'est tres drôle d'avoir une poussarde et je m'y intéresse énormement.

By the bye I ought really to defray the columns of Punch for a whole month at least, with the combination of mother & father-in-law, doctor & nurse. The adoration which that infant finds in its grandpa and grandma is something refreshing.

Et nunc majora canamus—What a horrible thing about Thackeray. Out of my own friends & family nothing could have shocked me more; parole d'honneur it haunted me for three days; I had intended to go to his funeral but was prevented; of all the unexpected things!

Tuesday

I had intended to write you a long letter, mais vlan! The infant had its first stomach ache (just like a little prince of Wales) and the uproar didn't cease; je m'y ferai; I shall grow callous to the most pathetic appeals.

'L'enfant paraît: adieu le ciel et la patrie,
Et les poètes saints! La grave causerie
S'arrête en souriant'

for which overhaul your Victor Hugo.

When are you likely to come up? The dowager Miss du Maurier will make her appearance in February, D. V. The noble Tammy will also be in London, and there will be cakes & ale.

I suppose you are hard at work; *I* am; I am now illustrating another book of Mrs. Gaskells, 'A dark night's work'; have you seen Sylvia's Lovers? This will be better; I am also going to illustrate a long tale in the Leisure Hour; they are so pleased with my drawings in the Sunday at Home.

Tu conçois si je pouvais prendre la place de Gilbert dans ces deux journaux, c'est une affaire de 500 par an.

Poynter has just returned from Dover and is working for the Dalziels. Aleco has been dreadfully ill. On Saturday I am going to a grand evening party at Lewises' to which my wife was also invited. Il paraît qu'il y aura de la bougie et que ce sera magnifique. I will now shut up & write again soon—pray give our united kind regards to your sister & believe me

Yours ever

K

[January, 1864]

My dear Mamma,

Every thing is going on splendidly; Pem has vanquished the difficulties of the commissariat department, though not without pain, and the little giant's energy of suction is terrific. It is a wonderfully fine child; about that there are not two opinions; you should see the delight of its maternal grandpa and grandma. I do so wish you were here, I believe you would be quite as enthusiastic. It has not taken notice yet. The shape of the head is perfect; and its chin and mouth, il faut les voir; the eyes are still swollen but of a lovely blue; the stains which gave us uneasiness are fainter, it appears that Pem was born with exactly the same, and yet the purity of her complexion does not leave much to be desired. Yesterday like an old muff she began to cry because of this mulberry colour on the little Busson's nose and forehead—and lo and behold, identical spots came out on her face in the very same places; and I have perceived that when a publisher or editor sends me a message which puts me in a maze a faint mulberry tinge reveals itself on my own conk. Donc ça ne sera rien. She's got a whopping big pair of feet, very narrow and well shaped however; but were not Isabel's feet your despair till she was eleven or twelve? I recollect them well enough, and if Clytie-Maud(!) takes after her Aunt in that respect when she is grown up I shall be well satisfied.

Her voice when she is not screaming too loud has the sweetest tones imaginable. The nurse brings her to me every morning in bed, that I may lick it with 'the fasting tongue'—I enjoy the operation so much that I shall persevere till it reaches the age of discretion. The nurse and Doctor are both excellent, although the former is always regaling us with her experiences, all the kids she has helped to bring into the world seem to have been born with guinea pigs climbing up their backs, or a fried sole with the brown skin upwards on the cheek; and it was she who put Pem in such a funk yesterday and me too. The Doctor said it was a very long and painful labour; almost as bad for me as for Pem I can assure you.

Enfin c'est très amusant d'avoir un enfant, and we are lucky in having a girl, which we had longed for. The day it was born I wrote to Tom A., the godfather, as I did to you, and the old trump wouldn't wait for the post but sent a telegram in latin, and this morning he has written such a charming letter.

Pem in spite of headache (no doubt the result of the chloroform of which the nurse disapproved, preferring a 'nat'ral labour'), is very well indeed, and looks deuced pretty and delicate; she will soon be up again please God.

And now my dear Mamma I will write no more today; for indeed engravers are inexorable in spite of a father's feelings, and I've got to work like bricks at another book of Mrs. Gaskell's.

I expect to hear from you to-morrow, and will write again the day after. Give our best love to Aunt Isabel, and accept the same yourself old granny.

Your ever affectionate son

Kicky

Tom wants to know if the Baby has inherited the light colour, long upper lip and jambe de cour of the Bussons, or whether it traces it's peculiarities to the Clarkes or Wightwicks. Also whether it has given any signs of the extraordinary talents which are expected from it.

[January, 1864]

My dear Mamma,

Although I have very little news to tell you, I write a few lines fearing you should wax uneasy.

The grandchild is going on superbly getting all over as fat as a pincushion. The ugly marks are getting less defined in outline and lighter in colour, and we hope they will soon disappear altogether and then it will be a very pretty child; it has a turn up nose, and blue eyes and such a mouth and double or rather treble chin. A very tall baby with beautifully formed limbs.

Pem has been downstairs these two days but still feels weak, and has much pain when nursing my voracious little daughter for its gums are like other people's teeth.

I've been working like a nigger these last few days, doing some more of those little drawings for the Cornhill. I guess I shall have to go on working like a nigger now, eh?

The baby is to be called Beatrix Isabel, godmothers Isabel and Mrs. Bell, godfather Tom Armstrong.

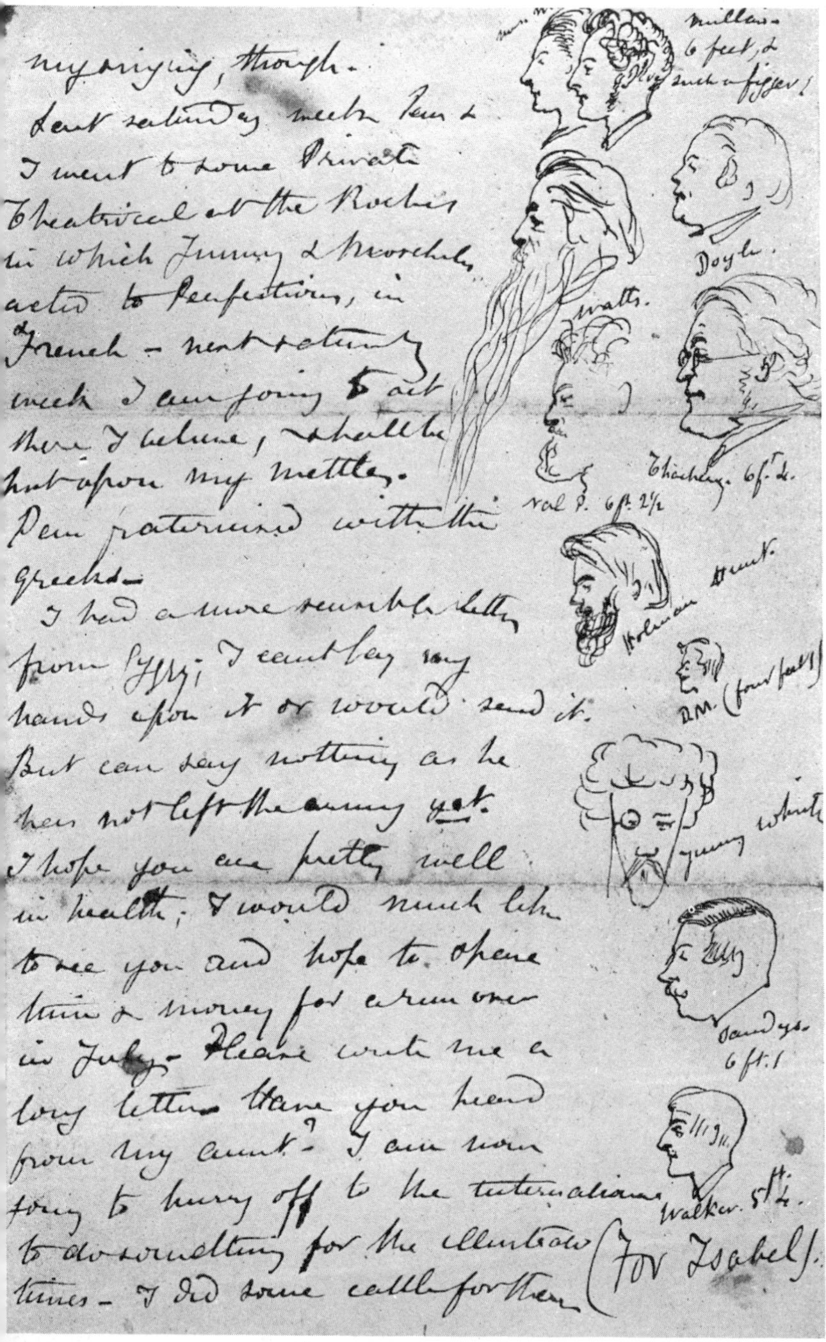

my origin, though.
Last saturday week Pem & I went to some Private Theatricals at the Rocks's in which Jimmy & Moscheles acted to perfection, in French — next saturday week I am going to act there I believe, & shall be put upon my mettle.
Pem fraternised with the Greeks —
I had a more sensible letter from Lizzy; I cant lay my hands upon it or would send it. But can say nothing as he has not left the army yet.
I hope you are pretty well in health; & would much like to see you and hope to spare time & money for a run over in July — Please write me a long letter. Have you heard from my aunt? — I am now going to hurry off to the International to do something for the Illustrated Times — I did some cattle for them

AT LITTLE HOLLAND HOUSE

Profiles of Millais and his wife, Richard Doyle, Watts, Thackeray, Holman Hunt, du Maurier, Whistler, Frederick Sandys and Frederick Walker; from the letter to Ellen du Maurier, *p.* 158

It is now post time so I will post this, and if there is anything about the pictures I will write again tomorrow

yours ever

K.

I feel so damned excited I can't draw a stroke and I've got to crowd a whole month's worth in the next postscript.

subject of my next sketch for Punch.

THE WEDDING

A humorous forecast; postscript to the letter to Tom Armstrong, *p.* 182. The figures from l. to r. are Tom Armstrong, du Maurier, Emma Wightwick, Mr. Punch, Mr. Wightwick

Mr. Wightwick a grandpa

We advertised for a nurse and have engaged a Norfolk girl who can neither read nor write, but seems as if she will turn out very well. The baby is three weeks old today and looks more like 3 months.

I hope Isabel will enjoy her stay in London enough to wish to remain there, and then she and you could settle somewhere not far off; I know you will feel very lonely while she is away, but anyhow not worse than when she was in Malines, and I flatter myself we shall fatten her up better than they, and if she goes back again to remain in Dusseldorf she will decide Sam by her plumpness. I hope she will take a liking to her little niece and goddaughter.

I've not heard from Eugène; I wonder whether he got my letter. It was sent to Provins without naming the department.

Tom Armstrong has sent up two pictures for exhibition

which are now here. I am much afraid they won't sell although there is immense improvement and parts of them are really fine painting.

I shall not write you a very long letter; I have next to nothing new to tell, and am so sleepy I can hardly hold my pen, for I got no sleep last night—that young lady has a fancy for turning night into day, and makes a hideous row if she is not talked to and amused from 3 till about 7 a.m.

I hear Mr. W. has written to Isabel. Next week I will send a fiver for the journey. We have not heard from Aunt Georgie; where is she?

So now my dear Mamma with best love

Your ever affectionate son

Kicky

[February 1864]

My dear Tom,

The Potter is here in safety; I of course know nothing about Potters, but there's no doubt about this being a devilish fine thing; I should have said Van Dyck in my ignorance of Potters. To-morrow, Sunday, I go to Lewis and straightway invite him to lunch with me some day next week, and make the article about it, en tout bien tout honneur s'entend—on est pauvre mais honneêeete! I will not hold out a great hope of his buying it, for he has not a single picture by an old master. I will then try (in case of not succeeding with Lewis) Gambard. Espérons que nous viendrons à bout de le vendre.

Everything is flourishing in the establishment, barring myself who am suffering agonies from toothache; the babe is growing in virtue and accomplishment and we are beginning its education. 'Train a child in the way it should go, and it shall come back to thee after many days'—isn't that the proverb or psalm or something?

My sister is still in Dusseldorf, confined by stress of weather. She wrote today to say she would start Monday or Tuesday via Dover and Calais.

No particular news. Jones, Boyce, Walker and Lohengrin (Lundgrün) elected members of the old water colours—S. Solomon ejected. Jimmy has painted or nearly painted a chinese woman which Gambard has bought for 100£—I hear it's very fine. Legros is making his fortune. Jimmy and Haden à couteaux tirés; quarrel about Joe, in which Haden seems to have behaved with even unusual inconsistency and violence; for he turned Jimmy out of doors vi et armis, literally, without his hat; Jimmy came in again, got his hat and went and said goodbye to his mother and sister. It appears he had told Haden that he (Haden) was no better than him (Jim)! Hinc illae assaultae et batteres, for it positively amounted to that. Frazer told me this, and I've not mentioned it to any but you; it's a deuced unfortunate thing and there is little chance of ever a raccommodement. The best of it is that Haden has dined there, painted there, treating Joe like an equal; travelled with them and so forth, and now that Joe is turned into lodgings to make place for Jim's mother, and Jim is living in respectability, Haden turns round on him and won't let Mrs. H. go to see her mother at a house which had once been polluted by Joe's presence. Droll, eh? I wonder Jim cannot agree with Haden, knowing him so well—I always get on capitally with him. I say with a deferential air and rather timidly: Mr. Haden, doesn't it occur to you that snow in reality, is of a fine jet black colour? And he answers heartily in the affirmative—but by jove, he won't stand bullying or chaff.

As for Jim I am told that he stands in mortal fear of Joe, and that he is utterly miserable; I met him lately and he certainly wasn't very nice to me, and seemed to have grown spiteful and cynical et pas amusant du tout. I fancy the Joe is an awful tie.

Take warning by this, O ye who rail at the domestic hearth, the 'domus and the teasing and pleasing wife'.

The Greeks are a providence to Jimmy and Legros, in buying their pictures.

What do you think, for a piece of news—Watts is going

to be married on the 20th to Ellen Terry, sister of the lovely Kate of that Ilk. I saw E. Terry at St. James's and was not particularly struck; but am told she is charming and only 17; Watts about 30 years older. They are going to live at Little Holland House!

And now old chap I will shut up; I do hope you will be up in Town soon; haven't seen you for 18 months.

Give our united kind regards to your sister; I am going to have my carte de visite taken as soon as I get a new set-out of clothes; as now I look par trop père de famille. There is a man called Winfield Junior, who has been taking large photographs of several of the fellows in 15 and 16 century costumes and they are splendid—you should see Lewis, Leighton, Calderon, Prinsep, Walker! Quels grands seigneurs!

I will write about Lewis v. Potter.

The missus will be awfully disappointed if you don't come and stand godfeyther.

91 Great Russell St.
Sunday
[February, 1864]

My dear Mrs. du Maurier,

Kicky received your letter and will answer it very soon, but in the mean time I thought you would not mind having a letter from me. We do hope Isabel will do all she can to be in London before Friday, as on that evening we are invited to a party at Mrs. Wylie's, who was a Miss Major, of whom you have heard us speak, and on Saturday the Greeks have asked us to dinner, and of course Isabel has an invitation to both, and it would be such a good opportunity to introduce her to all these people which we so much wish to do. You will be pleased to hear baby is getting on very nicely, and that I had begun to use the bottle you speak of about 10 days ago, by universal advice, particularly too as she was rather too much for me, and was preventing me getting up my strength. She only has it twice a day and I nurse her about 4 or 5 times. By my doctor's advice she takes Hard's farinaceous food, and it seems to agree with her very well. I should so like you to see her, she is a dear little thing, and if her marks will only go away, which everybody seems to look upon as a certainty, she will I think be very pretty. I am sorry to say she disturbs us terribly sometimes at night, but we are now going to adopt a different plan, and let her sleep in the servants' room and be brought to me when necessary. Kicky has been suffering very much from neuralgia, and is now taking quinine for it, which I believe is the only remedy, he takes much more exercise than he used, in fact a day seldom passes without his going for a walk.

My dear Mamma,

The baby suddenly requires her Mamma's attention, and as it is nearly post time I finish this. Pem has told you how anxious we are to have Isabel here on Friday; I hope she will be able to manage it.

We are both of us rather seedy today having passed two sleepless nights. What a lesson in patience a baby is!

On Saturday a letter came for Isabel from Isabella Lewis inviting her to lunch today; I took the liberty of opening it as Isabel wasn't here to answer—thinking it might be something important. Isabel had better not write to them until she's in London. I don't know whether it is quite right her accepting T. Malvany's escort, is it? Fancy what those people would say who found fault with her travelling to Paris etc.—damn 'em.

I hope she'll manage to enjoy her visit; she'll get fattened anyhow, and won't lack for invitations what with our friends and what with the Lewises.

As soon as she arrives I will write you longer, in answer to your very jolly letter which I had been expecting for some time. I am so sorry about your not getting on well with the people in No. 16. It would have been very nice to board somewhere.

And now my dear Mamma I will wish you goodbye for the present; I will try and send you some nice sketches of the baby in my next.

With best love

from your ever affectionate son

Kicky

I sent Eugène 20 fr. a fortnight ago.

[March, 1864]

My dear Mamma,

I have been expecting a letter from you every day and shall wait no longer—indeed I should not have waited as long, but I've not had time to write once this last fortnight.

Isabel got a long letter from you the other day and says that you are well. She has been staying with the Lewises ever since Friday last and I've neither seen or heard from her—I only hope she'll pick up a husband there, only not after the Mirehouse pattern. I suppose there's no chance with Master Sam, who in spite of his independent means seems tied to his Mamma's apron strings. That would be the best arrangement for Isabel, and I do wish it could be brought about, since he has caught her fancy. All her sympathies besides and affections are with the Dusseldorf people, and she would be No. 1. She's a rum girl—nothing seems to interest her—and she takes a kind of pride in boring herself everywhere, except she says in Dusseldorf where she is happy all day long according to her own account. Quant à moi, je ne m'en mêle plus, and trust that time will cure this kind of morbid abrutissement. Everybody I see around me has some kind of interest or other in what surrounds them, and I've no doubt if you and Isabel were over here she would be like the rest in course of time. That all her friends in Dusseldorf are kind hearted and nice people, very fond of her is very true; but she could find just the same over here.

The baby is getting on splendidly and is a regular little giant; it is laughing and cooing nearly all day long, and I needn't tell you we are very fond of it. I sometimes go up and see it take its morning bath, a performance it enjoys exceedingly. Such a brawny mottled little lump of fat and so tall! The marks are gradually getting paler on the lip and nose, but it will be a twelvemonth I daresay before they disappear entirely. I suppose Isabel wrote you all about the christening. My Aunt came in and of course fascinated everybody. I quite sympathise with you in thinking she is no fit companion for Isabel, but it's no use saying so. Isabel is coming to stay here next month. I'm afraid she'll bore herself like the very deuce as there is not much excitement going on just now. Last Tuesday we went to the Bells' at Kew and next Saturday we are all going down to see the Univ. Boatrace at the Majors. I wish all these people and Isabel would take to each other. Tom Armstrong is going to remain in London a little while; he is constantly here. What a delightful companion he is—more so than ever, for his health is improved and his temper better; of all the kind hearted unselfish fellows! I think he is still very nuts on Isabel, who can't bear him; I must say I am very glad she doesn't reciprocate, for he will never be in a position to marry.

I am very hard at work doing a long tale for the Leisure

Hour. I aspire to take Gilbert's place on that paper and the Sunday at Home—should such an arrangement come to pass, adieu all anxiety about money. The last two days I have been rather seedy from the coming spring; I am taking quinine and shall be right again in a day or two. Pem is very well I'm happy to say; a great devourer of meat and swallower of stout, for Miss Beatrix is a formidable feeder. Did you get my last drawing in Once a Week? The drawings I mentioned didn't come out in the Cornhill after all, only a little initial.

Tom has pasted all my proofs of wood drawings in a large book; they look gorgeous; it took us two long evenings, Pem and I cutting and Tom pasting. I have certainly improved. These things are arranged more or less in chronological order and each drawing seems better than the last. I 'eat my heart out' as Leighton says (of himself) to make progress and the missus is as anxious as I am. I hope the bull-pup (so Armstrong calls the baby) will have a love for art, though I do not wish her to be an artist.

Sometimes she looks so ridiculously like that little portrait you have of me as a baby. She will have her mother's complexion and the dark blue eyes, but I fancy she will imitate me in the nose and mouth. Last Sunday the servants took her out and went and had her photographed as a little surprise for us. I have not seen a proof yet, but suppose it will be some hideous daguerreotype.

What an extraordinary thing about Louisa's husband—I suppose Isabel has told you all about it. Louisa seems to be a not inconsolable widow, with about 700 a year, according to Isabel.

My Aunt has been staying with the Vincents and is going to stay with them again. They have got into very bad odour in their neighbourhood—their house being full of men all day and sometimes nearly all night according to my Aunt's account and yet she goes there and wants Isabel to call on them. I of course begged Isabel not to do so; from what I can make out fellows don't take their wives there, and it sounds very disreputable. As for my Aunt she will compromise herself some day, that is very certain. She is such a fool besides being a humbug. I really can't make her out, but really think she wants a little looking after.

And now my dear Mamma I will shut up, I've got such a racking toothache. I hope you will soon write. Tom is going to write to you. I hear you are at daggers drawn with your neighbour, Mrs. Smart, who must be a very unpleasant woman. Isabel hasn't shewn me your letter—she tells me her Sam is very ill.

Pem sends her best love and I am your ever affectionate son

K

Saturday
[April, 1864]

My dear Mamma,

Got your jolly long letter, which makes up for having had to wait for it such a time.

About Eugène, I will answer his letter; he is as mad as a March hare, and you may as well leave him to me; I will see what he says, about the money he wants in October, and if his reasons are sound, and truthful sounding, why I suppose I must send it him. I only hope that he will not get leave of absence and devote the money to a trip to London; I could fancy nothing more disgusting—but however there is no fear of that.

The baby is flourishing tremendously; Squire, our Doctor, says it's the finest specimen of an infant he has ever seen. Pem on the other hand is so dreadfully weak and thin that I am getting rather anxious for the weaning; that is to take place next month, when we go for a month to Clovelly in North Devon, by excursion tickets; and I hope to see Pem fill out a little. You can have no idea how engaging that baby becomes, she is such a wonderfully good-tempered child, but a regular little tyrant, insists on being noticed and played with by somebody or other the whole day; her two little bottom teeth have come through and the top are cutting. She's a general favourite, and it's great fun to see her fraternise with the men who come here; the other evening the big Val Prinsep insisted on nursing her, and we were so afraid for his black trousers. Tom, godfeyther, seems to delight in her and as for the grandfather and grandmother over here, you should only see them. Underneath us there's our landlady's soap shop, and that seems to be a great region of delight to Tricksey.

I hope to hear of your getting other lodgings, altho' you will find it difficult to suit yourselves so well as regards pleasantness of aspect and so forth, but Mrs. Sharp must be such an unbearable nuisance from your account that it is perhaps better to make the sacrifice. You are strange people in Dusseldorf to associate with such a person. Enfin, I suppose it's an excitement comme un autre. Sam Perrot called with Isabel's dress—it hasn't come back yet. I haven't invited him to dinner, for several reasons, from Isabel's description of him, our wineless Bohemianism would not impress him, indeed Isabel gave him rather an unamiable character, worldly, insincere and what not—and then, I do not wish the old P. lady to think that I encourage the Busson-Samitic alliance; though when that is achieved I will open wide the arms of friendship, and if necessary kiss all the family.

By the bye, I think that if Isabel were just to write a few words to Maman bellemère it wouldn't be amiss, would it, after staying there a month.

I am very delighted that you should think Isabel has received so much benefit from her trip. I think so too; she was very seedy when she came, as it appeared to me, both in mind and body; dull and bored and interested in nothing; whereas she grew to be considerably lively. My impression is that if she lived in England altogether she would be a totally different person. From what I can gather, Dusseldorf with its feuds, Sharps, broken hearts and sentiment, combined with a very relaxing climate and insufficient nutriment will become a hateful place to both of you unless Isabel's wishes meet with a speedy fulfilment.

On Tuesday next we go to Sarah Haselwood's wedding.

What a match for a poor governess! Henry Kingsley called the other day and seems a very first-rate fellow, par exemple il n'est pas beau; he makes 6 or 700 a year by writing, and has a first-rate position—that great fellow, his brother Charles, is to marry them.

I have been getting through a good deal of work and am told that I improve. I don't improve fast enough to please myself though. I want very much to paint in watercolours, and hope to do something in Clovelly. I suppose you have read everywhere about little Fred Walker's unparalleled success; seven, eight hundred pounds offered for little watercolours, a couple of feet square, and more orders than he can paint. If he doesn't get spoilt, what a grand little fellow he must be; only 25! and such a nice lad, so modest. Whistler is getting on very well now, wonderfully so considering that he is the great genius and innovator, the sort of fellow who dies in a hospital, while centuries after he has a statue put up. The other night I went to a bachelor's party to meet Rossetti and Swinburne at Simeon Solomon's. Such a strange evening; Rossetti is the head of the prœraphaelites, for Millais and Hunt have seceded; spoilt so to speak by their immense popularity; whereas Rossetti never exhibits and is comparatively unknown; this strange contempt for fame is rather grand. He is also a great poet, and his translations from the early Italian poets are the finest things in their way that have been done. As for Swinburne, he is without exception the most extraordinary man not that I ever met only, but that I ever read or heard of; for three hours he spouted his poetry to us, and it was of a power, beauty and originality unequalled. Everything after seems tame, but the little beast will never I think be acknowledged for he has an utterly perverted moral sense, and ranks Lucrezia Borgia with Jesus Christ; indeed says she's far greater, and very little of his poetry is fit for publication. If you like I will copy one of his very mildest which has been

Swinburne reciting

published, namely Faustine, and send it you. These strange creatures all hang in a clique together, and despise everything but themselves; and really I don't wonder. Swinburne's French poetry is almost as fine as his English. The other day at Jones's he was asked to write verses for four pictures of the seasons Jones has just painted, and in *twenty minutes* he had produced four beautiful little latin poems! Tom and I felt like two such bourgeois that night, so healthy and human; didn't get home till three, and wasn't it jolly just after this strange but gorgeous nightmare of an evening, to wake up and find a healthy innocent little baby weighing over 20 pounds.

Ce qui n'empêche pas that genius of this magnitude is a very divine and extraordinary gift, to be bowed down to and worshipped.

Tom Armstrong is painting a picture which promises to be very good indeed—a lady in a riding habit and a little girl asleep. He improves very much and I think his sojourn in London will do him great good, and I only hope he will prolong it ad infinitum; he is with us every evening or nearly so. He will very likely come to Clovelly.

I wish you could see your granddaughter now as she is sitting opposite on Pem's knee, she's making such a merry uproar, first a shout, then "adada", then a low lackadaisical moan which ends with a merry grin and a violent revolution of arms and feet, and exhibition of what is not generally shown in society. Her favourite position is to lie back, catch hold of her toes and swing about, utterly regardless of decency, I must say. We are so longing for the little pet's first word. There's nothing like a child for fun and fascination is there; I only hope there won't be one every year. I'm afraid it will be very difficult not to spoil her; I intend to let Pem do all the scolding, which she says is very unfair.

You will have received by this time the first instalment of my Leisure Hour drawings; they improve as they go on, and there are 27 of them. I have just done a drawing for Mrs. Gaskell's new tale of Wives and Daughters in the Cornhill, to appear next month. I am also illustrating all her works; je ne manque pas d'ouvrage, but am very slow; I am making up for years of lost time by the pains I take, you see. What a stunner I might have been! but it's no use thinking of that. Poor old daddy, he didn't twig the latent spark. Alfred Taylor in his notes on life says that for those who do not achieve great fame, Providence provides generally compensation at home, and from my observation of men he seems pretty right; perhaps by the time great fame comes to me, Pem will be blown up in a railway accident and Tricksy will run away with a private soldier. If so I am content to wait. You shall have the first tooth—and eke your great grandchild's first tooth, for I believe you will live to claim that if you come and live in England and give up sauerkraut and sausages.

How about it, old lady?

Your affectionate son
Kicky

Sunday Aug. 14
at Miss Anderson's,
West Pier, Whitby, Yorkshire

My dear Mamma,

I am at last able to write to you. I had expected a letter in answer to my last before starting, but suppose the fearful hot weather has made you disinclined to write.

We are now settled for a month or six weeks in the most beautiful place I ever saw, in very nice cheap lodgings on the quay. Whitby has been beautifully described by Mrs. Gaskell in Sylvia's lovers, as 'Monkshaven', and is very little altered I daresay from the time old Robson, Sylvia's father, was hanged, which part of the story was founded on fact. Just opposite on the other side of the narrow harbour the old red houses rise over each other against the side of the cliff, and above is the splendid old church and the ruins of a magnificent abbey, founded in the 6th century etc. I can't tell you how we are enchanted with the place or how much we wish you and Isabel were with us. It is beautifully warm, but Pem and I are going through our acclimatisation period

—she's got cold in the stomach and I have a beastly big boil over my left ear which draws my face so much to the left that I'm always turning round to follow it. I had to work very hard to leave and have 8 drawings to do in a hurry now for two books of Mrs. Gaskell; then I suppose will come the Cornhill and then I shall have a little time for watercolour painting. We wanted the change immensely, I especially; I was getting as I was at Bonn, hot weather doesn't suit me. As for that darling baby she *is* flourishing; keeps me laughing the whole day; to-morrow we are going to have her photographed to send you—the first as Isabel has probably told you was a failure. Pem thinks her beautiful in the face—I am not in any way blinded by fatherly love, such not being in my nature. She is not regularly beautiful for she has a good imitation of my nose and upper lip, but stunning large blue eyes and a beautifully shaped chin, head, neck etc., her arms are the largest I ever saw in a baby and most splendidly shaped. She is very tall, her legs do not promise calves, nor her feet a very high instep, so you see the little creature is not perfect; but what delights me is the immense strength, jollity and facetiousness it's got, and its intelligence which beams out of its face. It's never a moment without kicking up a row, and always laughing and chuckling, the most fatiguing baby to nurse. Some times it has a reflective mood which it indulges by lying on its back, and taking her feet in her hands quite regardless of the presence of strangers. Everybody is very fond of her and I don't wonder at it. Two Sundays ago it had a violent attack of Diarrhoea and frightened us awfully; Tom went off in a hansom for the Doctor, who told us he was sent for in time or it might have been serious. Now it has already got brown and does not show its marks so much—I suppose it will take a year before these entirely vanish. Tom godfeyther is as proud of it as we are and almost as fond of it I think.

I am now going to tell you something which will make Isabel very angry, about her cloak, namely that when I was going to take it to Sam P. and return his call at the same time I found I had lost his address; so I must put it off till my return when I will go there or else send it by boat. So send me his address, it's somewhere near Mornington Road.

Tom has just sold two pictures, one for 30 t'other 15—the first is very good, by far his best, but it doesn't pay to sell it at that price. If he comes to London he will improve and paint firstrate things. He has just gone back to Manchester. I want him to come here but don't know if he will.

Pem and I take long walks in the afternoon. I am going to visit and sketch all the stunning places of the neighbourhood. How do you like my Leisure Hour drawings? You've received the second batch by this time; they will get better as they go on—27 of them. I finished the last the day before we left.

I received a letter from Gyggy, recalling to my memory the "*promise I made him*" of *a trip to London*!!! and full of messages to Emily Rhodes. No mention of his letter to you—the fellow's a lunatic—I am going to write to him. How very odd it is my Aunt never comes to see us. What's she been up to? is she married? Her last letter to Isabel was most mysterious—she was so full of affection for us when she did come that we thought it would be necessary to keep a bed in the house—"tante mais tante promettante et compromettante! tha-at's goo-ood, eh Isabel?"

Wednesday

Pem has just received Isabel's letter and enclosure; which was very honest but quite idiotic. Since I began this letter I've been a little laid up with the boil and swollen face but am now all right. Pem is in very good order. Poor baby cutting her top teeth and occasionally rather fretful. We're having a great wind today. Yesterday I sent off two blocks to London, which is not so bad. We like this place so much that next year I should like to spend the summer working here and will do so if it's at all possible.

Just been reading the book that charmed you and me so much in Malines, Mrs. Gaskell's life of Charlotte Bronte. Isn't it a jolly book; such fun now knowing many of the people mentioned. Fenn and Halliday have nothing whatever to do with Best. They are friends of Lewis's, artists. Halliday is clerk in the House of Lords, a very distinguished thing I believe. Poor Fenn has no chance with his eyes. It seems to be warming with Samivel. Carry Dickson's nose out of joint—let us hope that it will soon come to a head like my boil. Glad to hear Mrs. Sharpe is cut. Glad to hear Sam refused to vote, though I don't know what he was to vote about but feel sure he did a noble thing in abstaining. Pem will write to Isabel in a few days to answer her jolly letter. The Malvany's will be a great loss to Isabel.

Take care of yourself old lady and write soon to

Your ever affectionate son

K

Pem sends best love to both.

91 Great Russell St.
Sunday
[September, 1864]

My dear Mamma,

We were at Whitby when we received your last jolly letter, announcing your intended change of dwelling and projected little trip up the Rhine. I was so taken up with work that we couldn't write you a proper long letter before the 23rd., and this is the first leisure since our return. You will also have got back to Dusseldorf and your new lodgings. I fancy you will regret your charming look out on the Uf-garten, but congratulate you nevertheless on getting into a new place, for I know you well enough to understand that Mrs. Sharpe's neighbourhood must have been most insupportable to you—and I hope you will pass a comfortable winter.

We got back to London on the 27th all of us much benefited by our trip although I was seedy enough for the first month; I am so delighted with Whitby that if possible I should like to spend 3 or 4 months there next summer, and paint watercolour pictures. I began one which would have turned out a stunner had I had time to finish it, and fortunately nothing sells like a watercolour if it's only

"KICKE AND HYS CHUMMES"

An imaginary forecast of married life; slightly reduced from a pen and ink sketch.

EMMA DU MAURIER WITH HER SECOND CHILD AND ELDEST SON, GUY

Slightly reduced from the original pencil drawing

decent; indeed I know that if once I succeed in doing them I shall very much increase my income. I have been hard at work since my return for Smith and Elder, illustrating books of Mrs. Gaskell's and the Cornhill, and have plenty of work before me I am happy to say. One great disappointment I had on returning to town was to find that my drawings in the Leisure Hour had not found favour with the penny public, who it appears prefer a more diluted kind of article. The publishers however like them in spite of opposition and as far as I can see wish to go on with them. I took great pains with them hoping to go down with the 'many headed beast' and hope to do so still.

I enclose another photograph of Tricksy, who is improving every day; everybody admires her tremendously, and there's no doubt she is getting very pretty as well as big and fat and healthy.

I go up after dinner to see her take her bath, and it's as good as a play. We put her about a yard from the bath and she crawls to it; puts her hands on the top and lifts herself up on her legs with a sort of chuckle at her own cleverness, and casts a longing eye at the water—then she puzzles how to get in, lifts up one leg to get it over the side and then losing half of her support tumbles down on her little posterior and looks round in the most helpless and pathetic manner. She has lately acquired a trick of imitation which is very amusing; if anybody coughs for instance she thinks it's done for her own special amusement and makes the most ridiculous imitation of a cough you ever heard. She's a beautiful little figure and her hair is beginning to grow nicely; the marks are disappearing and becoming quite unnoticeable. Her eyes are like Pem's but I think the rest of her features are like me. I don't know what I was as a baby, but if I was the most reckless highspirited and destructive little devil she takes after me in that respect.

We made some very nice acquaintances at Whitby. First the Leeches, with whom we got quite intimate—I had met them before but only on slight occasion. Leech is one of the grandest and most delightful men I ever met; not at all funny as you would fancy him to be, though, but the most simple hearted modest fellow in the world. He has two very charming children aged 9 and 10; the little girl Ada has fallen violently in love with Tom Armstrong, as indeed have all the family, for we left them in Whitby together. Mrs. Leech came to call on us the day after our return to town and I daresay we shall see a good deal of them. Poor Leech is in a desperate bad state of health, a confirmed hypochondriac, and I think that if he does not take great care of himself he will go mad. He works all day from 10 till five and at his age he ought to be resting; but I fancy qu'il a mangé son pain blanc as Gyggy says, and has lived all his life beyond his income, and now finds himself with two growing children to provide for, a warning example to successful artists. They have a beautiful house in Kensington. We also fraternised with the Thomsons; I don't know if you have heard of Henry Thomson the surgeon who two years ago went over to operate on old Leopold for the stone, and received the largest fee ever given to a medical man, 4,000 pounds. He would be one of your heroes if you knew him. His father was a small shopkeeper in Croydon, and brought him up to the shop. When his father died he kept on behind the counter till at 8 and 20 he had realised sufficient money to go to London and begin his studies; late as it was he worked hard and here he is at 44 at the very top of his profession, and in manner, information etc. one of the most delightful men in London. We dined with him last week. He now wants to give up his profession and turn artist for he has great talent and delights in the society of artists. His wife was Kate Loder, the pianist, a very plain woman but almost as jolly as he. I have a great belief in these late successes which are most encouraging to a man of my age. I do hope I shall be a first rate chap at 44, and if I keep my health I think I shall. Little Walker who is only 25 will never I think surpass what he has done; he's a second Wilkie, who woke one morning and found himself famous; aussi il le mérite bien. His watercolours are of a perfection! Tom Armstrong is now in Manchester. He was painting an out of door picture of 3 children in Whitby which Leech admired very much. It had fine qualities of painting but I think it will be a long time before he sells; there is always a something wanting, grace or charm or whatever you like to call it.

Smith and Elder are publishing an album of drawings by Leighton, Millais, Sandys, Walker, Noel Paton, Thackeray and me, which we have done for the Cornhill at one time or another; and last Sunday at Lewises' I met Millais who was in a terrible state of indignation; he has written to Smith to protest against this exploitage of work and wants me and the others to do the same. So that the grave question of artistic property being protected is broached at last. It is indeed unfair to think that perhaps the sale of these drawings, Millais' especially, will be bringing in a regular income to the publishers, and that the artist shall not benefit by it, and Millais swears that if he spends 500£ in going to law it shall not be done. This question has been occupying us draftsmen on wood, and I hope something profitable may turn out of it. I wish you would find out how Richter manages with his publishers, for nearly all his drawings have been illustrations to a periodical which have afterwards appeared in a separate form as '*Album—Richter*'. That fellow who keeps the *Austellung* would tell you so get Isabel to ask how it's managed—I mean the fair haired pimply young man in the book shop adjoining.

I enclose a few lines to Miss Malleson about her watercolours. They are very clever for a first attempt, and she may get to do very good work; as for selling these of course there is not much chance as there is not enough of subject, and parts are very weak. But I would certainly advise her to stick to it. I shewed them to Lamont, a very clever watercolour painter, and such was his verdict—you should see Poynter's landscapes in watercolour. . . .

Saturday
[October, 1864]

Dear & respected Tummus,

I intended to have written before this, but have been so

hard at work & so used up in the evening that I haven't had the pluck, besides which I haven't had any very particular news.

When are you coming? I should have thought you would have been here before this. You were invited to dinner at the Greeks last Sunday in their new house at Kensington—such a stunner! We dined there; nobody else, but lots of spartans & macedonians in the evening. Also Tammy & Jimmy. Jim is painting a large picture with the smallest Miss Spartali in it as a Chinese. I am told he has quarrelled with Legros; money matters, but as I don't know for certain what the particulars are I won't mention them. But Ridley said that if Legros' version of the affair to him was correct Jim had behaved very shabbily.

Friday yesterday week we had a *dinner party*; the Bells, Miss Poynter & Tammy, with Poynter & Miss Solomon in the evening; wished you'd been there; it was very jolly. Poynter has brought two more stunning watercolours from Wales, but I think I told you in my last.

The day before yesterday I went to borrow Tammy's priest uniform, & saw his picture. The old man is very stunning & the girl pretty. But old Tammy doesn't seem to have done much work—it's true he's been drawing a lot on wood. He is much worried by his Clifton affair. The old Governor is such a narrow-minded old idiot, & the mother doesn't know her own mind—so that affairs are not a bit more advanced than they were.

Yesterday afternoon I went to see Leech. Poor fellow he is dreadfully ill evidently, & I was really shocked to see how weak & thin he was; these last three nights he got quite funked, his sufferings were so great. I have a presentiment that he will not be able to do the almanac or that if he does it will nearly kill him. Your little sweetheart looked very lovely. They asked after you, ça va sans dire; you are a great favourite evidently.

I am doing a new tale in the Leisure Hour and have already done 4 drawings; also 2 for London Society which I have given to old Robinson to his intense 'satisfaction'. I have moreover just finished a drawing for Dr. Guthrie's new pious periodical the Sunday Magazine; tu vois que je n'y vais pas de main morte. I am now drawing all these things straight on the block, and I think that in boldness of execution & character they are better. I have also been using pencil and am curious to know how Robinson will pull himself of it.

Next Tuesday we go to the Marks's & Tuesday after to 'Dots' (Coyne). Only had a glimpse of Keene since our return—he was looking very thin.

We've given warning to Pears for March, and are of course quite undecided about where to go. Du reste nous avons le temps. Been in correspondance with Gyggy, who says everybody loves him, and as for his mother, 'c'est sa réligion'.

My aunt I hear is engaged to marry a surgeon in the Guards, a Dr. George I believe. We have neither seen nor heard of her. I suppose she has just got back to Dusseldorf. Your Goddaughter is flourishing and has cut another tooth —in all 5. She's as noisy & jolly as ever, and is getting quite a wig.

How jolly Whitby was! I look back upon it with pleasure & fond regret. Let's repeat the dose next year. But I say old chap I hope you're coming soon; tu nous manques joliment. Besides it will be I am sure for your good, and I hope you won't give up the idea of living in London. Let's hear from you. With love from the Missus & kind regards to all your family

Ever yours
Kick

P.S. Now going to your friend Delevignes', and ain't we going to treat ourselves to a bottle of sherry for to-morrow, just.

[December, 1864]

My dear Mamma,

I write a few lines for fear you should get anxious, but have not yet time to send you a proper letter. In a week or so I will. When you see Punch's Almanac, you will understand my not having time to write, considering it came besides my regular work.

We were much shocked to hear Isabel had been so ill; she has indeed had a bad time of it, poor girl.

I have plenty of news, and shall be able in my next to entertain you as your last letter deserves. I will now merely say that I am regularly on the staff of Punch and have taken Leech's place at that sacred dinner table on Wednesdays. I have been working all day and in the evening and barring a cold, which I am getting over, was never better—there's no doubt work suits *my* complaint.

Trixy is growing apace, more impudent and more engaging every day. More of her in my next.

As soon as my accounts are paid at Xmas, I will send you a 10£ note. We have given warning here, and are going to move into a house at March. This is most expensive and not room enough—ought to get a good house for the money.

Tom wrote a long letter to Pem in answer to one of hers, for I had no time to write. He will not be up till after Xmas, and then will settle in London for good. I wish you and Isabel would come to London; we could manage I feel quite convinced with economy and so forth. Isabel doesn't say how affairs are getting on zusammen, so we can't make out whether it is to be or not to be. If not to be, I don't suppose you will much care to stay longer in Germany.

I can't make out my Aunt a bit. What has she been up to do you think? She didn't spoil us with over attention when she was in London.

I will now shut up to send to the post. I shall have got through the thick of my work by next week and will then (as I have observed before, I believe) write you a long 'un.

With our united love to yourself and Isabel

My dear Mamma, your ever affectionate son

K

Xmas-day

[To Tom Armstrong] [1864]

Mong share amee,

Je n'avvy par le tong de taycreer plew to; songsar, jenny par bezwang de te deer ke je lory fay. I have been pitching into blocks morning noon & night, and hope to have a goodly show of the proofs to exhibit when you come to town. I hope you liked the Almanack generally & the D.M.s in particular; the Bouverie Street people are much delighted with it, and considering the hurry & so forth I think it looks pretty well. Keene's drawings are to my mind above all praise; that one of the patent traction crane seems to me one of the most perfect bits of wood execution I ever saw, & so is the one 'I swallered the call'. Millais' block is very pretty, & so is Walker's, though I confess, from some admirable unpublished caricatures I saw by the latter, I was a little disappointed as far as humour is concerned. The other 3 unsigned drawings are by a man called Eltze. There was to have been another drawing of mine but it was not done in time & came out in the ordinary number, where it looks rather inexplicable & out of place. Tenniel's headings are also very jolly. Enfin, I shall not know till Wednesday to what extent it has sold, and am very anxious on account of the prominent part my sketches play in it. I have however received many flattering compliments & so forth, but the proof of the almanack is in the selling. I have a notion I shall be of great service to Punch when I get a little into the habit; vedremo.

The Wednesday dinners are a great institution & very jolly. Old Mark I like immensely, the most genial old fellow that ever lived; Shirley Brooks is a deuced amusing fellow, but rather snarling & sarcastic; Sir Tom de Taylor, very jolly too, but so beastly well informed that he rather imbeasts one at times; the nicest of all is Percival Leigh I think, and old Evans whom we call Pater, next to whom I sit. The dinner gets uncommonly jolly towards cigar time; the other day we all stood up on our chairs to drink success to the Almanac with 3 times 3. The first time we dined at the office after poor Leech's death 2 or 3 weeks ago, they drank my welcome in a very warm & friendly manner I thought, and old Pater turned up the tablecloth where I sat & I saw carved on the table J.L ça m'a fait un sacré effet. He told me to carve 18  54 i mine; but I preferred to wait a little. I also saw further on W. M. T., & D. J., besides the names of all the others, so that this old oval table has quite a prestige for me.

Tenniel is a delightful fellow though very quiet—Burnand very amusing, Horace Mayhew often very drunk; bon enfant mais bête. Silver rarely opens his lips, at which I wonder for he's got lots to say for himself. Our dear old stiffnecked Keene doesn't get quite in tune with the others, and I think these dinners haven't as much charm for him as for this child. Il est vrai qu'il en a depuis longtemps l'habitude. It's quite possible for fellows to talk like an angel & write like poor Poll; not that the conversation is of a very angelic nature generally, but it would be a most mistaken idea to judge of these fellows from the letter-press of Punch, et voilà ce que je ne puis pas comprendre. I get quite fascinated by little bits of recollections which are constantly cropping up about the fellows who are dead & gone; they very often talk of Leech & make one love him more than ever. Somme toute I wish you were one as I am sure you would like the fellows very much. In conclusion, ye dinner very good also ye clar't.

I must now give you what news I can about the fellows. Legros as you may have seen in the Times is married. He called here the other day, and talked very bitterly of Jimmy, whom he says he can never see again. There has been some money quarrel between them and according to Legros Jimmy's conduct has been most shabby; audi, of course, alteram partem. But he was especially bitter about Jimmy's conduct à propos of his (Legros') marriage, for it appears Master Jim chaffed him on all occasions in a very disagreeable manner; je vois ça d'ici, and when poor Legros was trotting out his sorrows I could not help thinking "Arcades ambo!" Mrs. Coronio took the cue from Jimmy, and was very rude to Legros on one occasion, which he shut her up, & consequently is less *well seen* there than he used to be; however he has plenty of work for the next 17 months, copying Lady Somebody's pictures; we are going to call on the young ménage after the 7th. He spoke of Rossetti as his best & most useful friend.

Jones poor fellow has given up all idea of building his house; he has had lots of trouble & not done a stroke of work for 4 months—his wife's confinement & scarlet fever, & his own horrible funk about it have quite knocked him up. He's looking out for a house in Kensington, and Poynter is going to take his rooms. Poynter is drawing for Dalziels; he looked in yesterday for a wonder, more chevalier de la triste figure than ever—I can't make him out. He has just had 3 little watercolours swept away by Gambard for 100£, and is doing very well; he is painting a large oil colour of Roman ladies at the circus for the academy; I haven't seen it. Walker has two very clever sketches in the Winter W. C. Jones's studies for decoration in red chalk have been much raved about; I was disappointed, and thought that the finest things there *by far* were two farmyards by Boyce; I never saw anything so solemn & so grand; one a red tiled barn right across & the foreground filled with miry straw in which little black pigs are wallowing, *lovely*, my dear fellow; makes a large frame of pretty little farm studies by Birket Foster which occupy the place of honour on the same screen & monopolise all the attention, look rather foolish I can tell you. Walker has however just painted a pendant to his Spring called Autumn which I have not seen, but am told is far finer than everything he has done—800 guineas I believe; no wonder he wears a sealskin waistcoat, about which I dream at night, wishing it was a little wider across the chest & belonged to me. Tammy often looks in of an evening; very anxious to get plenty of work on wood. He has been doing some drawings to Esmond on paper to shew to Smith & try and get an illustrated edition of it to do; I have not seen them, but he has the costume, knows the period & they ought to be good; I hope it will work but have misgivings. Old Bill is doing some drawings for Swain.

I hope you will be here in time to go to Mrs. Smith's party (did you get the invitation all right?) Don't you think that your stay in London did you good? Looking back on your work I am convinced of it. Your notion of going to an academy at night is excellent; just the very thing you want, though we shall be deuced sorry not to have you smoking the cigarette of peace in our hospitable mansion. But I think you ought to draw draw draw till all is blue, for you can paint as well as anybody. Old Keene has reached his great perfection through this; for years I believe he has spent his two hours at the Langham, and his early drawings which I have been looking at in old Punches have just the faults of your paintings; a certain ungainliness which came from his difficulty in imitating nature engrossing all his attention, & not letting him think of anything else. Now he draws so easily that he can do it by feeling in the same way that a good sportsman will shoot a snipe, more by the feeling of his gun with relation to his hands & shoulder than by taking aim with his heye. Old Keene is more than 10 years older than you, and the drawings I refer to were done six or seven years ago.

K

[January, 1865]

My dear Mamma,

I hoped to write to you before this, but have been prevented by the usual cause, i.e. work. I had put off my regular work to do the almanac, and got up arrears of blocks almost a yard high to fill up within a given time etc. etc.

First I must tell you that Tricksy walked unaided across the nursery on her birthday, and it was a great treat to see her; she wears a huge pair of knickerbockers over her petticoats to keep them clean and her appearance is very comical; I wish you could see her. She is as large as an ordinary child two years old, and full of life and energy; 8 teeth and her hair curling beautifully; the marks have not disappeared quite, but do not interfere with her beauty; she is very bright and intelligent and getting very fond of her mamma and me—likes to put her arms round my neck and kiss me which is very nice. You recollect the kind of thing I've no doubt—altogether she's a regular little pet, and a credit to the drainage of Bloomsbury.

I hope that Isabel has got strong again; T. A. writes that you intend to come nearer England this summer, either France or Belgium; that is indeed good news. Tomorrow I send in my Punch a/c and as soon as it is paid I will send you the 10 I promised; I had hoped to do so now but have had rather an expensive week from Charlotte Blyth's wedding, of which more further on. I had also had some thought of taking a week's holiday and going to see you before the end of this month, but fear I shall have to put it off till the spring or summer. I have never been so long without seeing you before, and feel as if I should rather like to, as you may imagine.

I hope you will write to me as soon as you get this and tell me all about your plans of moving that I may discuss them with you. It would be nice indeed to be able to go and spend a day or two with you without all the expense of that terrible long journey and the 10 or 12 days absence from work which it necessarily entails.

I wish Isabel had been here to see her beauty Charlotte married yesterday; she did look beautiful and no mistake as a bride. The husband is a very nice fellow although rather young; he has just bought a practice at a small place called Ingatestone, in Essex, and there's no doubt they'll get on famously.

How did you like my almanac drawings? They've been very much admired I can tell you. I wish I could shew you one or two letters I got, and tell you what some people tell me. To believe some of them poor dear Leech was all very in his way but nothing like the great man I'm expected to turn out. If I could hope that in another 30[1] or 40 years I should have such a funeral as his, I should look forward to a future indeed. I am regularly on the staff of Punch now which is a very good thing besides being a very pleasant

[1]He died thirty-one years later.

one; and I've no doubt that when I get into the reins, in a few months or so, they will find DM a very useful person, and pay him accordingly. Espérons-le toutefois; for as far as work is concerned I have more than I can do, but as I cannot work fast and well at the same time my only chance of increasing my income is by being paid at a much higher rate. The Wednesday dinners are very jolly and I think I am rather a favourite, being the juvenile of the lot; besides which they think me still juveniler. One of their principal men, Shirley Brooks, who used to write the Essence of parliament and is a very smart fellow very kindly asked us on New Year's Eve to his house where we had an uproariously jolly night, all the rest of the people being intimate friends of his and his wife's. Tom Taylor I don't like quite so much; Mark Lemon is an old darling and so is old Evans etc. Going to dine there today.

We are going to leave our house in March as it is getting too small for us, and Pem is in a great state of mind about where to go to; we have seen a very jolly house for 70£ in Tavistock Place, that dreary street which leads straight from Tavistock Square to the beastly street of Wharton.[1] The price is certainly very fascinating but is in terrible want of repair; but a most comfortably built house—and then there is the terrible question of furniture, that we shall of course have to do gradually.

Poor T. A. writes in a great state of despondency. He has not succeeded in selling his two last pictures and consequently fears he will not be able to come up to London.

Thursday

Couldn't send this off yesterday.

You must look out for a ballad of mine which will appear I believe in next week's Punch, illustrated all down the side. If it is understood I should like to do a series on different social matters of the day and eke political. Shouldn't I like to do political cuts for Punch some day; ça viendra j'espère

[1]Wharton Street, of unhappy memory. See footnote, p. 5.

without any damage to that jolly fellow Tenniel. Shirley Brooks wants to get me into the Garrick—I belong to one club to which I never go, and which I shall give up if I get into the Garrick. If I make anything like a hit in Punch I've no doubt I shall devote a great deal of my time to it, and try and force myself now and then to go out more; for Pem and I are terrible stay at homes of an evening and shirk going out tremendously. I of course can't settle what I shall do this year yet; for Smith (and Elder) have made to me sub rosa a mysterious proposition; they want to buy me exclusively for some new thing, but will not tell me yet what it is to be; I have however reserved my freedom to draw for Punch, and to fulfil a year's engagement with London Society which will end next October. Whether I shall accept this proposal when the whole is made known to me I don't know, for it is always a bore to be tied down—on the other hand Smith & Elder are royal fellows to pay. Keeping health and all I hope to double my income next year, and I am wonderfully well now; everybody tells me they never saw me look so well before. I get a little more walking and so forth and intend to patronize Chiosso's gymnasium; for I am afraid the profile of my figure will soon give signs of rising about the waistcoat; c'est que j'ai passé la trentaine! sans en avoir l'air.

I will send you my new tale in the Leisure Hour, probably the last I shall do for them, though now they want me at any price, and tell me to make my own charges after this.

We hope to get a long letter from Isabel or yourself and to hear that Isabel is all right again, and whether there are any chances of that little match coming off.

And now my dear Mamma with our best love to both I will shut up.

Your ever affectionate son

K

[February, 1865]

My dear Mamma,

I must give the usual cause for being such a long time

without writing, the quantity of work I have had to do. I suppose you have seen how I've been coming out in Punch; my things have been very much liked; and my position is getting pretty well fixed by this time, and with health and hard work I may look forward towards getting tolerably well off some day. Punch doesn't as yet pay me very liberally, but it suits my book of course to take great pains in spite of that, so that soon I hope I may command what price I like. I am going to make a strike for an extra guinea on the large blocks in a few weeks. I can see they are very well pleased with me; Old Evans has just sent me all the Punches from the beginning (1841) beautifully bound and gilt edged; such an array, and such fun to look over; it's great fun to look at the drawings Leech did 16 years ago, when he was my age, and compare. My drawings go down among artists tremendously, and that is what I care most about. That one of the croquet players made quite a little sensation I can assure you.

All this à propos of Punch, when I have other things to talk about. Why doesn't Isabel write to us about your proposed move towards the coast; the subject is not uninteresting to us; Tom says you are thinking of Calais. Most absurd, you would be miserable. Now talk of Boulogne if you like; it is a charming place, and you need only know whom you like; there is at least some amusement going on, and some people to look at. Then there is Dieppe, Honfleur, lots of charming places all along the French coast from Picardy to Brittany, every one of them better than that filthy hole Calais. Brussels is nice too. I wish you would write to me a long letter about it and give me your reasons and so forth. I second the motion of your coming nearer enthusiastically, and wish you would come nearer still, i.e. London or near it.

I hope to go and see you in May or June, in fact have quite made up my mind to do so; for a week or so. How nice if you lived in Boulogne; I, or sometimes all of us, could go from a Saturday or Friday till Monday and not pass this long period without seeing each other. My advice is go to Boulogne, there will be money enough if you want it, so don't be too anxious on that score. If you came to Boulogne, we should all go there this Summer, including Tom Armstrong; he and I would make a painting excursion into Normandy perhaps and come back and join you after. I don't think you would find Boulogne a bad place to winter in either—Enfin, think it over.

Your little granddaughter is in a very flourishing state; there is a very good back view of her in Punch seated at table taking her tea. We are getting fonder of her than ever; she is very intelligent; I send her for my boots, or a block or to ring the bell or shut the door etc. We are very lucky in having an excellent nurse for her; one great reason I want you so much to come near the coast is that it's the only chance of showing her to you unless you suddenly become a millionare.

To-night I am going to Lewis's whose evenings are getting more and more gorgeous; half the peerage will be there tonight, and very likely the Prince of Wales. Last time (a month ago) Harold Power, the son of the celebrated Irish Comedian who went down in the President, and I, acted and sang a little French piece together, Les deux aveugles, musique par Offenbach, and it was so successful that we are going to repeat it to-night, it is very funny and the music charming. Our costume is something wonderful, as we get regularly up for it with paint and old clothes et tout le tremblement. I should like you and Isabel to see us. Pem knows it by heart as we have rehearsed here over and over again while she played the accompaniments.

Lewis's choir is now by far the best in England and the

music they sing magnificent; I know of nothing I enjoy so much as those evenings. He is certainly a princely fellow. Baker is coming to dine with me and I am going to take him as a kind of return for his having invited us down to Brighton a fortnight ago; I had a day's hunting with the harriers there and by jove wouldn't I like to hunt once a week or so.

Friday

I began this last Saturday and haven't had time to go on with it since. We've been getting furniture for our new bedroom; we have another floor given to us, and so need not move for a good while to come. In fact I don't wish to move now till I get into a regular good house to pass the rest of my days in, somewhere in the country D. V. and bring up a numerous family in fear of the Lord.

Last Saturday was a great success, There was a notice of our performance in the 'Musical World', I will try and get it to send to you. On Tuesday we dined at Little Holland House again; Joachim was there; they insisted on his playing Adelaide, and Pem played the accompaniment; there's an honour; she did it very well too. He afterwards played the pizzicato to 'Deh! veni alla finestra' while I sang. What a charming fellow he is, and what a musician; the Michael Angelo of the violin.

Isabel's love affairs seem to run smooth enough; I send you a little sketch which I flatter myself is very good, shewing Isabel and Samuel 20 years hence, waiting to be married till he has provided for his sister's grandchildren. I think he will dessiner himself when he hears you are going away, and if he doesn't it will be as well for Isabel to get another chance somewhere else.

Tom is getting on with his pictures; I hope they will get in and sell. Yesterday he dined with Val to meet Millais at the club; Millais is one of the hangers this year and it's always well to have friends at Court. He told me to send his love, and say that he will soon write.

Last Friday we spent the day in Essex at a place called Ingatestone, with Charlie and Charlotte Franklin (née

Blyth). He's got a very nice house with no end of rooms, large garden, stables etc. for 30£ a year. They have spent on the furniture etc. a thousand pounds; his practice is worth about 500 a year; and he already is a great favourite; fancy this boy of 23! She was looking so lovely; her sister and (sister-in-law) Jessie is coming to grief; they have three children and James Franklin, her husband, is in debt and has to sell out to pay; what the deuce will become of them I don't know.

(From the press)

'The twins are expected early in May' (Daily Telegraph)

'We are told that a celebrated artist not a hundred miles from Bl—msb—ry expects an important addition to his family in April'—(Evening Star)

I am looking out for a long letter from you; every line of your letters is interesting so make it as long as you can; you know you've plenty of time; ce n'est pas comme moi.

I should like to hear how Master Eugène is getting on; have you heard from him lately?

Moscheles I hear is getting rich; he has set up a painting academy.

And now my dear Mamma I will bid you goodbye for the present, or this letter will never go. In two month's from today I hope to be with you, or say two months and a half; write soon. With best love from everybody to everybody

Your ever affectionate son

Saturday
[May 13th, 1865]

My dear Mamma,

Just a line to say that Pem was delivered of a boy to-day at 2 o'clock; it has been a terrible labour worse than the first as the child is so enormously large; much larger than Tricksy. She is dreadfully faint and exhausted; the pains began yesterday evening at half past ten; she has however just had half an hour's sleep which has done her much good. I have not seen her yet, but cannot delay this longer on account of the post.

There is no post to-morrow, but I will write again on Monday.

With best love to Isabel.

Ever your affectionate son

K

Wednesday

[May, 1865]

My dear Mamma,

Everything has been going on famously. We are looking out for a letter from you.

Pem's rapid recovery is quite astonishing, considering that there was flooding to a very alarming extent, and that the child is so enormous in size—like a child six weeks old.

He will be a good-looking fellow; quite a different sort to Tricksy though; I shall be proud of him. It's the greatest fun in the world to see Tricksy with him; I can't describe to you what a delightful child Trixy is getting to be; so full of life and romping spirits and such original tricks of her own; and never two days the same; and she's growing so pretty; I wish you could see her.

I will not write any more; I am so pressed with work and all that I can't write a long letter now, but it doesn't much matter as I shall see you D.V. in less than a month. I will manage to meet you in Malines on the 12th or so and we'll go lodging hunting in Brussels. Shan't we have a lot to talk about. Best love to Isabel, who won't know Trixy when she sees her.

Your ever affectionate son

K

Trixy, from her hands and feet will be a large and tall woman, like her mother—Guy Louis, in spite of his gigantic proportions, will not depass me.

Chez Madame Francy
Grand Pont No. 3
Malines.
[16 June, 1865]

My dearest wife,

Fancy my rage—Here I am at Malines and find a note from my sister saying they will not be here till to-morrow! How stupid—I do so wish I had started Sunday next. What the devil to do with myself in this beastly hole where I've spent so many miserable days I don't know.

The journey was very slow altho' there were some very nice people on board. I'll never travel alone again if I can help it—it's wretched work. The best thing to do now is to take a long walk. I do so wish you were here.

It seems very strange to see these good people again—they don't find me much altered—only fatter.

I hope you are all getting on well. How I should like to think you were starting for Kew.

Be sure to let me have a letter from you soon telling me all that is going on at home; I should like to receive one to-morrow but suppose I shan't.

I shall now post this that you may be sure to get it to-morrow morning—and go and walk off my beastly vexation—for I *am* vexed and no mistake.

Kiss my darling little Trixy for me and also t'other tho' he won't very much appreciate the compliment, and with many kisses for yourself my darling

Your ever loving husband
Kick

Saturday
[17 June, 1865]

My own dearest Husband,

I have this moment had your letter, it was very vexing getting there before your mother and Isabel, but my darling it won't oblige you to stay longer I hope, I couldn't stand it really. I miss you so terribly. I hope you find the rest is doing you good. Try and walk as much as possible and go to bed early. I am afraid this will not reach you until Sunday morning although I answer your letter at once. I hope I have put the right address, but I can scarcely make it out, so put it plainer in your next. I'm glad you don't like travelling alone, I must go with you next time, however many babies there are. We are all very well, but the house is so wretchedly dull without you my old pet. Tom came in as he came from the boat, and in the afternoon I went to Grosvenor H. for an hour or two, and in the evening Joe came and spent half an hour with me and brought me some beautiful roses. I met Miss Osborne as I walked to Mamma's, she was very amiable as usual. Yesterday I had an affectionate letter from Mrs. Dalrymple asking us to dine there on Sunday and telling me that Mrs. Jackson was going to send us an invitation for Friday next to a hay-making party. She said she hoped we should go and take with us our eldest *Babe*. I have written a nice letter saying how sorry I am we shall not be able to go. I called on Mrs. Beddowe and Miss Solomon yesterday, both out, the latter out of town, when I came back I found Mrs. Haden had been. Joe came to say goodbye and Tom called and then came in at 9 o'clock and stopped until 11. I had got Fraser and he read the Academy notice to me, he was delighted at what was said about him, it seemed quite to put him in good spirits; he is going to the Leech's this evening so I shall be alone, to-morrow I dine at Grosvenor H. I wish the Jacksons' party had been the following week, when we could all have gone, including Isabel, it would have been very jolly.

Try and write to me as often as possible, my dearest, it is the greatest pleasure I can have now and above all things be home on Sunday.

Give my best love to your mother and Isabel and Believe me my dearest Husband

Always your most loving Wife

Pem.

Malines.
Sunday
[18 June, 1865]

My dearest wife,

I was delighted when I got your letter saying all was right—it didn't come till twelve and I was getting very fidgety. We are now going to Brussels; Mamma and Isabel got here yesterday morning—Mamma looking very well only the old lady has lost all her top teeth and it makes her speak just like Mrs. Smith! Isabel is looking very thin indeed.

There is no chance of our stopping over Sunday; indeed we think of leaving Thursday as my Mother will be left in a boarding school in Brussels and the plan at present is that Isabel will go over to fetch her in 3 months' time and they will settle somewhere in or near London. We have been talking lots about you and the kids, and I don't think you will have to fear any want of affection in your Mother and sister-in-law. I shall have lots to tell you which of course I can't write now. I am very glad the D.'s and J.'s have beeen so amiable.

When you write next address to Hotel Windsor, Brussels.

You don't say anything about the kids so of course they're all right. I suppose the little maid is with you. I daresay you miss me old chap, for I do you more than you think I dare say.

Tell Tom that Malines is simply *the most lovely place* in all creation; pale green and red houses and over-hanging gardens on sleepy canals etc. etc. Indeed I have a great mind to come and work here for a month with the kids and you; I could make lots out of it, you really have no idea what a place it is.

We are now going to pack up and the next day or two will be a great bustle, but I shall find time to write you a line each day.

(N.B. the most beastly thing in the world—a wifeless bed in a Malines Hotel.)

Kiss the dear kids. Love to Carver (the old lady thinks

Carver one of the most charming women going; tell Carver it's because she doesn't know her as well as I do).

Universal love to Tom. A kiss on your right eye, your left and your mouth and somewhere else where it's very nice.

Your ever loving husband

K

London, Friday evening
[June, 1865]

My dear Mamma,

For a wonder we are alone this evening, and I am able to write to you in consequence; Isabel is staying at the Rhodes' where she has been since Monday; Tom is not well and has gone home early for fear of catching rheumatics in the night air.

We are all well at home, altho' Tricksy is much plagued with her teeth; it makes her fretty; the eye teeth and some of the double ones. Guy Louis, who was christened last Thursday (Val and Marks and Ellen Levy for sponsors) is flourishing.

I didn't get much of your last letter as Isabel left for the Rhodes' the very morning I came back from Oxford and took it with her of course. On Friday last I went down to Oxford, to meet Tenniel, young Charles Dickens and 3 others to row back to Windsor; one of the most splendid holidays I ever recollect, and I wish I could do it a little oftener—you will soon see I hope some burlesque account of it in Punch like the hunting. The weather for the first two days was lovely; on the third it poured, but we caught no harm rowing—70 miles; ce n'est pas mal.

I heard from Gyggy a little while ago; he is at last doing the only thing that may get him on, and out of his present melancholy position, altho' he will have to run a small risk. He is going to Mexico; in his first letter he told me of it and asked for a little money; I didn't believe him but sent him 20 francs; I shall probably send him a little more before he sails—on the 8 or 12th, that is if I hear from him again.

He seems in famous good spirits, and sanguine about the epaulette. When he last wrote he was at Castres (Tarn) 12 chasseurs. They land at Vera-cruz, whence they start in half an hour, on account of the fever. He writes with his usual inconsistency, first telling me that they sleep on deck with their horses (hardship No. 1) and next that they do the journey on foot from Vera-cruz as they don't take any horses with them (hardship No. 2). Now he has some chance of retrieving himself from his idiotic and disgraceful failure, and I hope he may succeed in doing so. He writes in quite his normal style, mixed with a little sentiment.

Do you recollect a Mr. Clarke with whom my father had some business just before his death? He has hunted me up and wants to know whether we have administered and here's what for, so he says: It appears that he and my father conjointly bought an invention from a certain Frenchman, called Lallemand (and whom I recollect) for the making of paper out of peat; that they took out a patent for the same and that now somebody else is working it and profitably; he wants to sue them for compensation but cannot do so alone—and it is necessary that the next of kin of his late partner, namely yourself, should either administer to my father's estate, or else by letter to him renounce such administration, thus leaving him to sue the parties in question at his own risk, he being then sole administrator. In this case he says whatever chance may befall him, we don't suffer; on the other hand if he succeeds in getting compensation (amounting he says to 800£ or 1,000£) you have a right to half of it legally. Whether this is true or not I can't tell; however it doesn't much matter to us, for even if you did get 4 or 500£ it would be walked off with by the poor Governor's creditors. I will as soon as possible however enquire from Baker, or some other lawyer, what are the real laws in the matter and let you know. He's a fishy sort of beggar I think and not enormously to be trusted.

I am glad to hear that the food is better at Mlle. what's her name. Isabel has wonderfully improved in appearance since her stay but has been suffering again from her teeth;

she is going to Underwood on Tuesday to have one out.

I suppose she has written to you about our proposed trip to Felixstowe; we are going there on the sixteenth for a month or six weeks; it isn't a pretty place or a very amusing one, but one of the healthiest spots in England, and I hope we shall all get as strong as horses. By the time we get back we shall be looking forward to seeing you over here; to end your wanderings to and fro on the earth in I hope a peaceful manner, by being godmother to Trixy's eldest child (she will marry young).[1]

I am working very hard, and according to all accounts, getting very popular; I have recently struck for higher wages with Punch; I used to charge 4 and 3 guineas, and asked in an imperial manner for 6 and 4, saying that I could not work for them at a lower wage (*what* a lie!) What should I have done had they refused! You may imagine my anxiety during three days until I got a letter, and a most amiable one, saying it was all right and that I only asked for my dues. And it came in time I can tell you; for in spite of my apparent success, I have to work slowly and painfully enough—Enfin je crois et j'espère que ça marchera de mieux en mieux. (Harrow and Oxford for Master Guy Louis.)[2]

The Publishers of Punch, the Evanses, are seemingly very sweet on me, and we are sending each other invites to call and all that kind of thing; a good sign for the future I suppose, if my career is to lie that way; it is not the highest unfortunately, but a paying one I suppose, and leads the way to immense popularity if one is lucky and does one's best.

Poor T. A.'s tide has not come to turning point yet and his affairs look very gloomy; and yet he is improving very fast.

I suppose Isabel has told you there are not many marrying men flying about in our waters; she abuses all our friends, and she and Pem have great fights about it.

[1]He was right. Trixy married when she was twenty.

[2]In point of fact it was Marlborough and Sandhurst.

And now old lady I will bid you goodbye—Pem sends her best love. Hoping to see you soon

Your ever affectionate son
K

[June 1865]

Dear Tom,

What dost thou that thou tarriest across the pond? All day long & every day have I waited for thee. Yester-eve, when the earth was wet with rain and the shining flags reflected the policeman opposite thy dwelling, as he stood watching for one that cometh not (haply thyself), I called upon the Lady of thy Land; she wasteth with an unfulfilled longing that thou shouldest come back.

Little news have I, who write these words in sorrowing haste! She who bore me thirty summers back is still alive & kicketh right merrily! She who bears me all day long & every day walks as ever in health & comeliness; but ah me, she who bore her who bears me is weak & pale, & sallow as an autumn leaf! She whom she who bears me bore (and whom thou didst vouch for) beareth herself right lustily; so doth she who with thee did vouch for her whom I named last! My son also aileth not! How art thou? and Oh! when shall we kill the fatted fullgrown calf?

For Evermore I toil, as is my wont!
See'st thou in foreign lands
The labour of my hands?
Write if thou lik'st them . . . if thou dost not, don't!

Oft have we gone at eve, of late, among strangers whom thou lovest not, wishing that thou wast also there with knife in meat & wine in horn: lingering late by the side of friths, bathing in brooks! The last of all the Fridays of this my life, I broke bread at Sir Valentine's, where he abideth newly; a lothly dwelling! a goodly feast! O'Neale, The Knight of Creswick, Christie the Man's son, and many others! Grant sitteth over the forty for evermore; for 'he that seeth land' saw it not!

Thy brother cometh oft.

I have moreover eaten the salt of James, the James that

whistleth! We are friends. I marvel much at the cunning work his fingers have woven on the stretched cloth. The two damsels in snowy samite! and many a scape of sand & sea & sky which he hath lately wrought on some distant coast—I know not where.

Sweetly did the minstrels sing at Moray last week—Drunk got I.

The women of my house do send their love!
The daughter of my house doth send a kiss!
And, for a stampt and duly posted dove
Bearing an olive branch, I send thee this.

K

Just over five years had passed since that summer day in 1860 *when Kicky had borrowed ten pounds from his mother, and left Dusseldorf for London. It was now June of* 1865, *and his dearest hopes had been fulfilled. He was married to the woman he loved, he had two children, his one eye had not failed him, his success was established not only as an artist in his profession, but as a much sought-after personality in the artistic and social world of his day.*

From now until his death, thirty years later, he was never to know failure, nor financial worry. His mother and sister came to settle in London near him (his sister later married Clement Scott, the dramatic critic), and even his brother Eugène, the luckless Gyggy, left the army, married and raised a family of three, who with Kicky's own children often figured in the pages of Punch *during the next twenty years.*

Success never spoilt Kicky's nature. Whether it spoilt his art is another matter. To illustrate, and joke about, London Society week after week for twenty years required concentration of a special kind. Punch *gave him security, and fame—but what if there had been no* Punch? *Would illustrating have been a phase only, and would he have become a great painter? No answer to that question.* Punch *claimed him. But in the later editions we look in vain for those exquisite initial letters, those figures of fantasy, those creations of his imagination, that we find everywhere in his early work; even in his early sketches, drawn on the back of an old envelope, and preserved, for sentiment's sake, by his mother or his wife.*

The hungry young man, anxious, uncertain, lonely, and in love, became the successful illustrator, the contented husband, the happy father. The dreamer vanished. The practical artist took his place.

Yet not entirely. Whoever reads the novels, Peter Ibbetson, Trilby, *and* The Martian, *written in late middle-age, knows that Kicky the dreamer had not died. That sense of the past, that haunting mal du pays, that agony for childhood, youth, and the days that used to be, which he inherited from his French father and bequeathed to his own children, fill the pages of his books with phantoms, so that his readers are caught up in the web of his nostalgia, and suffer with him.*

This volume of letters ends with the one written to Emma, when he visited the Paris Exposition of 1867, *and which foreshadows those novels that were to come from his pen more than twenty years later.*

Friday-Saturday
id est midnight

Dearest Pem,

Altho' I have written to you once today I write again instead of writing in my diary as this can be pasted in after, and at the same time it will gratify your conjugal feelings by letting you know all your faithful hubby's doings as they come to pass.

After leaving the blackguard guinguette where we lunched and posted our letters, we walked thro' the lovely Tuileries to the Place de la Concorde, where we took a bus to the Pont d'Iena which leads to the Exposition. The weather was intensely hot and bright and what with that and the preceding fatigue I couldn't get into the proper key for enjoying the familiar drive. We went into the Exposition and chiefly confined ourselves to the outer buildings which are most delightful; especially the Algerian and Japanese women so like the pictures we know. After paying demi francs here and there and doing absinthes and beers now and then we went twice round and inspected the restaurants of all parts of the world. Spiers and Pond's young ladies I am sorry to say did not come up to my expectations. Deutsch and I got on very well; his amiability is irresistible; but funnily enough we didn't get to talk with anything like geniality until we got into an argument about Jesus Christ going to visit the leper, of all things in the world—and that we would have done just as comfortably in Great Russell St. At 6 we dined at the Diner Europière as we were very hungry and casually minded—so our dinner, which was excellent, cost us five francs a head.

After this we went again among the inexhaustible outer courts—darkness had come on and the whole scene was a blaze of light and confusion of noises and crowds of merry people. A French crowd is most genial and full of charm. We coffee'd at an Algerian place where four Turks played barbarous music, and had some beer at a café chantant where the beer was vile. It was now about 8.30 and we were very tired, so we proposed to go home, and crossed the bridge with that intention. The lights of Paris and Passy were shining just before us in thousands and I made out the lights leading to Passy Grand Rue. This was too much for me and I dragged poor Deutsch to Passy; up the Rue Basse where I saw our old house gleaming in the moonlight or starlight, I forget which, but looking so sweet and melancholy that I immediately went half crazed as you know is my habit under such circumstances. Close by was the attic where my father lived and that I mentioned to you the other day, and the crowd of recollections was quite overpowering to me. I lost all sense of fatigue, and longed to be rid of dear little Deutsch, whose remarks did anything but chime in with my feelings; how could they? Down the Rue de L'Eglise every shop and door of which I seemed to recollect; fancy looking into a window where exactly 20 years ago Isabel used to take lessons in French grammar from an old lady, and seeing a life-size portrait of Lord Dundreary there! Then the unsympathising Deutsch, poor fellow, and I went into the Grand Rue and enquired after our old grocer, Guénier, a household word to us then, and a good one to give credit. Guénier has been dead these five years; and as Deutsch said the place knew me no longer. The Daunergues have disappeared. The U. D. had an ice at a café to wake him up, and we took a bus down the Avenue de St. Cloud by the Arc de Triomphe and the faubourg du Roul to the Madeleine. Now this bus took me by a house in the Rue de la Tour where we lived just 4 and 20 years ago, and then by the corner of the Rue de la Pompe where we lived for 3 years after.

U. D. had by this time fallen asleep, poor fellow; but in passing this corner which I have dreamt of distorted and exaggerated quite lately I thought I should go quite crazed —I was as one in a dream and yet awake, with all facetiousness knocked out of me. "Where are my schoolmates gone", as the Governor sings. Alas! the galleys, the guillotine and what not, and I! alas! married! All this time U. D. was swinging about from side to side in a way that interfered with my enjoyment, so I woke him up to show him the school where I was reared; the dear little chap didn't say damn it, or anything of the kind, but fell asleep again like a baby. I sought for sympathy from the driver and he gave me as much as I could have wished for, and prepared me for a great shock—namely that the old school had been pulled down two years ago to make room for a large hotel! And there was a big flaunting white house on the place where stood the delightful little red-bricked buildings I have drawn in one of the first few pages of my blue sketch book. This was very painful. Where the deuce are *those* school mates gone? For I've been in many schools about here in one way or another. The coachman gave me then a history of all the changes that I saw and wondered at as we drove along, and I never enjoyed a chat so thoroughly, for by this time another fellow had got up between me and Deutsch and D. slumbered peacefully on him. When we got down I gave the driver a franc at which he was apparently charmed and surprised. I wanted D. to go home and leave me to stroll about as I was then far too excited to sleep, but he insisted on coming too. So we went down the Rue St.

Honoré into the Palais-Royal, up the Rue Vivienne and the Galerie des Panoramas to the Boulevard—every step of the way most enchanting to me, and finished the evening at an open air café on the Boul-des-Italiens where D. tret me to Ponche and I him to Groseille.

The scene on the boulevards too lovely; crowds upon crowds of people who seem to have nothing in the world to do but enjoy themselves. And we enjoyed ourselves in spite of fatigue and overpowering heat. And now my duckums, goodnight. God bless you and the dear kids; knowing it will please you I am going to look at the 3 photos before I put the light out: I have now looked at them —and they look very well.[1] I am very anxious to hear from you, and trust you are all well and happy. Love to Maman Bellemere.

Saturday

Pemkids, God bless you.

Breakfasted at the hotel—weather lovely and hot. Looked over the directory for old schoolfellows and so forth—found Froussard, receveur des contributions directes, 36 Quai de Béthune. Walked off with Deutsch, who is game to go anywhere, to the Quai de B. which is in the Marais, Louvre, Seine, Notre Dame de Paris, all most lovely in the sunlight, seen thro' blue spectacles. Found the Quai de Béthune; heart beat to meet my old schoolmaster and friend, Froussard; but it was another, Louis Froussard, not even of kin; beastly French directory had put no christian name. Then Deutsch insisted on going into the Morgue—fortunately no dead bodies today. Then loafed round Notre Dame, and thought of Victor Hugo's romance—all the romantic surroundings, old houses with rusty iron balconies etc. swept away. Crost over to Quartier Latin, did an absinthe poivrée with a cigarette, and then to see Anker at our old studio, 53 Rue Notre Dame des Champs. Anker had left, but we found the portress, Madame Vinot, her husband and the two sons now grown up—anything more charming than their reception I can't conceive. The house had been dull

[1]The du Mauriers' third child, Sylvia, had been born the preceding November.

and dead since les 'anglais' had left; ce joli M. Armstrong, ce beau M. Rowley et M. Lamont, et monsieur Poynter and I. They felt my biceps and mourned over my lost eye like a mother. How charming French people of this class are! Deutsch was quite delighted. Then to the Rue de Bayeux to see Aunt Louise—Deutsch very kindly waiting outside for it is a convent of young she-orphans. Madame la Supérieure took me up to the dear old Aunt[1] who is really wonderfully little altered. She was delighted and covered me with kisses; it is 9 years since we last parted at Malines. She was delighted with your portrait my dear Pem (so by the bye were the Vinots who said I had good taste) and with Trix and Guy. She was much pleased to hear of my having put the stone up to Daddy, her brother. Then with Deutsch for a swim at the Pont Royal baths—at least *I* swam and *he* waded. Deutsch is great fun in a state of nature, so white and plump, like a little white Hercules. Dined in the Palais-Royal, 2.75 a head—coffee'd at Tortoni's and went to see the Famille Benoiton, 4 fr. places. Old Benoiton (Parade) was delightful, and all acted well, but was disappointed with the piece on the whole. Maudlin appeals to French pit sympathy now and then, about mother and child. Think I like Caste better—over at nearly 12—dreadfully thirsty, went to a café and drank 5 bocks de bière between us. Bonsoir Madame, bonsoir mes enfants.

Sunday

Much distressed at not getting a letter, but reflected I couldn't very well—D. didn't get any either. Breakfasted together here—weather lovely but so hot! Walk to Palais-Royal where we took bus to the Pont de Grenelle, and went to bathe in the baths where I learnt to swim, and where I first went with a child's delight 5 and 20 years ago. You can fancy my delight in plunging in, knowing what a crazy chap I am about these things. Talked with the proprietor who recollected Melchior Froussard well, but didn't know what had become of him. After dallying about together like Hercules and Antinous, we'll say, walked into Passy,

[1]Louise Busson du Maurier, his father's sister.

and this afternoon has been more exciting to me than any I ever spent; for after revisiting all sorts of old places and having reserved the Rue de la Pompe for the last I saw a schoolfellow of 25 years ago serving in a little grocer's shop belonging to his mother; I recollected his mother's face directly, Madame Martin Léard, and he and I warmly greeted each other to Deutsch's intense amusement. He was 5 years old when I was externe at the pension Pelieu, now Charonnat, and didn't recollect me in the least, nor should I have known him; personally he is not interesting—indeed very much the other way, so I soon bid him farewell, to go and look at the outside of the house where I lived from 8 to 11, and which is to me the dearest of all these Passy dwellings. What was my luck to find 'Maison à Louer!' I have never put foot in it since we déménagéd 22 years ago! I got the porter to take us in, and upon my word the sensation was so powerful as almost to bring on diarrhoea. Every room unaltered, but so small to what I'd expected—the staircases the same, balusters and all, and so familiar I could scarcely think I'd ever left. They want 3,000 fr. a year. We then paid 1,000. I should so like you to have been there. The trees in the Avenue have grown to twice their size and block out the old view from the garret window; they have cut down the famous apple tree, and shortened the garden, but two lilac bushes remain with the Perron just as they were. Outside the garden an avenue used to lead to a large park—through this park the Passy Railway now runs, and every available space on the side has a little stucco villa upon it. I plucked a piece of ivy from the gate that used to open from the Avenue into it, and which has been shut for many years and walled in, but it is the same rusty gate, ni plus ni moins.

By this time I was no longer quite myself, and Deutsch's indefatigable good nature in trudging about with me through the hot sun shall never be forgotten. We then went to No. 66 Grand Rue, the cabinet de physique of old Louis XVI, where we went for a year after. Here again was an apartment to let, not ours, but the attic. We went over it, a charming little furnished place for 300 francs a month, and the idea forcibly took possession of my mind that I should like to go and bring you all over here for a month, if I can get Bradbury and Evans to allow me an extra 10 a week for the said month for which I will do Paris for them thoroughly well, only a *page* a week instead of a half page. I will think of this again tomorrow when I'm less excited about it; and write accordingly. How you would enjoy this lovely Passy, and the gaiety and geniality all around—and what fun we might have.

Then D and I walked through the lovely Bois de Boulogne to the Mare d'Auteuil which has been brutally modernised and prettyfied, and took a bus from Auteuil thro' Boulogne to St. Cloud. It was now 6 and we dined very happily at the Tête Noire. I'm getting very fond of Deutsch—and our dinner was very pleasant; he confided to me his great wish to be married and many other things I will tell you. After this we went to a 6 sou ball which was very dreary, loafed about the park and finally took the boat back to the Tuileries. What a river it is! Up the Rue Vivienne to the Boulevards, beer and home.

And now ducky, missing you very dreadfully (I mustn't say how much in a diary you know) and looking at your photo which seems quite strange, I will say goodnight, and God bless you and Trixy, and Guy, and Sylvia.

Monday

Up late and rather tired from yesterday's walking and excitement—breakfast at Hotel. D and I went to call on Brandon—he was not at home. Then for a delicious bathe at the Bains Deligres. Then in omnibus to the Exhibition where we did the picture galleries, loafed about and finally dined—after which we went to see Chang and Chung. Had a long conversation with these two worthies and exchanged autographs. Deutsch, who had never seen Chang, was so smitten with his beauty and stateliness that he could talk of nothing else. The picture galleries were very fatiguing. We got home at 12 or so and like two fools sat up discussing in my beastly bedroom till 2 o'clock. It was a great delight to get your letter on getting home and to find all was right. I suppose Sylvia is only suffering from sudden change to Ramsgate. I hope to find a letter to-morrow.

Tuesday

Tremendous storm of rain all night. I got up rather seedy and deaf of one ear. Went with D. to the Bridge when I left him to go to the Exhibition, while I took a turn again for the last time all over Passy, as the sensations I get by doing so are priceless and worth all the exhibitions in the world, including pictures. Explored well every street or nearly so, and almost every porte-cochère, corner, pillar, post and what not brought back a souvenir. It seemed so funny to think of my having a merry English wife and kids all the while at an English watering place, while all the former part of me which I had evoked was so French.

Did not meet any more schoolfellows in grocer's shops, I regret to say, but saw some names unaltered over shop doors—notably one Bouchez, Boucher, which is a curious coincidence I used to notice when quite a little kid.

It is now 2.30 and I have returned into modern life again as you will see by the envelope where I am writing this. I am going to post this and look out for Master D. who has fallen in love with a lovely little Welsh barmaid at Spiers and Pond—prettier than Mrs. Poynter and much sweeter. I promised her I would put her in Punch. I am glad the Poynters are coming altho' I don't suppose we shall forgather very much. I intend to leave this to-morrow evening as I am getting very homesick, and moreover spent with fatigue and excitement. To-night we are going to see the Grande Duchesse, by Offenbach.

With kisses to all and yourself included

Your ever loving Husband

Kicky

I suppose I shall be with you sometime Thursday afternoon or evening.

P.S. What wife ever got a longer letter?

APPENDIX

APPENDIX

Notes, Mainly Biographical

Page 1

"*Tom*", so frequently mentioned in these letters, and to whom many of them are written, is Thomas Armstrong (1832-1911), who was perhaps du Maurier's closest friend outside his family. They first met in Paris, and by New Year's Day, 1857, were sharing a studio with T. R. Lamont ("the Laird" of *Trilby*) and Poynter at No. 53 Rue Notre Dame des Champs.

Armstrong exhibited at the Academy regularly after settling in London, but he was never very successful as a painter, and possibly he found his true *métier* when in 1881 he succeeded his old friend, Edward Poynter, as Director of the Art and Science Department at the South Kensington Museum, a post he held for seventeen years.

The *Memoir* of Thomas Armstrong, published in 1912 (Martin Secker), contains his reminiscences of du Maurier and Whistler during their student days in Paris.

Page 3

Reade was Samuel Read (1815-83), water-colour painter, who at this time undertook the duties of what would now be called "art editor" of *The Illustrated London News*. He was a close friend of Charles Keene whom he had known in early days at Ipswich.

John Leech (1817-64), had been working for the engravers since 1835 and contributed regularly to *Punch* since its beginning in 1841.

Towards the end of his life, after the publication of *Trilby*, du Maurier told an interviewer that Leech's drawings in a *Punch Almanack*, which he came across by chance while staying in Malines, were at any rate one cause for his decision to cross to England and try his fortune as an illustrator. But after his return to England (du Maurier added), "Leech no longer shone as a solitary star in my little firmament. A new impulse had been given to the art of drawing on wood, a new school had been founded, and new methods—to draw straight from nature instead of trusting to memory and imagination."

Leech was one of the most popular illustrators of his day, but he belonged essentially to the older school of Cruikshank and "Phiz", who were primarily caricaturists. Their aim and methods were quite different from those of the young illustrators, such as du Maurier and his contemporaries, who flourished during the 'sixties.

Mark Lemon (1809-70), was the genial corpulent editor of *Punch*, of which paper he had been one of the founders in 1841.

Herbert Ingram (1811-60), had founded *The Illustrated London News* in 1842, and in 1860 he was also owner of *The Illustrated Times*. Du Maurier was to contribute drawings to both of these papers.

Carrick was probably J. M. Carrick, a minor illustrator of the 'sixties.

Page 4

Du Maurier had first met *James Abbott McNeill Whistler* (1834-1903), about 1857 in Paris, when they were fellow students working under Gleyre. By 1860 Whistler had more or less permanently settled in England and at the date of the letter was living at an inn near Wapping Pier, occupied with the famous series of etchings of the lower Thames.

Charles Keene (1823-91), is perhaps the greatest master of black-and-white who has ever worked in this country. Today he is mainly known by his drawings as reproduced, very inadequately, in *Punch* over a period of forty years. In 1860 he had been recently elected to the staff of *Punch*, and kept his studio in Baker Street (over Elliott & Fry's), walking to and fro daily from the house in Hammersmith, where he lived with his mother and sisters.

Many years later, in the course of a lecture, du Maurier referred to his close friendship with Keene during the years following his return to England:

"With all my admiration for Leech it was at the feet of Charles Keene that I found myself sitting. We were much together in those days, talking endless shop, taking long walks, riding side by side on the knife-boards of omnibuses, dining at cheap restaurants, making music at each other's studios. His personal charm was great, as great in its way as Leech's; he was a democrat and so was I, as one is bound to be when one is impecunious and the world is one's oyster to open with the fragile point of a lead pencil. His bohemian world was mine—and I found it a very good world and very much to my taste—a clean, honest, wholesome, innocent, intellectual, and most industrious British bohemia, with lots of tobacco, lots of good music, plenty of talk about literature and art, and not too much victuals or drink."

"Willy" O'Connor had been a fellow student with du Maurier at Gleyre's studio in Paris.

Whistler's 1860 Academy painting, "At the Piano", depicting his half-sister Mrs. Haden and her daughter, had been rejected by the Paris *Salon* in the previous year. In July, 1939, the picture was sold at Christie's for £6,405, and is now in America.

John Everett Millais (1829-96), was at this time (1860) working more for the engravers as an illustrator than with his brush, though his painting, "The Black Brunswicker", was one of the successes of the 1860 Academy. In 1853 he had been elected A.R.A.

Sir Charles Lock Eastlake (1793-1865), had been elected P.R.A. in 1850.

Whistler's brother-in-law was *Francis Seymour Haden* (1818-1910), surgeon, and etcher of genius. In 1847 Haden had married Whistler's half-sister, Deborah. At this time the Hadens were living at No. 62 Sloane Street.

Barge Yard, Bucklersbury, in the city of London, was where du Maurier spent three years (1853-6) in a private laboratory, fitted up for him by his father who was ambitious for his elder son to become a scientist. For an entertaining account of the *dolce far niente* existence led by du Maurier and his companions in Barge Yard, see *The Martian*.

Page 6

Edward John Poynter (1836-1919), had shared the studio at 53 Rue Notre Dame des Champs with du Maurier, Lamont, and Armstrong. In 1860 he had his studio in Grafton Street, and was having a hard struggle to earn a living, but his Paris contemporaries always had faith in his ultimate success. He was elected P.R.A. in the last year of du Maurier's life.

"*Old Ionides*" was Alexander Ionides, whose father had become a British subject. Ionides was a wealthy merchant who had formed a fine collection of pictures and prints—it was he who bought the sixteen plates of Whistler's etchings of the lower Thames—and his house on Tulse Hill, Norwood, was at this time a centre of entertainment for du Maurier and his contemporaries. The son, Alecco ("the Greek" in *Trilby*) had known du Maurier in Paris: Luke, the second son, became an intimate friend of Whistler and later of Burne-Jones. The family are referred to in later letters as "the Greeks".

Luigi Gordigiani (1806-60), "the Italian Schubert", was a composer whose work was in favour at this period. He wrote over three hundred *canzonette* and *canti populari* for voice and piano: "delicious melodies of a sentimental usually mournful cast, based on the melodies of old Italian national tunes, often set to words of his own." (Grove.)

Stradella probably refers to the opera of that name.

Adelaïde is the famous song by Beethoven.

Mdlle. Artot is Desirée Artot (1835-1907), the celebrated soprano singer. At this time she was appearing "with great applause" at Philharmonic and other concerts in London.

Page 7

"*Bill*" is Lionel Charles Henley, whom du Maurier had first met in Düsseldorf. A few months after the date of this letter they were sharing lodgings in Newman Street. Henley contributed drawings to a few of the periodicals during the 'sixties, but he was better known as a painter. In 1879 he was elected a member of the R.B.A.

Giuglini, so rapturously admired by Isabel du Maurier, was Antonio Giuglini (1827-65), who had first appeared in London in 1857. At the date of the letter he was singing at Drury Lane and Her Majesty's. His life ended in a lunatic asylum in Italy.

John Sims Reeves (1818-1900), the famous tenor, was born at Woolwich, the son of a musician in the Royal Artillery. Three years before the date of the letter he had achieved perhaps his greatest triumph at the Handel Festival at the Crystal Palace in *Messiah* and *Judas Maccabaeus*.

Page 9

"*The beast Gilbert*" refers to *Sir John Gilbert* (1817-97), who at this period was, after Birket Foster, the illustrator most in favour with the engravers. Gilbert was a prolific illustrator. He had regularly contributed drawings to *Punch* from its first issue on July 17th, 1841, but severed his connection after the editor had complained that he did not need a Rubens on his staff!

Page 10

The *Bells*, who are frequently mentioned in the letters, were Robert Courtenay Bell and his wife Clara, a sister of Poynter. At this time they were living in Torrington Square, Bloomsbury.

Page 11

"*Munro the sculptor*" would be Alexander Munro (1825-71), who contributed to the carving of the stone on the Houses of Parliament.

Page 12

The British Lion was a short-lived periodical published by Nathaniel Cook, a proprietor of *The Illustrated London News*. Du Maurier received his guinea—his first payment—but before the drawing was due to appear this particular British Lion became extinct.

Page 13

The Illustrated Tennyson is the famous Moxon edition, first published in 1857.

Page 14

Bradbury and Evans were the proprietors of *Punch* and of *Once a Week*. "*O.A.W.*" refers to *Once a Week*, first issued in the previous year. This magazine was destined to loom large in du Maurier's life during his early years in London. What are almost certainly his first published drawings had appeared on September 29th, 1860 (Vol. III).

No comparable periodical in this country maintained a more consistently high standard of illustration. At this time, besides du Maurier, Millais, Sandys, Pinwell, Walker, Burne-Jones and Whistler were among its illustrators.

Page 15

Tom Jeckell (*or Jeckyll*) was an architect whom du Maurier had known in London during the 'fifties before he went to Paris. It was to Jeckyll that Leyland, the Liverpool shipowner, in 1876 entrusted the decoration of his dining room at 49 Princes Gate—before Whistler got at it. The story of "the Peacock room" need not be told here except to say that Whistler's escapade was perhaps the main contributory cause of Jeckyll's mental derangement and early death.

Page 21

The "*emigration*" to Berners Street from the "*abject hole*" in Newman Street was recorded by du Maurier many years later in *The Martian*. The following passage relating to "Barty Josselin" in the novel may be taken as directly autobiographical:

> "And there at Berners Street he worked all day, without haste and without rest, and at last in solitude; and found he could work twice as well with no companion but his pipe and his lay figure, from which he made most elaborate studies of drapery in pen and ink; first in the manner of Sandys and Albert Dürer, later in the manner of Millais, Walker and Keene. Also he acquired the habit of using the living model for his little illustrations. It had become the fashion; a new school had been founded with *Once a Week* and *The Cornhill Magazine*, it seems; besides those already named, there were Lawless, Poynter, not to mention Holman Hunt and F. Leighton; and a host of new draughtsmen, most industrious apprentices, whose talk and example soon weaned him from a mixed and somewhat rowdy crew."

But from the letters it appears that du Maurier's stay in Berners Street was not for long. In a month or so he returned to Newman Street, but to a different address, and with Henley as a less exacting house companion than Whistler.

Richard Buckner was a fashionable portrait painter whose name is today almost completely forgotten. He worked and flourished from 1842-87: his portraits were compared favourably with those by Millais, and his charges were commensurate with the popular opinion of his abilities.

Page 22

The Iris refers to a drawing, much admired by Whistler, published in *Once a Week*, Vol. III, November 17th, 1860: it is the first "characteristic du Maurier" in the artist's earlier manner, and was exceptionally well engraved by Swain. The inept verses entitled "Non Satis" which the drawing purported to illustrate became a byword with du Maurier who frequently quoted from them.

Du Maurier's full-page drawing for the Christmas Supplement of *The Illustrated London News* was reproduced on December 22nd, 1860 (page 591) and is of exceptional interest. It depicts many of the young artist's friends and acquaintances in a series of gay bustling scenes conceived and carried out in the manner of Leech and Doyle. At least two self portraits of the artist may be discerned and a brilliantly executed little vignette of the contemporary Whistler.

Page 24

"*The Levies*" were the family of Joseph Moses Levy (1812-88), who in 1855 had founded *The Daily Telegraph*, the first London newspaper to be sold at a penny. Levy had eight children, of whom the eldest, Edward Levy-Lawson (1833-1916), became in 1903 the first Lord Burnham. In a later letter (1862) du Maurier refers to the wedding of Edward Levy (as he then was called) to Miss Webster.

Page 26

The bedside drawing, "*On her death-bed*", which Whistler "went on about", was published in *Once a Week*, Vol. IV, May 25th, 1861. This is the earliest of the great designs which du Maurier contributed to this paper, and shows the artist under the influence of Sandys who himself was influenced by Dürer and Rethel.

"*Annie's head*": Whistler was at work on his second painting of the Haden household, "The Music Room", later re-named "Harmony in Green and Rose". "Annie" was the daughter of his half-sister, and a great favourite of the artist. She is seen again in "Annie Haden", one of the great portrait etchings of the world.

Page 27

"*Serjeant Thomas*" ("serjeant" is a quondam legal rank) was a lawyer who opened a print shop in Bond Street. A fervent admirer and patron of Whistler, he allowed the artist to print the etchings of the lower Thames on a press installed in his house, and there the plates were bitten while Thomas plied the artist with excellent port. The inevitable quarrel eventually ensued: "I wrote to the old scoundrel", said Whistler, " and he died in answer by return of post—the very best thing he could do."

Delâtre was a printer whom Thomas brought over from Paris to help and advise Whistler in the printing of his etchings.

Page 29

George Cruikshank (1792-1878), had been working as illustrator since 1810, and was completely out of sympathy with the new school of wood engraving.

Samuel Lucas (1818-68), was the first editor from 1859-65 of *Once a Week*. A friend of Thackeray, he is described by a correspondent in *The Times Literary Supplement*, August 23rd, 1947, as "one of the most brilliant editors in a period of great editors."

Page 31

Abraham Solomon (1823-62), exhibited "game and costume" canvases at the Academy from 1841-62. His style is perhaps sufficiently indicated by the titles he chose for his paintings: in 1857 his Academy exhibit was called, "Waiting for the Verdict", and in 1860 his picture "Drowned! Drowned!" won popularity. Solomon's younger brother, Simeon, and sister, Rebecca, both of whom are mentioned in subsequent letters, were also artists.

Page 33

"*Cimabue*" is Frederic Leighton (1830-96), afterwards Lord Leighton, P.R.A. He is called "Cimabue" after his painting, "Cimabue's Madonna carried in Procession through the streets of Florence", exhibited at the Academy in 1855, which first brought him into prominence.

"*Lewis the Linendraper*" is Arthur Lewis, partner in the firm of Lewis and Allenby in Regent Street, and a popular host of his day. At this time he was living in Jermyn Street, where he conducted a choir—"the Jermyn Band"—of which both du Maurier and Keene were members. Later he was to marry Kate Terry, sister of Ellen. Lewis was an amateur painter and etcher of distinction who exhibited for many years at the R.A.

Giovanni Battista Pergolese, Italian composer (1710-1736). His operetta, *La Serva Padrona*, is regarded as having determined the form of comic opera until the time of Rossini.

Page 36

"*Phiz*" was the pseudonym of Hablot Knight Browne (1815-82), a prolific illustrator, especially of novels by Dickens, Lever, and Ainsworth.

Frank Bellew contributed drawings to *Punch* from 1857 to 1862, many of them dealing with incidents in the American civil war. After 1862 he worked for some years in America.

"*The Duke of Omnium*": a character in Trollope's *Framley Parsonage*, which was then (1861) appearing as a serial in *The Cornhill Magazine* with illustrations by Millais.

Page 38

Sir John Tenniel (1820-1914), was a member of the *Punch* staff for fifty years and designed over two thousand cartoons for the paper. His illustrations for the two *Alice* books (1865 and 1871) can hardly have been happier, but his style, though admirably adapted for his work as cartoonist, was unsympathetic and unsuitable for the ordinary run of serial illustration, and it is curious that his work should have been (as du Maurier suggests) in favour with editor and engraver. In 1861 he was illustrating a long serial story *The Silver Cord*, by Shirley Brooks, in *Once a Week*.

Pagr 41

Henry Silver bequeathed to *Punch* an interesting diary recording conversations held at the weekly dinners during the time he was on the staff (1856-70).

Enrico Tamberlik, tenor singer, born in Rome 1820, died in Paris 1889. He had first appeared in England as *Masaniello* in 1850, and remained a member of the Royal Italian Opera Company in England until 1864. He retired in 1877 to Madrid but occasionally sang in public until his death.

John Chandler Bancroft was an American, the son of the historian and American Minister in London. He was on intimate terms with du Maurier and Tom Armstrong, both of whom he had first met at Düsseldorf. Bancroft returned to America shortly after the time of this letter. He was a craftsman in wood and made a remarkable collection of oriental china and prints. He died in Boston in 1900.

Page 50

Frederick Walker (1840-75), whose work on wood at this period is so often mentioned with despair by du Maurier in these letters, is today mainly remembered for his accomplished *genre* paintings in water-colour. Like many of his contemporaries, he began his career as illustrator, and was long regarded by du Maurier as his most formidable rival in winning the favour of editor and engraver. His first contribution to *Once a Week* had been published in Vol. II on February 18th, 1860, some seven months before du Maurier's first appearance. But it was his illustrations to Thackeray's serial, *Philip*, in *The Cornhill Magazine*, 1861-1862, that first brought him into prominence.

In an article published in *The Magazine of Art*, August, 1890, du Maurier wrote:

> "Frederick Walker, then (about 1860) quite a boy, leapt into fame by his illustrations in *Once a Week* and *The Cornhill Magazine*. I can find no word to express the admiration I felt for them as they appeared one after another, each better than the last—an admiration that left no room for any petty feeling of personal envy. He 'made school', as the French say, in wood draughtsmanship. Putting aside the charm of his composition, the grace and naturalness of his figures, the sweetness of his landscapes, the exquisite deftness and dexterity of his manipulation (those effective little cross-hatchings that are to be found more or less in almost every wood-cut executed since his time), he was the first to understand, in their 'inner significance', the boot, the hat, the coat-sleeve, the terrible trousers, and, most difficult of all, the masculine evening suit. Even Millais and Leech, who knew the modern world so well, could not beat him at these."

Matthew J. Lawless (1837-64), illustrator on wood, was an Irishman educated in England. Throughout his brief career he remained faithful to the pre-Raphaelite tradition.

Page 52

Enrico Delle Sedie (1824-1907), operatic baritone singer, was the son of a Leghorn merchant. "Though possessed of so little voice as to gain the sobriquet *Il baritono senza voce* he made up by dramatic accent and purity of style." (Grove.)

Marietta Alboni (1823-94), a famous contralto singer.

Giovanni Mario, Cavaliere di Candia (1810-83), was the greatest operatic tenor of his generation. He married *Giulia Grisi* (1811-69), for many years operatic *prima-donna* in London, Paris, and St. Petersburg. At the date of the letter Madame Grisi had recently signed an agreement binding her not to appear in public within a term of five years.

Page 53

"*. . . a report that Jimmy Whistler is dying.*" After Whistler's labours at Wapping and Rotherhithe on the etchings of the lower Thames he carried his mistress "Jo" off to Brittany, where he began his famous portrait of her known as "The White Girl". Here, according to one report, he was poisoned by the quantity of white lead necessary for his work, and became very ill. He was sent by his doctor to recuperate in the Pyrenees, where he was nearly drowned when bathing and rheumatic fever ensued.

Page 63

This letter has been wrongly dated. It should have been dated August 1862 and placed accordingly. The error was detected too late for rectification.

Page 64

Schenck had been a friend of du Maurier and Felix Moscheles in Antwerp and Malines—they were known to each other as "Rag", "Tag" and "Bobtail". In a lively little book which Moscheles wrote in 1896* he quotes an interesting letter written by Schenck during the Antwerp period:

> "As du Maurier's eyes, though better, will most probably not allow him to resume his profession as a painter, we have determined to try our fortune together in Australia. . . . He hopes to obtain employment by drawing sketches, caricatures, etc., for the Melbourne *Punch* and other illustrated papers. You know how eminently suited he is for that kind of work, and we hear that an artist of talent of that description is much wanted out there, and would be sure to do exceedingly well."

* *In Bohemia with du Maurier* by Felix Moscheles (Unwin, 1896).

Page 65

"*My tale and illustrations*" refers to an illustrated article, entitled "Recollections of an English gold mine", written by du Maurier for *Once a Week*, Vol. V. September 21st, 1861. The recollections were based on his experiences during the summer of 1854 when engaged by the directors of a gold mine company to go down to Devon to assay the alleged ore. This article marks the first appearance of du Maurier as author.

Du Maurier's work at this period was strongly influenced by *Frederick Sandys* (1832-1904), who was proclaimed by Rossetti as the greatest of living draughtsmen. Sandys produced only twenty-four drawings on the wood, but they are among the most important of the period. He inherited his father's scientific interest in the methods and technique of the old masters, but the master who most inspired his work was undoubtedly Dürer. Although closely associated with the pre-Raphaelite circle he was never a member of the Brotherhood.

Page 67

Pamphilon's was a restaurant in Argyle Street discovered by Charles Keene and much frequented by him and his companions.

Page 68

"*My friends in Edinburgh*" refers to the publishers and editor of *Good Words* which, established in 1860, was printed by Messrs. Strahan in Edinburgh and edited there by Dr. Norman Macleod.

Page 72

Henry Stacy Marks (1829-98), artist, the son of a coachbuilder, began his career as a student of heraldry so that he could paint crests and coats of arms on the panels of carriages. Elected R.A. in 1878, he was chiefly known for his paintings of birds, which won the admiration of Ruskin.

"*A fellow called Leigh*" was Henry Sambrooke Leigh (1837-83), the son of J. M. Leigh, director of a famous art school in Newman Street. H. S. Leigh was a journalist who translated and adapted many French operas for the London stage.

Thomas Morten (1836-66), was an illustrator on wood who, like too many of his contemporaries, died before his work received the recognition it deserved.

George Walter Thornbury (1828-76), poetaster and art critic to *The Athenæum*, supplied innumerable verses to the periodicals of the 'sixties—doggerel often redeemed by the splendid illustrations accompanying them.

Edward Dutton Cook (1829-83), was a novelist and dramatic critic.

Page 76

"*The Trident*" was Captain H. R. Howard, so called because he signed his *Punch* drawings with the device of a trident.

Page 80

"*Dry Point*" was, as du Maurier later discovered, the pseudonym of Henry Stacy Marks, who on Keene's recommendation had been engaged as art critic to *The Spectator*. Marks wrote of du Maurier in the article:

> "Mr. G. du Maurier has not been sufficiently long before the public to estimate him truly, yet his drawings have a pleasant silvery look, and exhibit refinement and gentlemanly feeling. If he continues to improve as he has lately, *Punch* will have found in Mr. du Maurier a great acquisition."

Page 81

The "*serial in three numbers*" for which du Maurier had just done a drawing was a story entitled "The Admiral's Daughters" by A. Stewart Harrison. Du Maurier's three illustrations appeared in *Once a Week*, Vol. VI, December 28th, 1861, January 4th, 1862, and January 11th, 1862.

Page 83

Charles Hamilton Aïdé (1826-1906), was a man of universal talent who knew everyone during his bland, accomplished career. In 1867, while staying with Aïdé in the New Forest, du Maurier recorded in his diary: "I am beginning to feel a very warm friendship for Hamilton; a more sincere affectionate and unselfish fellow doesn't exist, and he is a thorough gentleman (hateful word to describe a jolly thing)." Aïdé's mother was a very beautiful old lady whom du Maurier often used as a model for *Punch* drawings.

"*My Lord of Ardwick Place*" refers to Tom Armstrong. Ardwick Place was at this time his address in Manchester.

Page 84

Mrs. Blackburn was a celebrated illustrator in her day. Landseer said that in the drawing of animals he had nothing to teach her. Her contributions to *Good Words* are signed "J.B."

Thérèse Tietjens (1831-77), opera singer, of Hungarian parentage. From 1858 she made England her home, appearing at Her Majesty's and (after 1867) at Drury Lane.

Page 85

The letter beginning "My dear Mamma" has been wrongly dated. It should have been dated October, 1862, and placed accordingly.

Page 86

"*I will send you my Kettle-drum which has been much praised....*" The drawing called "A Kettle-drum in Mayfair" was published in *London Society*, Vol. II, September, 1862. "Kettle-drum" was a period term for "an afternoon tea-party on a big scale"—thus Mr. Eric Partridge in his *Dictionary of Slang*.

Page 87

The letter to "My dear Tom" has been wrongly dated. It should have been dated October, 1862, and placed accordingly.

Page 88

The serial in *Once a Week* was "Santa; or A Woman's Tragedy": the two illustrations with Hampton Court backgrounds were published on September 13th and 20th, 1862 (Vol. VII).

Mason was probably a son of Judge Mason (died 1859) sometime American Minister in Paris. In his student days Whistler had made use of Judge Mason for procuring him invitations to the balls at the Tuileries which he attended in a borrowed dress-suit.

Page 90

The "*new periodical*" was *London Society*, which reproduced many illustrations by du Maurier between August 1862 (Vol. II) and June, 1868 (Vol. XIII), the date of his last contribution. The magazine never attained the artistic standard of *Once a Week*—it was a different kind of paper, being "smart" and topical rather than literary—but it was representative of its period. The London Bridge drawings did not appear until March, 1863 (Vol. III); the delay in publication is explained in a later letter.

Page 91

Valentine Cameron Prinsep (1838-1904), known to his friends as "Val", had first met du Maurier at Gleyre's studio in Paris. He was a man of Herculean proportions—always a great attraction for du Maurier. (The character and physique of "Taffy" in *Trilby* was partly based on Val Prinsep.) Elected R.A. in 1894, Prinsep as painter was a weak derivative of Leighton: possibly his interests were too dispersed to enable him to become a great artist. In 1884 he married an heiress, the daughter of F. R. Leyland, a shipowner of Liverpool, whose "Peacock room" in his home in Princes Gate, as decorated by Whistler, became notorious.

At the date of the letter Val Prinsep was living in Charlotte Street, but he was often at Little Holland House, the home of his parents.

Page 92

Thomas Reynolds Lamont (1826-98), known among his intimates as "Tammy", though he figures curiously little in these letters, was and remained one of du Maurier's closest friends from the Paris days. Thirty years later, when du Maurier romanticized the scenes of his youth in *Trilby*, he modelled the character of "The Laird" on Lamont, giving him however an execrable French accent for which Lamont humorously threatened libel proceedings, as did Tom Armstrong likewise for being left out of the novel altogether.

Page 93

To "*Entertaining Things*" du Maurier contributed two indifferently engraved illustrations (December, 1861, and January, 1862). First published by Virtue in January, 1861, the paper expired in May of the following year: the bound copies in the British Museum are probably the only ones now extant.

Page 95

Du Maurier's "first invasion of the sacred precincts of *The Cornhill Magazine*", of which Thackeray was then the editor, was unsuccessful, but from 1863 he became the most constant and valued of the magazine's artist contributors, illustrating long serial stories by, among others, Mrs. Gaskell, George Meredith, and Thomas Hardy. His first contribution was reproduced in April, 1863.

Page 96

The *Swains* and the *Dalziel brothers* were the most skilful wood engravers of the time. Many of the most representative books containing wood engravings of the 'sixties were planned and distributed by these two firms, the members of which not only commissioned the illustrators whose work they engraved but regarded many of them as their *protegés* and friends.

F. Smallfield was an illustrator and etcher of some distinction.

Page 97

"*Hogg Jim*" refers to James Hogg, editor of *London Society*.

Page 99

Little Holland House was the Kensington home of *Henry Thoby Prinsep* (1792-1878), Indian civil servant and scholar. Prinsep was one of the most popular London hosts of the time, and in his "rambling combination of two old houses in a spacious garden", as the *D.N.B.* describes it, he entertained constantly and lavishly. Ellen Terry in her reminiscences described the house at this period as "a paradise where all the women were graceful and all the men were gifted."

George Frederic Watts (1817-1904), lived with the Prinseps at Little Holland House for twenty years. After the lease expired in 1871 he built the present Little Holland House in Melbury Road, which partly stands on the site of the older house.

Page 101

"*The Langham*" was the Langham Sketch Club in All Souls Place, successor of the Old Artists Society, which Keene regularly attended until the end of his life.

Page 104

Whistler's picture, "*The Coast of Brittany*", or "*Alone with the Tide*", was exhibited at the Academy in 1862.

"*Jo*" was Joanna Heffernan, the daughter of a bohemian Irishman ("a sort of Captain Costigan" was one description), who always referred to Whistler as "me son-in-law". Jo was a woman of little education but of keen intelligence and of great charm. At first their relationship was the casual one of artist and model, but she soon became a necessary part of Whistler's existence, and had accompanied him to France in the summer of 1861. Her copper-coloured hair enchanted not only Whistler but also Courbet, who painted her at least twice ("La Belle Irlandaise" and "Jo, femme d'Irlande") at this period.

Page 105

The "*Woman in White*" was Whistler's portrait of Jo, known as "The White Girl", which became the most famous of Whistler's early paintings. Rejected by the Academy, the picture was first shown in a London gallery where an incurably literary public considered it as an unsuccessful attempt to illustrate Wilkie Collins's *The Woman in White*, the popular novel of the day. In 1863 "The White Girl" was exhibited in Paris—in the "Salon des Refusés" where, with Manet's "Déjeuner sur l'herbe", it created a *succès de scandale*.

"*Ridley*" may be M. W. Ridley, Whistler's first pupil and a disciple of the master.

Page 107

J. D. Watson (1832-92), was a sound draughtsman, examples of whose competent but rather uninspiring work are to be found in many of the periodicals of the 'sixties.

Page 110

Mrs. Sartoris was Adelaide Kemble (1814-79), who had appeared as *Norma* at Covent Garden in 1841. In the following year she married E. J. Sartoris, art critic, and closed her career as a professional singer. Mrs. Sartoris was a friend of Leighton whom she had first met in Rome in 1853. The Sartorises lived in St. James's Place.

Shirley Brooks (1816-74), succeeded Mark Lemon as editor of *Punch* in 1870. Later at any rate he and du Maurier became good friends.

Page 114

At this time the work of *Edward Burne-Jones* (1833-98), was little known to the general public. As a painter he only came into his own with the opening of the Grosvenor Gallery in 1877. It seemed likely at the date of du Maurier's letter that he would become one of the great illustrators on wood of the period; but, apart from two drawings published in *Good Words* in 1862 and the following year, a few unimportant book illustrations, and one contribution for Dalziel's *Bible Gallery* (not published until 1881), he abandoned working for the engraver until many years later he produced the designs for the Kelmscott Press.

In 1860 Burne-Jones had married Georgiana, one of the five daughters of the Rev. G. B. Macdonald. (One of her sisters married Poynter, and another Lockwood Kipling, the father of Rudyard.) At the date of the letter they were living in Great Russell Street, and were about to set forth on a journey to Italy with Ruskin.

Page 116

Joseph Swain engraved all the *Punch* blocks from 1843, two years after the paper's foundation, until 1893, when he retired after reproduction by "process" had taken the place of wood engraving. (See also above.)

Page 118

"*Ernest*" was Ernest Delannoy, an obscure painter with whom Whistler had struck up a friendship at Gleyre's during his student days in Paris and who had been Whistler's companion on the expedition to Alsace during which the famous French set of etchings was produced. Whistler had brought Ernest with him to England in 1857, but almost at once his friendship for him had begun to cool. Ernest, who was a complete bohemian, found London *trop triste* and returned to Paris, starvation and eventually, according to some reports, death in a lunatic asylum.

Page 119

Tom Taylor (1817-80), author and playwright, was on the *Punch* staff for thirty-six years, in 1874 succeeding Shirley Brooks as editor. For many years he was art critic for *The Times*.

"*The delightful and refined author of Rita etc.*" was Adelaide Kemble (Mrs. Sartoris).

Page 121

"*Plinth*" refers to Thomas Plint of Liverpool who had just died: the sale of his collection of pictures at Christie's in March, 1862, was the most important of the season. Plint was a patron of Rossetti, and had given Burne-Jones his first commission.

"*The Carpenter's Shop*", now at the Tate Gallery, had been exhibited at the 1849 Academy under the title, "Christ in the Home of his Parents". Millais was then aged twenty. The picture had been subjected to violent press criticism, notably by Dickens, who referred to it in *Household Words* as "mean, odious, revolting, and repulsive".

Page 124

Haden, it should be remembered, was a surgeon as well as an etcher of genius.

Page 126

Charles, 3rd Earl Somers (1819-83), had married, in 1850, Virginia Pattle, sister of Mrs. H. T. Prinsep of Little Holland House. The dinner party on Wednesday, 9th April, 1862, was at No. 7, Carlton House Terrace, where, about six years earlier, Watts had adorned the walls of Lord Somers's dining-room with a series of frescoes representing "The Elements". These frescoes, the work of the artist's best period, are as fresh and compelling today as when they were painted. They were discovered under the wallpaper by the Germans just before the last war when the building was part of the German Embassy. At present they are in danger owing to proposed demolitions and rebuilding.

"*Dicky Doyle*" was Richard Doyle (1824-83), *Punch* artist and designer of the present cover, who had, however, severed his connection with the paper in 1850.

Page 127

Sir Coutts Lindsay was a wealthy banker and man of taste. In 1877 he was one of the founders of the Grosvenor Gallery and in consequence was savagely attacked by Ruskin in *Fors Clavigera*.

Page 128

Traer was Haden's assistant and now and then a model for Whistler. He died in Paris in the spring of 1867. Du Maurier recorded in his diary: "Whistler wants me to subscribe to the bringing over of poor Traer's body, which of course I will do."

Page 133

Thackeray's novel, *Philip*, was at this time appearing as a serial in *The Cornhill Magazine* with illustrations by Fred Walker.

Page 139

"*Jimmy has just done a first-rate drawing on wood for O.A.W.*" Only six wood engravings by Whistler were published, and four of them he contributed to the 1862 volumes of *Once a Week*. The first, to which du Maurier is probably referring, appeared in Vol. VI on June 21st, 1862: "The Major's Daughter", as it is called, depicts a girl on board ship pensively looking over the sea—a lovely and very characteristic thing.

Page 142

Mrs. Dalrymple was one of the seven sisters of Mrs. Prinsep, the daughters of James Pattle of the East India Company. Another sister was Mrs. Cameron, the celebrated photographer. According to Ellen Terry, Mrs. Prinsep, Lady Somers, and Mrs. Cameron were known as "Beauty", "Dash", and "Talent".

Page 152

"*. . . your finger not yet healed.*" In *Memorials of Edward Burne-Jones*, by his wife, Volume I (Macmillan, 1904), the following relates to the engraving accident which befell Miss Wightwick:

> "Du Maurier brought his handsome fiancée to see us, and she and I took counsel together about practising wood-engraving in order to reproduce the drawings of the men we loved. I had begun it already, but she, though eagerly interested, had scarcely seen the tools required for the art. I can recall du Maurier's distress when she drove a sharp graver into her hand one day."

Page 156

Edward Levy (1833-1916), who in 1903 became the first Lord Burnham, married in 1862 Harriette, daughter of Benjamin Webster, actor-manager. In 1875 Levy assumed the additional name of Lawson.

Page 158

"*Mrs. Millais*": in 1855 Millais had married Euphemia (or "Effie") Gray, who had been the wife of Ruskin.

Page 164

The "*young parson*" was probably Stopford Augustus Brooke (1832-1916), who in 1859 had been appointed to the curacy of St. Mary Abbots, Kensington, where he remained for four years. According to the *D.N.B.*, "shortly after his marriage [in 1858] Brooke resolved to search for a field of larger opportunity, but though his reputation as a preacher was already considerable, his religious views, judged by the standard of the day, were dangerously broad, and for a short time he was without employment." In 1880 he seceded from the Church of England. He produced many works on English literature and was an amateur painter of distinction.

Page 170

"*Leighton drawing on wood*": George Eliot's *Romola* was then (1862) appearing as a serial in *The Cornhill Magazine* with illustrations by Leighton.

Page 174

"*Mellon's concert*": Alfred Mellon (1821-67), conductor of the Musical Society and of the Promenade concerts which for several seasons were given under his name at Covent Garden.

Page 175

Du Maurier's sketch books at this time contain many caricatures of the dark saturnine features of *Philip Hermogenes Calderon* (1833-98), a painter of Spanish extraction who came to England at the age of twelve and remained for the rest of his life. From 1853 he contributed regularly to the Academy, mostly vast historical canvases which were very popular. In 1887 he was elected Keeper of the Royal Academy with an official residence in Burlington House. A good portrait of "The Doge", as he was called, by du Maurier may be found in *Punch*, September 28th, 1868.

Page 176

"*My Lord Dundreary*": this probably refers to du Maurier's drawing, "Lord Dundreary married", which was published in *Punch*, October 25th, 1862.

Page 178

"*I was at a lecture of Professor Owen's . . .*" Sir Richard Owen (1804-92), the celebrated geologist, was at this time lecturing at the Royal Institution.

Page 180

"*The competition is getting tremendous*". A list of prominent Victorian painters who at this time were working for the engraver for magazine and book illustration would include Millais, Rossetti, Holman Hunt, Ford Madox Brown, Burne-Jones, Leighton, Arthur Hughes, Orchardson, Poynter, Watts, and Marcus Stone.

Page 185

"*. . . goes into ecstasies about Florence Claton I am told*". *Florence Claxton*, with her sister, Adelaide, supplied a few commonplace illustrations to the periodicals of the 'sixties.

"*The Story of Elizabeth*", by Miss Thackeray, was at this time appearing as a serial in *The Cornhill Magazine* with illustrations by Fred Walker.

Page 188

A drawing, from much later memory, of "the little girl in the brown boots by the Foundling Hospital", as she appeared in 1853, is reproduced in *The Martian* (1896). Here is du Maurier's description of their first encounter, as related in that novel:

> "One morning, as I carried Ida's books on her way to school, she pointed out to me three girls of her own age, or less, who stood talking together at the gates of the Foundling Hospital. They were all three very pretty children—quite singularly so—and became great beauties: one golden-haired, one chestnut-brown, one blue-black. The black-haired one was the youngest and the tallest—a fine, straight, bony child of twelve, with a flat back and square shoulders; she was very well dressed, and had nice brown boots on arched and straight-heeled slender feet, and white stockings on her long legs—a fashion in hose that has long gone out. She also wore a thick plait of black hair all down her back—another departed mode, and one not to be regretted, I think; and she swung her books round her as she talked, with easy movements, like a strong boy.
>
> 'That's Leah Gibson', says my sister; 'the tall one with the long black plait.'
>
> Leah Gibson turned round and nodded to my sister and smiled—showing a delicate narrow face, a clear pale complexion, very beautiful white pearly teeth between very red lips, and an extraordinary pair of large black eyes—rather close together—the blackest I ever saw, but with an expression so quick and penetrating and keen, and yet so good and frank and friendly, that they positively sent a little warm thrill through me. . . .
>
> And finding her very much to my taste, I said to my sister, just for fun, 'Oh—*that's* Leah Gibson, is it ? Then someday Leah Gibson shall be Mrs. Robert Maurice'."

The passage is directly autobiographical. For "Ida" read "Isabel"; for "Leah Gibson", Emma Wightwick; and for "Robert Maurice", George du Maurier.

Page 196

"*. . . I am illustrating Warren's beastly book.*" Du Maurier contributed seven illustrations, engraved by Whymper, to *Passages from the Diary of a Late Physician* by Samuel Warren (Blackwood, 1864).

"*Eleanor's Victory*", a story by Miss Braddon, was running as a serial in *Once a Week* (1863), Vols. VIII and IX.

Page 198

George Smith (1824-1901), was the publisher—Smith & Elder—who established *The Cornhill Magazine* for Thackeray, and later founded *The Dictionary of National Biography*.

Page 199

"*The sensation tale*". This refers to du Maurier's illustration for "Mokeanna; or the White Witness", published in *Punch*, February 28th, 1863. "Mokeanna", by F. C. Burnand, was a series of stories parodying the sensational style of the day, each story being accompanied by a drawing which imitated the manner of Sir John Gilbert's illustrations for *The London Journal*. Millais's illustration appeared on March 21st, 1863.

Page 200

Edward Askew Sothern (1826-81), actor, first appeared in the part of *Lord Dundreary* in a play, "Our American Cousin", by Tom Taylor, at the Haymarket Theatre in November, 1861. *Lord Dundreary*, as portrayed by Sothern, became the talk of London, and the play ran for 496 consecutive performances.

Page 204

John Brett (1831-1902), was a painter who treated his subject with a more than pre-Raphaelite minuteness of detail. His best known picture, "The Stone Breaker", (1858), was exhibited recently at the Tate Gallery.

Tom Taylor was at this time art critic of *The Times*.

"*Old Westminster Bridge*" was one of six etchings by Whistler exhibited at the 1863 Academy. But du Maurier may be referring to Whistler's oil painting, "The Last of Old Westminer", depicting the old bridge in course of demolition, which was also exhibited.

Page 205

Adelina Patti (1843-1919), the most famous soprano coloratura singer of her day. She had made her début in England two years previously in "La Sonnambula" by Bellini, and from 1861 to 1884 she sang every season at Covent Garden. Her career extended over a period of 56 years. At the date of the letter (May, 1863), she was appearing in Rossini's opera, "Il Barbiere di Seviglia".

Page 207

William Michael Rossetti (1829-1919), brother of D. G. Rossetti, was at this period art critic to *Fraser's Magazine*. He was then living with his brother in Cheyne Walk, the *ménage* including Swinburne and Meredith.

"*Millais' Moonlight*". This refers to "The Eve of St. Agnes" painted at Knole and exhibited at the 1863 Academy. The painting was bought by Val Prinsep and is now in the Victoria and Albert Museum.

Page 208

"*A splendid piece of colour*". According to Tom Armstrong, Whistler once mentioned his mother to fellow students in Paris. Lamont exclaimed, "Your mother? Who would have thought of you having a mother, Jimmy!" "Yes, indeed, I have a mother, and a very pretty bit of colour she is, I can tell you."

Page 210

Alphonse Legros (1837-1911), painter and etcher, first met Whistler in Paris and followed him to England where he stayed for the rest of his life. (His remark on being naturalised, "now I can claim to have won the battle of Waterloo", is his only recorded witticism.) Fantin-Latour (1836-1904), came to this country at the same time but soon returned to his native France. "The Society of Three", as they called themselves, were inseparable at this period. In 1867 Whistler and Legros had the inevitable quarrel and finally parted company. Towards the end of his life Legros became head of the Slade School of Art.

"*The Night Watch*" (at Amsterdam), is one of the most famous of Rembrandt's paintings.

Page 210

The "*bachelor's paradise*" was Moray Lodge, a house which still stands but may soon be demolished. Arthur Lewis's Saturday and Sunday parties here were among the most convivial and entertaining of their day. "Music at 8.30; Oysters at 11", announced the invitation cards elaborately designed by Fred Walker, a frequent guest, as were indeed nearly all du Maurier's contemporaries and friends. Here sang "The Moray Minstrels", a highly trained choir of which Keene was a constant member; and here du Maurier heard the finest musicians of the time. Years later he described one of these parties in *Trilby*, where Arthur Lewis is represented as Sir Lewis Cornelys, and his house called Mechelin Lodge.

The United Arts Club had just been established in Tenterden Street, Hanover Square, in a house with ceilings decorated by Angelica Kauffman.

Page 212

"*The Sunday at Home*". Nine of du Maurier's most distinguished illustrations are interred in this forgotten magazine, all of them published in 1864.

Page 215

"*I have also to illustrate Mrs. Gaskell's tale, 'Sylvia's Lovers', for Smith and Elder. . . .*" This, a one-volume edition, with five illustrations, published in 1863, was the first of many novels by Mrs. Gaskell to be illustrated by du Maurier. The artist greatly admired Mrs. Gaskell's work, and his drawings for her books show how sensitively he understood and interpreted the charm of her stories.

Page 216

"*Jimmy and the Rossetti lot . . . are as thick as thieves, etc.*" The quotation is an adaptation of La Fontaine's fable, "La Querelle des Chiens et des Chats, et celle des Chats et des Souris" (Book XII—Fable 8).

"Ces animaux vivoient entre eux commes cousins.
Cette union, si douce et presque fraternelle,
Edifioit tous les voisins."

Page 221

Thackeray had died suddenly in the early morning of Christmas Eve, 1863.

Page 226

Gambart was a wealthy picture dealer with a gallery in London and a house in Nice. He was a friend of Sarah Bernhardt and an early patron of Millais and Walker. Du Maurier met him at Arthur Lewis's parties.

Page 227

Jones is Burne-Jones.

George Boyce (1826-97), was a landscape painter of the David Cox school.

Egron Lundgren (1815-75), was a Swedish painter who had worked in England since 1853.

The Society of Painters in Water Colours was familiarly known as the Old Water Colour Society.

"*A Chinese woman*". This was Whistler's portrait of Christine Spartali, known as "La Princesse du Pays de la Porcelaine", and later to hang in the famous "Peacock Room" in Mr. Leyland's house in Prince's Gate,

"*The 'domus and the teasing and pleasing wife'.*"

. . . domus et placens
Uxor . . .
House and wife of our choice.
(Horace, *Odes*, 21.)

Page 228

Watts was then aged forty-seven, his bride sixteen. They parted company in the following year, and in 1877 Watts obtained a divorce. Kate Terry, who later was to marry Arthur Lewis, was at this time the more famous of the two sisters.

Page 235

Henry Kingsley (1830-76), whose best known novel, *Ravenshoe*, had been published in 1862, married his second cousin, Sarah Haselwood. *Charles Kingsley* (1819-75), his more famous brother, was the Christian Socialist and author of *Westward Ho!*, *The Water Babies*, etc.

Simeon Solomon (1840-1905), was the youngest member of the family whom in a previous letter du Maurier referred to as "among the kindest of his acquaintance". Like his brother, Abraham, and sister, Rebecca, he was an artist. His studio, where the party referred to in the letter took place, was in Howland Street. He had exhibited at the Academy since the age of eighteen and by 1864 had already made his mark both as painter and illustrator on wood. To *The Leisure Hour* of 1866 he contributed a series of drawings depicting contemporary Jewish life and ritual which Burne-Jones described as "the most imaginative work he had ever seen". Swinburne was a warm admirer, declaring that more than one of his poems was inspired by a Simeon drawing. He had many influential friends who were attracted by his charm, looks and good humour.

Such was Simeon Solomon in 1864; but a few years later, owing partly to adverse press criticism of his later work, his career suddenly collapsed. He refused commissions and no longer painted. All attempts to help him failed: he had gone under and preferred to remain under. For a time he was an unsuccessful pavement artist in Bayswater, but eventually drifted to St. Giles's workhouse, where he became more or less a permanent resident. Swinburne described him as "a thing, unmentionable alike by men and women as equally abhorrent to either —nay to the very beasts—raising money by the sale of my letters to him in past years." On a night in May, 1905, he was found insensible in the street and taken to hospital. He died three months later in the workhouse dining room.

At the time of the letter *Dante Gabriel Rossetti* (1828-82), was living with his brother William at Tudor House, 16 Cheyne Walk, Chelsea, with Swinburne and Meredith as temporary inmates. In 1861, sponsored by Ruskin, he had published his translations of the early Italian poets. As a painter he had already produced what many consider his most inspired work, and his second phase as artist had not yet begun. In 1862 he had lost his wife in tragic circumstances.

In April, 1864, the date of du Maurier's letter, *Algernon Charles Swinburne* (1837-1909), was practically unknown outside a small but dazzled circle of friends. In 1862 *The Spectator* had printed "Faustine" and a few others of his poems, but they had made little stir, and du Maurier's opinion that the poet's genius would remain unacknowledged seemed at that time to be justified. But when Moxon, exactly a year after the date of the letter, published *Atalanta in Calydon*, its success was instant and overwhelming; and on the publication of *Poems and Ballads* in 1866 Swinburne became the most talked of man in England.

On December 1st, 1866, du Maurier contributed to *Punch* some verses which brilliantly parodied *The Ballad of Burdens*. Years later Swinburne wrote in a letter to du Maurier: "Your *Ballad of Blunders* I read when it appeared. I am certain no one enjoyed or appreciated it more—if so much. It was perfect."

Page 241

"*The Leeches*". In a lecture which du Maurier delivered on "social pictorial satire" in March, 1892, he referred to this first Whitby visit:

"My brief acquaintance with Leech began in 1860, but I had not many opportunities of improving the acquaintance till I met him at Whitby in the autumn of 1864—a memorable autumn for me, since I used to foregather with him every day, and have long walks and talks with him—and dined with him once or twice at the lodgings where he was staying with his wife and son and daughter—all of whom are now dead. He was the most sympathetic, engaging, and attractive person I ever met: not funny at all in conversation, or ever wishing to be—except now and then for a capital story, which he told in perfection. . . ."

Page 242

Sir Henry Thompson (1820-1904), was a remarkable man. The only son of a general dealer, he became the best known surgeon of his time, a pioneer of cremation, and an authority on diet. He was also a student of astronomy; a collector of china (Whistler helped to compile and illustrate the catalogue of this collection); and a talented artist who exhibited regularly at the Academy between 1865 and 1868. He wrote at least two novels under the pseudonym "Pen Oliver", one of them illustrated with twenty full-page drawings by the author. In his house at 35 Wimpole Street, where he lived from 1851 until his death, he entertained the best known men of the day. His dinner parties were known as "octaves" because they began at 8 o'clock, consisted of eight courses, and eight guests attended them.

Page 243

"*An album of drawings*" was *The Cornhill Gallery*, published in 1864, and reprinted in the following year, containing one hundred engravings, all taken from *The Cornhill Magazine*, of which (among others) twenty-eight are by Millais, twenty-seven by Walker, twenty-five by Leighton, two by Sandys, and three by du Maurier.

Adrian Ludwig Richter (1803-1884), Professor at Dresden Academy, was known for a series of illustrations from German life, scenery, and literature, which he furnished to the wood engravers from 1835 onwards. These engravings were published periodically in Albums.

Page 244

The *Spartalis* were relations or connections of the Ionides family. Christine (later the Countess de Cahen) and her elder sister Marie (who became Mrs. Stillman), were the daughters of the Greek Consul-General in London. They were both of extraordinary beauty with full red lips and masses of black hair. Swinburne seeing them at a garden party said, "They are so beautiful I feel I could sit down and cry." Tom Armstrong described the occasion when he and his friends—including Whistler, Legros, Rossetti, and du Maurier—arriving one day in a cab at Tulse Hill met these two girls for the first time: "We were all", he wrote, " *à genoux* before them, and of course every one of us burned with a desire to try to paint them."

"*I am told he (Whistler) has quarrelled with Legros. . . .*" The final break did not come until 1867 after which they never spoke to each other again. In April of that year du Maurier recorded in his diary: "Row between Jimmy Whistler and Legros last Friday, in which Legros was knocked down by a blow in the eye, but plucked out some of Jimmie's hair; *c'est gentil*!"

The tale for *The Leisure Hour* was called "The Awdries and their Friends", with thirteen illustrations which appeared weekly from January 7th to April 1st, 1865. The two drawings for *London Society* were reproduced in Vol. VI, Christmas number 1864.

"*Old Robinson*" was the engraver who engraved these drawings—and very skilfully.

Page 245

Joseph Stirling Coyne (1803-68), was a busy journalist and dramatic author, well known in his day. He had been an original contributor to *Punch*, and was one of its founders in 1841, but he soon severed his connection with the paper. Douglas Jerrold, referring to Coyne's somewhat uncleanly appearance, once remarked, "Stirling Coyne? *I* call him Filthy Lucre!"

"*We've given warning to Pears*". The rooms in Great Russell Street were over the offices of Pears' Soap.

Page 247

"*The Bouverie Street people*" refers to *Punch* which then, as now, had its offices in that street.

Fritz Eltze contributed drawings to *Punch* from 1864 to 1870.

"*Old Mark*" is Mark Lemon, then editor of *Punch*. (See also above.)

Percival Leigh (1813-89), had been elected to the *Punch* staff in 1841, the first year of the paper's publication, and he contributed regularly until his death forty-eight years later.

Evans was one of the proprietors of *Punch*.

"*J.L.*" is Leech who, according to custom, carved his initials on the table after his election to the staff in 1854.

Page 248

"*W.M.T.*" is Thackeray; and "*D.J.*", Douglas Jerrold (1803-57). Jerrold was a regular contributor from 1851-57: his "Mrs. Caudle's Curtain Lectures", illustrated by Keene, appeared in 1846.

Francis Cowley Burnand (1836-1917), succeeded Tom Taylor as editor in 1880, and during his twenty-six years in the chair greatly increased the paper's reputation.

Horace Mayhew (1816-72), for a time acted as Mark Lemon's sub-editor. Elected to the staff in 1845, he was a prolific contributor.

Page 251

The funeral of John Leech took place at Kensal Green on November 4th, 1864. Describing the scene du Maurier wrote:

"It was the most touching sight imaginable. The grave was near Thackeray's, who had died the year before. There were crowds of people, Charles Dickens among them. . . . When the coffin was lowered into the grave, John Millais burst into tears and loud sobs, setting an example that was followed all round; we all forgot our manhood and cried like women! I can recall no funeral in my time where simple grief and affection have been so openly and spontaneously displayed by so many strangers as well as friends—not even in France where people are more demonstrative than here. No burial in Westminster Abbey that I have ever seen gave such an impression of universal honour, love and regret. 'Whom the gods love die young'. He was only forty-six."

Page 252

The "*ballad*" was "L'Onglay a Parry", published in *Punch*, January 14th, 1865: verses written in Cockney French, a form of speech in which du Maurier was always amusingly inventive.

"*Shouldn't I like to do political cuts*?" This was probably not intended to be taken too seriously, for du Maurier was never interested in politics, and more than one *Punch* colleague has told of his indifference when the discussion at the weekly dinner turned to the subject of the cartoon: how, putting a napkin over his head, he would say, "Why don't you talk about something sensible—like pretty women or big dogs? While you clever old cockalorums are settling the cartoon, *moi je vais faire dodo*."

Page 255

Harold (or *Hal*) *Power*, a popular bohemian in his day, was the son of Tyrone Power (1797-1841), the Irish comedian. Hal Power's son, also Tyrone (1869-1931), was well-known on the American stage, and his grandson is the present Tyrone Power, of film and stage fame.

Page 256

Joseph Joachim (1831-1907), first appeared as a violinist in public at the age of seven and became the greatest master of his generation. His success continued for over sixty years.

Page 262

"*Young Charles Dickens*" was the eldest son of the novelist.

Page 264

Guy du Maurier was to achieve fame in 1909 with his sensational invasion play, "An Englishman's Home". A soldier by profession, he was killed in March, 1915, near Ypres, commanding his battalion of the Royal Fusiliers. His mother had died in the preceding January.

"*. . . a good sign for the future if my career is to lie that way.*" Most of du Maurier's contemporaries, the young illustrators who contributed to the books and periodicals of the 'sixties, regarded their work for the engraver as a convenient way of tiding over a difficult period until they were economically in a position to fulfil what they considered their true *métier*—painting. Keene, Tenniel, and du Maurier were practically the only illustrators of their generation who remained faithful to black-and-white until the end of their careers. It is significant that all three were in bond to that exacting task-master, Mr. Punch.

Whether or not du Maurier would have become a great painter in different circumstances—if, say, *Punch* had not almost exclusively claimed his services for over thirty years—is a question which cannot be answered. But towards the end of his career du Maurier gave his own thoughts on the matter in an article he wrote for *The Magazine of Art*, in September, 1890:

> "If the illustrator in black-and-white confine himself to his own particular branch, he must not hope for any very high place in the hierarchy of art. The great prizes are not for him! But if he has done his work well, he has faithfully represented the life of his time; and for that reason alone, his unpretending little sketches may, perhaps, have more interest for those who come across them in another hundred years, than many an ambitious historical or classical canvas that has cost its painter infinite labour, imagination, and research, and won for him in his own time the highest rewards in money, fame, and academical distinction. For genius alone can keep such fancy-work as this alive, and the so-called genius of today may be made the scape-goat of tomorrow, so fickle and unsound a thing is popular favour. But how we look, and what we wear—the way we disport ourselves in the sight and hearing of those observers who are amongst us—all this has surely a perennial interest. We may not grow very rich or very famous, perhaps. But we may, if we try, find comfort in the thought that, for all we know to the contrary, our unsophisticated little black scratchings may still have power to charm and amuse, by virtue of the literal truth that is in them, when some, at least, of the Rembrandts, the Titians, Raphaels and Veroneses of this century shall have passed out of fashion and lost their hold."

Page 268

Du Maurier's companion on the visit to Paris was Emanuel Oscar Menahem Deutsch (1829-73), semitic scholar, and at this time assistant librarian of the British Museum.

Page 273

"*. . . . after which we went to see Chang and Chung*". These "two worthies" were young Chinese giants who at this time were showing themselves at the Paris Exhibition. Du Maurier had probably first seen them a year or so earlier in London, when they were on view at the Egyptian Hall.

INDEX

References in bold figures are to Biographical Notes in the Appendix